INTO THE DEEP

Tom Gunning

Senior Cycle Religious Education

A Curriculum Framework for Senior Cycle

VERITAS

Published 2007 by Veritas Publications
7–8 Lower Abbey Street, Dublin 1
publications@veritas.ie
www.veritas.ie

ISBN 978 184730 021 8

Theological Adviser: Patrick Mullins OCarm, STD

Consultant to the Programme: Maura Hyland
Designer: Niamh McGarry
Text Editor: Elaine Campion and Ruth Kennedy
Copyright Research: Ruth Kennedy and Caitriona Clarke

Printed in the Republic of Ireland by Microprint, Dublin

The author would like to thank all the teachers who piloted materials and in
particular the staff and students of Loreto Secondary School, Wexford.

Extracts from Smashed: Growing Up a Drunk Girl, Koren Zailckas, Ebury Press, 2006, reprinted
by permission of the Random House Group Ltd (pp.31–2,34–6,37,39); extracts from Between
a Rock and a Hard Rock, Aron Ralston, Atria Books (a division of Simon and Schuster), 2004
(pp.43–5,48–9); extracts from Over the Edge: A Regular Guy's Odyssey into Extreme Sports, Michael
Bane, Orion mass market paperback, new edited edition, 1998 (pp.57–8,); extracts from
Miracle in the Andes, Nando Parrado, Crown, 2006 (pp.136,138,141,143,144–5,146–7); Poem
by Wayne Dyer in The Power of Intention, Hay House, 2004 (p.168); extract from 'The Great
Hunger VI' by Patrick Kavanagh, courtesy of the trustees of the estate of the late Catherine
B. Kavanagh, through the Jonathan Williams Literary Agency (p.170); extract from Moving
Mountains, Claire Bertschinger, Doubleday, 2005 (pp.200–1); extracts from 'Canal Bank
Walk' by Patrick Kavanagh, courtesy of the trustees of the estate of the late Catherine B.
Kavanagh, through the Jonathan Williams Literary Agency (pp.236–7); extract from Chicken
Soup for the Teenage Soul II, Carol Gallivan, HCI Teens, 1998 (pp.194–6); extracts from Left to
Tell, Immaculee Ilibagiza, Hay House, 2006 (pp.212–13,214,217–18,219,); extract from The
Gift, Sally Rhine Feather and Michael Schmicker, St Martin's Press, 2005 (pp. 289–90);

Artwork courtesy of: Diana Wilson (p.2,102); Claire Doyle (p.2,102,160,206); Nicola Nolan
(p.160). Images supplied by Getty Images (pp.56,205,223,224,243,267). Images supplied by
the Bridgeman Art Library (pp.210,264,272,282). Stock photography courtesy of
www.sxc.hu.

CONTENTS

INTRODUCTION

Who are you? Who do you think you are? Who do your friends, your teachers, parents and classmates think you are? Everyone has formed some opinion of you, but how accurate are they? These may seem like obvious questions, but the answers are deep and complex. Only five or six years ago you were considered a child; now your adult personality and purpose are emerging.

Some people never discover who they really are because they live on the surface of things and never look any deeper. They act and think the way others would have them act and think in order to be accepted. Strangely, though, they are never accepted, perhaps because they are never really being themselves. They are never accepted for who they truly are on the inside. The journey to self-discovery is difficult because so many people want us to be like them, to behave the way they would have us behave, to become the person they want us to become. The alternative is to become the person we truly want to be, to look into ourselves and finally know who we really are as opposed to the person we pretend to be. It is a journey towards an authentic existence. It is a journey into the deep.

Many have made this journey. Jesus, for example, was completely authentic. Though his message and vision of things often annoyed and disturbed people, he never pretended to be anyone else.

The following is the story of a singer/songwriter who, through experience, discovered his true self. It is the story of someone who turned his back on possible 'success', fame and celebrity in order to be authentic. This is Pierce Turner's story. Haven't heard of him? Exactly.

' In my mid-twenties things were really going well for me in terms of my music career. Or so it seemed anyway. At the Glastonbury Festival I was second on the bill! Around that period in my life I was spending a lot of time in America (I live there most of the time now). I was living in New York, trying very hard to be successful and I have to admit that things were going well. A turning point came, though, when my manager sat me down and told me that things were really about to start happening for me in America. I was on the verge of a big record deal. I know that, for many, that sounds like a dream come true – Irish singer/songwriter making it big in the US. But my manager told me that he wanted to change my life. I looked at him and I thought, no, I don't want that. Sure, I wanted to be successful and I had ambition. But more than anything I wanted to be myself. I wanted to be myself as a singer and as a songwriter. I'll tell you why.

Pierce Turner

I need to take you right back to my teenage years, when I started to learn something important about myself. I remember looking in the mirror. I was overweight and spotty. I then looked at my brothers, who seemed popular with the girls. They must have been alright looking and as I was related to them I figured that I was better looking than this. Then a strange thing happened. I went to England for a short time. While there, I sorted out my weight and

into the deep

my face. I went to Carnaby Street and bought myself some clothes. I went home a man. When I walked down the town (Wexford) people didn't recognise me – girls looked at me. So this was what it was like for the brothers! As time went by, however, I learned that what I saw in the mirror wasn't the real me. There was someone else deep down inside me and I wanted to find that person. On the outside I was Pierce the photographer who walked around town with his portfolio. But my real obsession was music, though I would never have admitted that. I wanted to protect it – I didn't want anyone to take it away from me. Deep down I didn't think people would accept Pierce the musician.

I finally got the courage to do the music thing and even journeyed to Kerry to audition for a place in a band. I did my audition but unfortunately I didn't know what a minor chord was. I found out quick but I didn't get a place in that band. I remember another time trying to be myself. I got an outfit that I really liked and wore it down the town, but I could hear people saying, 'Where are ye going with the big head on ye?' I was finding it increasingly hard to be myself. Fortunately I had a mother who always encouraged me to be a free spirit. I was beginning to go public on the whole music thing, yet I was still longing to be someone else. At the time I wanted to be Bob Dylan and later, in America, I wanted to write the type of song that would become a number one hit. I hadn't the courage to be myself. I didn't know I could exist in the world as Pierce Turner the musician. I thought I had to be someone else, a Bob Dylan, whoever. But that was all a front – I just wasn't being real.

I remember my manager in America telling me that when I went out in front of an audience they would hate me and I would have to win them over. Well, I won them over, again and again, but these were only twenty-four-hour fans, not real fans. I wanted something else, something genuine and real, and I didn't care what the cost would be.

into

the

deep

I began to discover something about being a genuine musician, a real songwriter – to be successful as a songwriter, your songs had to be autobiographical, they had to come from who you were and your unique qualities. As long as I was trying to imitate others I was actually quite boring. When I began to write about my own experiences, my own life, I opened myself up and people could look inside. Now I was genuine and so were my fans. They were lifelong. And this is the strange thing: when you become genuine you attract people to you for the right reasons – you attract real friends.

If I'd let that manager in New York change my life I might have a huge fan base now. I don't know. I probably would sell more records and have more money. I might be famous, a celebrity even. But it wouldn't be me. I'd be living someone else's life, singing someone else's songs and playing gigs to audiences I didn't even know. I look back now and I'm glad I never traded my life for any of those things; fame, success (whatever that is) and popularity. I am who I am and that's what people seem to like. I don't wear disguises and nobody owns me. Most of all, and this is important, I actually know who I am. What you see is what you get. And the people who do listen to my music … they'll still be there the day after tomorrow.

(Pierce Turner)
www.pierceturner.com

into the deep

DISCUSS

1 Pierce Turner likes to write music that is true to who he is. People feel they can identify with his songs. Some say that many 'celebrity' and more popular musicians are less authentic because often they don't even write their own material and that therefore it's harder to identify with their music. What do you think?

2 Music helps Pierce Turner be authentic and have the courage to be who he really is. Many teenagers say they listened to more 'popular' music when they were younger but now they listen to the music that they can identify with. Many say their music reveals who they really are. Do you agree with this? When did you start to listen to the music you really wanted to listen to as opposed to music that just made you feel part of the group?

3. 'When someone asks to see my iPod I feel awkward because they might laugh at some of the music on it.' Does music reveal your true self? What does a person's choice of music say about them? Do you feel free to listen to the music you really want to listen to or would you be rejected by your friends if you did?

GIGGING WITH PIERCE

' I gigged with Pierce and now that I've read his piece it's made me think. A lot of people are afraid to be themselves and never discover who they really are because they are so busy trying to be like other people. Girls in particular (in my experience anyway) can be so fabricated and fake that they only live on the surface of things pretending to be somebody they aren't. Some strive purely to find out the latest gossip and be the first to tell their peers while others try so desperately hard to be the centre of attention that they are willing to go to any lengths to get it. They want to fit in and to be popular so badly that they shape their personality to suit what their 'friends' think. This might not be obvious to some but it does happen!

As a musician, I have learned from Pierce to stand up and be myself and to hell with everyone else if they don't like it! This is not only relevant when I'm

into

the

deep

playing music but in every aspect of life. Music and performing are very much a part of who I am and I think it is important that people can see this when I play live music. I express who I am by playing music that I love; others write songs, others buy certain types of clothes, etc. Whatever way you express who you are, be honest and true to yourself. One thing that I have found is that when you are honest and

genuine with yourself and who you are, you will meet other people who are honest with who they are also, people who are genuine and people who respect you. You will find that these are often the people that you will remain close to for the rest of your life. As Pierce puts it, people who are 'not just twenty-four-hour fans'!

So stand up, be yourself, and be proud. Be counted as an individual, not just as another face in the crowd!

(Rachel Clancy)

DISCUSS

1 At thirteen or fourteen many teenagers feel they have to go unnoticed by being the same as everybody else. Then some begin to wear the clothes they want to or the hairstyle they want to. An individual emerges. Do you think this is an important development in the life of a teenager? Do you think teenagers can become individuals or is there one big mass identity that everyone has to fit in to? Give reasons for your answer.

2 Some say that to really become yourself you need good friends around you. Bad friends want you to be the same as everyone in the group. Do you agree with this? Why do you think this is so?

3 If good friends help you to become your real and authentic self, what else helps?

4 Pierce Turner had genuine fans because he plays genuine music. People who are genuine and real have genuine and real friendships. What are the other advantages about being your true self? For example, does it help you make better decisions about your life when you know who you really are? Is it easier to take care of yourself?

COULDA, SHOULDA, WOULDA ...

There is a group of people known as the 'coulda, shoulda, wouldas'. They look back on their lives and think: 'I could have done that' or 'I would have done that' or 'I should have done that'. Opportunities missed, dreams unfulfilled, potential unrealised. It seems that near the end of our lives there is a clarity about what could have been done, the person we should have been, the stuff we would have done ... coulda ... shoulda ... wouldas haunt waking time and makes for uneasy sleep. And one thought haunts more than others ... I lived someone else's life ... I did not live my own ... if I had been truly me ... I coulda ... shoulda ... woulda ...

And so begins *Into The Deep*, a journey past the façade of who you appear to be to the God-given identity within. The single most fundamental insight of religious traditions has been that we, each and every one of us, have been created for a purpose. Each purpose is different and so we must be ourselves, authentic, real and genuine. The world needs us to fulfil our dreams and reach our potential. It is why we were created. So, whatever your name is, find your purpose and don't die wondering 'what if?' Don't die with your music still in you.

It's never too late ... the Jewellery Maker's tale

About six years before I retired from my office job I took a week's holiday and enrolled in a workshop learning how to make silver jewellery. I have always had an interest in visual things – shapes and colours – but never did anything about it. I found the week exhausting because my mind had to switch into a different mode. Also using things like saws, polishers and files was very different, but by the end of the week I had made five pieces of silver jewellery. It's never too late. The workshop was run by Cormac Cuffe, and he was a very encouraging teacher. I still attend the workshop.

This experience turned out to be very rewarding. I knew then that I would have an interest that would be both creative and stimulating and that is the way it has turned out. I realise that I am very lucky to have the time, energy and ability to do something I really love. People have said that the pieces are very spiritual. I don't know but it certainly is me being creative. Maybe that's what they mean.

I could of course think that it's a pity I didn't do this earlier in my life; perhaps I could have made a full-time career out of it, but what is the point? In the last few years of working nine to five, it was great to have an interest to 'escape to' and work at something that was satisfying to me. I found this gave me energy because it was coming from inside, from a deeper place.

There are many things you can do with silver. You can change its shape by hammering it; very satisfying. You can give it texture by putting it through a roller with a piece of fabric. You can introduce colour by using stones, precious or otherwise. There are lots of other options. Over the years you develop your own style. People ask me do I see myself in my jewellery. Not sure.

Since I retired I have been to Los Angeles three times, working at a conference selling my jewellery. It has been a great experience. You get to hear what

into

the

deep

people think of your work. I get a great buzz from this. And guess what? I'm retired.

This piece reminds me of the sea because of the texture of the sliver and the colour of the stone.

I made this piece from scraps of silver. For me it has a very organic shape.

I wanted to keep the shape of this piece very simple. I intended the cut out shape to represent a cross. Some people think it looks like an angel.

This piece is also made from scrap pieces of silver. Sometimes the shapes present themselves to you and you just go with it.

This piece I call 'eclipse'. I think the shape speaks for itself.

My jewellery is inspired by the shapes, patterns and textures found in the world of nature. Another influence is the spirals and crosses of the Celtic tradition. I like to think that they have an organic look and feel.

www.ibagnall-design.com

SECTION D

CELEBRATING FAITH

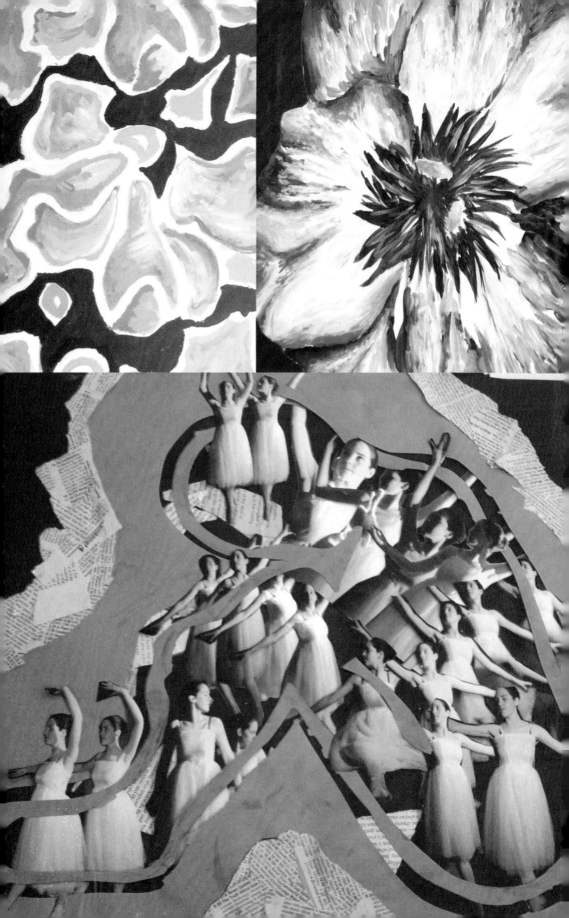

Chapter One

THE REALM OF THE UNSEEN

> We believe in one God,
> The Father, the Almighty,
> Maker of heaven and earth,
> Of all that is, seen and unseen.

(Nicene Creed)

THE PAM REYNOLDS CASE

The Church teaches that every spiritual soul is created immediately by God – it is not 'produced' by the parents – and also that it is immortal: it does not perish when it separates from the body at death, and it will be reunited with the body at the final Resurrection.

(Catechism of the Catholic Church (CCC), 366)

The phenomenon of religion is based on one central component: the belief that some non-material element must exist. Religions claim that there is more to the person than just the material body. Enshrined in religious belief is the doctrine of the soul. All religions believe that after death something survives the body to enjoy an eternal existence. But is there any evidence to back up the claim that after death some non-material part of us continues to exist? Obviously it would be very hard to prove such a claim, but evidence has emerged in recent years from the Pam Reynolds case. It is probably one of the most bizarre and intriguing stories ever to emerge from the world of medical science.

When Pam Reynolds was wheeled into the operating theatre of the Neurological Institute in Phoenix, Arizona, she would undergo one of the most pioneering surgical procedures ever attempted. Pam had an aneurysm, which was caused by a weakness in one of the arteries in her brain. If it ruptured, it would prove fatal. The size and location of the aneurysm meant that it couldn't be removed using traditional surgical methods. Instead, a procedure known as hypothermic cardiac arrest or 'standstill' would be performed. During this operation, Pam's brain would have to be drained of all its blood, while her heartbeat and breathing would have to be stopped. Effectively, during the operation she would be dead. Her chances of survival were dependant on her core body and brain temperature being dropped to sixty degrees. Once the operation was over and the aneurysm was safely removed, her vital signs would be fully recovered.

Four medical teams worked together so that Pam could be retrieved from the edge of death. They began by removing a large section of Pam's skull using a specialised saw called a Midas Rex. The surgeon, Dr Spetzler, removed the bone flap and began his journey deep into her brain. At the base of her temporal lobe and between the third and fourth cranial nerves, Dr Spetzler located the giant aneurysm. It was so large and invasive there was no doubt that hypothermic cardiac arrest would be required.

Brain surgery

Warm blood was removed from Pam's body into a cardiopulmonary bypass machine. Here it would be cooled before being returned to her body. Pam's heart was injected with high doses of potassium chloride and within minutes the last electrical spasms of her heart were extinguished. At 11.25 a.m., the most daring part of the operation began. The cardiopulmonary machine was switched off as the head of the operating table was tilted up. All the blood was drained from her body. Immediately the aneurysm sac collapsed and was removed.

into

the

deep

During this time, a special device called an electrogram was fitted to Pam's ears to check for brain activity. There was none. Pam was now effectively dead, except for the fact that her 'life' rested in the most advanced surgical machinery ever devised.

The Realm of the Unseen

It is at this point of the story that things really begin to get interesting. If religion is correct about its claim that something survives death, then where was Pam when the electrogram registered no brain activity? Where was Pam when she was dead?

According to Pam, when the surgery began she remembers hearing a musical tone, a natural D. The sound, she claims, was pulling her out of the top of her head. She remembers looking down on the operating table. In particular, she remembers looking at the Midas Rex saw, which she would not have seen when she was awake before her surgery (for obvious reasons: it wouldn't be a good idea to show the patient the saw that was about to open her skull!). She gave a detailed description of it and of the equipment in the room, though she didn't recognise what everything was.

When the electrogram registered no activity, Pam 'remembers' being pulled upwards, like in an elevator but really fast. She then recalls being in something that resembled a tunnel or vortex and her grandmother was calling her. She stated:

> I continued with no fear down the shaft. It was a dark shaft that I went through, and at the very end there was this tiny pinpoint of light that kept getting bigger and bigger and bigger. The light was incredibly bright, like sitting in the middle of a light bulb. It was so bright that I put my hands in front of my face fully expecting to see them and I could not.

into
the
deep

The Realm of the Unseen   5

But I knew they were there. Not from a sense of touch. Again, it's terribly hard to explain, but I knew they were there. **,**

(Dr Michael Sabom, *Light and Death*)

It would appear from Pam's account of what happened to her during the surgery that something did survive when she died.

DISCUSS

1 Do you think Pam's account is credible? Give reasons for your answer.
2 What do you think she was describing when she entered the dark tunnel?
3 Is there any reason why Pam may have made up the story?
4 If some part of Pam did survive her death, what do you think it was?

EXAMINING THE EVIDENCE

The Pam Reynolds case has important implications for religious belief because it would appear to suggest that after her 'death' Pam survived and began to enter another realm. While this could never be fully proven, it does provide evidence that there is more to us than the physical or material. It points convincingly to the religious belief that we are more than our physical bodies and we have a spiritual side to us. This spiritual and non-material element is perhaps capable of surviving death. However, before we jump to any conclusions, we need to examine the evidence.

into the deep

Was Pam really dead?

Surprisingly, this is a very difficult question to answer because medical experts are uncertain as to what exactly constitutes death. The most recent and accurate method of assessing whether a person is dead or not is based on the loss of whole brain function. It is known as the 'whole brain' definition of death. There are three clinical tests to assess 'whole brain' death, and during Pam's operation her brain was considered

dead by all three tests. However, there remains a problem: doctors can save people from death and even rescue some who are close to death but they cannot raise people from the dead. Because Pam didn't die, by definition, she was never dead. Yet, according to an interview with Dr Spetzler after the operation, he insisted that when there was no blood going through the brain, there was absolutely no activity. In his own words, there was 'nothing, nothing, nothing'. Unfortunately, there is no real answer to the above question. The readers will have to decide for themselves.

Did Pam really 'see' the surgical instruments while there was no brain activity?

Pam claimed to have been able to 'see' the Midas Rex saw that was used to open her skull. She was asked to give a description of this saw and she claimed it looked like 'an electrical toothbrush'. It's not what one might expect a bone saw to look like, but independent investigations confirmed her descriptions. Remarkably, the only time Pam could have seen it was during her surgery and at no other time.

Another interesting piece of information regarding Pam's surgery is her claim to have 'heard' a conversation between two of the doctors while she was under surgery. She claims they were remarking on how her veins and arteries were very small. The doctor in question, Dr Murray, noted in her post-operative report that Pam's arteries were indeed very small. What makes this point even more remarkable is that throughout the procedure Pam was wearing a pair of special earphones to detect brain activity. They would have prevented the patient from hearing anything about the operation. How Pam 'heard' that conversation remains a mystery.

The implications

The Pam Reynolds case has been examined and referred to in many journals and books because of its unique quality. It appears to be another example of what is referred to as a Near Death Experience. Near Death Experiences often occur when a person's heart stops beating during surgery, but they are quickly brought back. As we will see, people often report having had very strange experiences during the time when they lacked vital signs.

into
the
deep

Pam, however, wasn't just 'near' death, she was in fact as dead as any living person could be defined. She had flatlined. There was no breathing, blood pressure, heartbeat or brainwaves. There was no blood in her brain. According to Dr Michael Sabom who investigated the case, Pam had what he would regard as an *after death* experience.

As we mentioned earlier, the existence of a spiritual part to our identity is central to any religious claim. In recent times, however, scientists have taken a serious look at religious beliefs and, as with the Pam Reynolds case, evidence is emerging that supports religious claims.

The existence of the spiritual world or of our souls can never be proven, and certainly not from near death or after death experiences, because it is too difficult to define what actually constitutes death. Yet if we believe that Pam really did leave her body and begin to enter a spiritual realm, it demands that we ask ourselves some serious questions. People will admit that they might only think seriously about religion at certain significant moments in their lives, such as after a death, or in times of sickness or great need. One could be tempted to think that if the spiritual world does exist and we are connected to it, then it's really only a matter for when we die and is not really relevant to now.

Throughout this book we will gather evidence and stories from around the world which suggest in the strongest possible terms that religion is extremely relevant for living and not just for dying.

into

the

deep

DISCUSS

1   How do you react to the evidence stemming from the Pam Reynolds case?
2   In what way might it make people think about the spiritual world and their own spiritual identity?
3   A person's spiritual identity is clearly relevant when they die, but in what way do you think that same identity is relevant during the time when they are alive?

THE MEANING OF DEATH IN THE CATHOLIC TRADITION

**Lord, for your faithful people life is changed, not ended.
When the body of our earthly dwelling lies in death
we gain an everlasting dwelling place in heaven.**

(CCC, 1012)

All who are baptised in the Christian tradition are baptised into the death and resurrection of Jesus Christ. In baptism all are given the gift of everlasting life. Within the Catholic tradition death has a positive meaning because of Christ. Death is seen as the end of our earthly pilgrimage and when it is finished we shall not return to other earthly lives. A person dies once and there is no reincarnation.

After death the soul enjoys a continuing existence in the mercy and love of God. The Christian can view death as a step towards God and everlasting life in heaven. At the time of death the Church speaks words of absolution over the dying person, anoints them with a strengthening oil and gives them a final Eucharist (*viaticum*) as nourishment for the journey ahead. The Church speaks the following words of assurance of things hoped for to the dying:

> Go forth, Christian soul, from this world
> in the name of God the almighty Father,
> who created you,
> in the name of Jesus Christ, the Son of the living God,
> who suffered for you,
> in the name of the Holy Spirit,
> who was poured out upon you.
> Go forth, faithful Christian.

Chapter Two

RITES OF PASSAGE

> ❛ The only way you can understand your life
> is as a spiritual journey. ❜

In the previous chapter, we examined the idea that there is a spiritual world and we posed the question as to how relevant that world is. Does it concern the dynamics of dying or is it relevant to living? Can spirituality and religion make a difference to your life? How important is it? Ultimately, you must come to your own answer on that one. Yet as you sit in your classroom today, there is a particular reason why the question is being posed. You are a teenager and, whether you have realised it or not, for the past while you have been making a journey towards self-discovery. If you can accept the reality of a spiritual world and the notion that you are in some way connected to that world, then it may very well have implications for how you understand yourself and your place in the world.

DISCUSS

Can you identify ways in which teenagers seem to be interested in the spiritual world? For example, can you list programmes on TV that deal with the spiritual realm and are popular amongst teenagers? Why do you think teenagers are interested in such programmes?

ADOLESCENCE AS A SPIRITUAL JOURNEY

Whether you accept it or not, according to the most ancient wisdom and traditions, the teenage world can be best understood as a spiritual journey. We know that teenagers are interested in music, fashion, relationships, sport and their own personal achievements, but we now want to examine how the spiritual dimension of teenage life manifests itself.

If you don't believe that there is a spiritual dimension to teenage culture and life, answer the following questions. If your answers are predominantly no, then we're wrong, so have a little sleep for the rest of the class. If your answers are predominantly yes, then you may wish to read on and discover more about yourself.

into the deep

You may discuss these questions in class. Do they represent in some way the reality of your lives?

- Have you recently slammed a door or felt like slamming a door?
- Are you enjoying the privacy of your bedroom more and more?
- Would you like to put a 'Do Not Disturb' sign on your bedroom door?
- Do you feel you are withdrawing from your parents?
- Are you ever excited about doing risky things?
- Do you feel confused about your identity, about what clothes to wear, the look to have, the people you should really be hanging around with?
- Is there a sort of an emptiness inside you, like there's something you're looking for but just can't find?
- Have you felt a fury inside you, like you'd love to be able to go into a room and just trash the place? Do you ever feel like going berserk?
- Do you ever feel like running away from home?
- Do you want to change things, reform systems, regenerate what seems decaying and lifeless in society?
- Do you think teenagers are undervalued in society? Do you feel that adults never want to listen to your opinions?
- Do you ever feel like nobody really knows the real you?
- Do you want to change yourself?
- Finally, if you met a wise old sage who offered to bring you on a journey of self-discovery, what would your answer be – yes or no?

into

the

deep

THE PHENOMENON OF ADOLESCENCE

If your answers were predominantly yes to the above questions, then we could easily say that such feelings are typical of a stage of a person's life known as adolescence or being a teenager. The way some adults talk about adolescence would lead you to believe that it is an unfortunate time: it's 'a stage you're going through' and 'it will pass', hopefully quite soon. When you seem to be going through a problematic period, adults will sometimes tell you 'it's just your age'.

You may be rebellious, subversive and confrontational … the teenage rebel. For many adults, the sooner you become adults the better. Sometimes it would appear that teenagers are less inclined to do just that. Some 'teenagers' continue partying well into their twenties! It's becoming increasingly difficult to define when exactly a person actually reaches adulthood. When can we say with certainty that a person is no longer a teenager and is now an adult?

DISCUSS

1 Would you define yourselves as boys/girls or men/women?
   If the above question caused difficulty, discuss the reasons why.
2 What do you think defines adulthood? Do you want to become adults? Why?
3 Are adults good at helping you to understand what it means to be an adult? In what ways do they help you to become one?
4 What experiences make you feel that you're becoming an adult?

into
the
deep

During your discussions, a lot of issues may have been raised. It may have become clear that there is much confusion about what constitutes being an adult and also how you're supposed to get to that stage. It may be the case that you are not too bothered about becoming adults. It may very well be that when you take a look at the world of adults, you're disappointed by what you see. Adults may constantly tell you that a certain job and college course will make you happy – study hard, get to college, get the job and all should be well. They may tell you that a certain level of wealth and lifestyle will make you happy. While they might believe that, perhaps, deep down, you don't. Teenagers see things differently. It's possible that sometimes you see the truth and adults don't. Far from being problematic, this vision is actually vital and highly significant for any society.

> **DISCUSS**
> 1 Do you agree with the above statement that teenagers see things differently to adults? Why do you think teenagers might have a better vision than adults?
> 2 When should teenagers listen to adults? When is the adult vision of things better than the teenage one?

In this chapter, something new is going to be presented to you and it concerns an understanding of the state of adolescence. This information has been hidden for many, many years and has only recently come to light. It's time to meet The Berserkers.

THE BERSERKERS

> They went without shields, and were mad as dogs or wolves, and bit on their shields, and were as strong as bears or bulls; men they slew, and neither fire nor steel would deal with them; and this is what they called the fury of the berserker.

(Mircea Eliade, *Rites and Symbols of Initiation*)

The word 'berserk' comes from the 'Berserkers' who, quite literally, went berserk. The word translates from old German as 'warriors in bear skins'. The Berserkers belonged to older and more primitive Germanic societies, in which the challenge for the young person was to become a warrior in bearskin. In order to become such a warrior the youth had to leave behind his old identity as a child. This could only be accomplished through a prescribed set of ordeals and rites.

The ordeals included having to slay a wild boar or a wolf, or fight against an enemy unarmed. Once the youth killed a wolf, he skinned it and then wore it. By putting on the bloodied wolf skin, the youth assimilated the behaviour of a wolf and became a wild-beast warrior, or 'Berserker'. Berserkers were reputed to have been the fiercest of all warriors. They could emit strange sounds that completely freaked their enemies.

Needless to say, every youth wanted to become a Berserker, because nobody, absolutely nobody, gave them hassle. The Berserker possessed a unique characteristic known as *wut*, also known as *furor*. The annals of warriors record that *furor* was an immense fury that terrorised enemies and could even paralyse them with fear. The youth who eventually became a Berserker was a hero in his society because he protected the group from attack and brought security and peace to his land. The

Artist's impression of a Berserker

Berserkers were so fearsome that peace reigned. Other warriors who challenged them quickly turned and went home. The Berserker was rarely in a fight, for few would take him on.

into
the
deep

DISCUSS

1 The age of the Berserkers corresponds to what we would term adolescence. In what ways would you say Berserkers resembled today's teenagers and in what ways were they different?

2 Researchers realised that in primitive societies, people recognised that youths had particular characteristics beneficial for the group. What would you think are the advantages of adolescents for a society?

THE PLACE OF YOUNG PEOPLE WITHIN ANCIENT AND FORGOTTEN TRIBES

ASIDE

When we use the term 'primitive' in this text, it refers to cultures that have not been touched or affected in any major way by the 'modern world'. You may have previously heard the term used in a negative sense, indicating that something is not advanced or developed. As we will see in these chapters, primitive societies may not have been advanced technologically, but in some ways they have a lot of insights to offer modern society.

When primitive tribes such as the Berserkers were first discovered by people from modern societies, one aspect of their culture was immediately noticeable and very strange – there seemed to be no teenagers. There were teenagers in age, obviously, but people were either recognisably children or they were adults.

In fact, it soon became clear that what we term adolescence simply didn't exist in primitive societies and, to a large extent, still doesn't. In modern society, the journey from childhood to adulthood can take up to ten years or more. Childhood ends around twelve (perhaps younger) and adulthood begins when a person gets a job and is no longer dependant financially or otherwise on their parents. It is hoped that somehow along the

into the deep

way teenagers will pick up some of the skills that are needed for adult life. Often this process can be left to chance. Not so in a primitive society.

In recent times, researchers and anthropologists have become fascinated with the absence of adolescence in primitive groups, and it has led many to journey into the most remote regions on the planet to try to discover the secret behind this remarkable phenomenon.

What no modern mind could understand was how these societies seemed to transform children into adults without a prolonged period of adolescence in between. What was even more remarkable was that these societies suffered none of the problems that we associate with adolescence, such as rebelliousness,

Shan boy in northern Thailand undergoing Poy Sang Long initiation rite

vandalism, irresponsibility, promiscuity or addiction. Neither was there such a thing as crime, depression or mental illness. Something very interesting was going on with primitive groups and it was happening deep inside the most remote forests ever encountered by western researchers. What they uncovered would eventually tell us much about modern teenagers.

DISCOVERING ANCIENT RITUALS AND SECRET RITES

When westerners first visited archaic tribes, it was initially difficult to establish communication and trust. Most had to live with the group for many years before they were allowed access to the mysteries of the group. From the outset, one strange phenomenon was apparent.

into
the
deep

Anthropologists discovered that every couple of years a most fascinating event happened in the life of a tribe. Early one morning, the elders of the tribe visited the homes of boys who had reached puberty. Forcibly, they removed the children from the tents and brought them deep into the most remote parts of the forest. The mothers were distraught and often fought the elders. They wept openly because they would never see their 'children' again.

Weeks later, the young people would emerge from the forest radically different. They would have new names. They would resemble boys in looks only, but in every other way they would have been transformed into adults. They would be skilled warriors and hunters and would live with the men. Soon they would marry and start their own families.

Anthropologists in other tribes had witnessed the same process with girls. They too would be taken away and after a short time they would return as women. They would start their own home, have children and be skilled in medicine and nutrition.

> **DISCUSS**
> 1 How do you think the tribes managed to transform children into adults in such a short time?
> 2 When do you think teenagers should be recognised as adults and treated as such?

PRIMITIVE RIGHTS OF PASSAGE FOR MALES

 Initiation and death correspond word for word and thing for thing.

For years, westerners were forbidden to accompany the elders into the forest to witness the strange rituals. Eventually they gained entry, but when they ventured into the woods it became apparent that they were witnessing ancient rites of initiation – what came to be known as 'rites of passage'.

Initiation refers to the transition of the individual into a new state, and within the tribe this new state was adulthood. The boys would make their transition into adulthood by means of the most complex and bizarre rites imaginable. It is important to note that primitive tribes didn't want to get rid of teenagers. On the contrary, they realised that from around thirteen onwards, something highly significant was happening in the lives of young people – the adult was emerging.

We will now take you through the different stages that boys were brought through from childhood to adulthood.

A BLACKENED DARKNESS

 I have been to dark places. Am I the only one?

According to the elders of the tribe, it was only possible to turn a boy into a man by first destroying the identity of the boy inside. This wasn't fun. The process began when the boy was forcibly separated from his mother and familiar environment. When the boys first entered the forest they were understandably nervous. They were taken to specially made huts that resembled both wombs and tombs – a tomb for the boy to die in and a womb to give birth to the man. They spent much time buried in their huts in the darkness. Outside, drumbeats ominously foretold the ordeals that lay ahead.

Depending on which tribe the boy belonged to, he was covered with dirt and blackened earth to look deathly, ragged, dishevelled and unkempt. Alternatively, he was covered in white powder to look deathly or ghostlike. He was also forced to wear a mask, so that he could not catch his reflection. The blackness, darkness and ghostlike appearance symbolised one thing – the boy that once was no longer existed. The boy, the child, was dying.

into

the

deep

THE THRESHOLD ZONE

 Sometimes I haven't a clue who I really am
or who I'm supposed to be.

ASIDE

The term 'threshold' was used by the anthropologist Victor Turner to describe the condition of the neophyte, the name given to the boys when they were between two states. When you stand at a threshold, you are between two places – in effect, you are nowhere. You are in a ' twilight zone' between two worlds.

Victor Turner

In primitive tribes, that which couldn't be identified was often feared. The boy no longer existed, but as of yet neither did the man. If there was neither a boy nor a man, then nothing existed, and so the term 'neophyte' was used to describe the person. Because these neophytes 'didn't exist', they were sent off to be isolated and secluded. They had to endure the ordeal of isolation, while their sense of identity was in complete chaos. Sometimes boys were dressed as girls just to completely confuse them.

During this time, the neophytes became very confused. Everything around them was unfamiliar; they were even unfamiliar to themselves. Then something extraordinary happened inside the neophyte; it was like there was a vacuum inside them – they had absolutely no identity. This state of confusion was exactly what the elders wanted: if someone was confused about their identity, it would be easier to give them a new one.

into

the

deep

DISCUSS

1 Do you know any teenagers who dress differently? Are they unsure of their identity?

2 Try to discover other parallels between what neophytes went through and what teenagers experience today. If you discover parallels, as a class group discuss why you think they exist.

INITIATION INTO THE SPIRITUAL REALM

' Sometimes I get scared about the future. Do I have what it takes? '

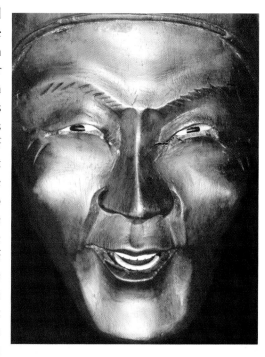

One very unusual aspect of the neophytes' seclusion involved their encounters with 'monsters'. The elders had two objectives during their rites of initiation: the first was to initiate the neophyte into manhood and the second was to initiate him into the world of the spirits – the spiritual realm. The modern reader must realise that, unlike in our culture, a child in a primitive society knew nothing about the spiritual world up to then. The elders devised a plan to entice the neophyte to think about the world in a new way – to realise that there was a completely different plane of existence known as the supernatural realm.

into

the

deep

When the young boys were alone in the forest, the older men dressed up as monsters and visited them. The hideous masks the men wore startled the boys into thinking about their environment in completely new ways. The next day they would plague the elders with questions about the night visitors and the elders would begin to tell them about the world of the spirits. The elders would later admit to being 'the monsters' and apologise for frightening the boys. We might presume it was at this moment that the neophytes developed a sense of humour!

DISCUSS

Do you ever remember being terrorised by adults with stories about ghosts? In what way did it affect the way you thought about the supernatural realm?

THE ADULT EMERGES

into
the
deep

What was it that actually enabled the neophytes to become adults? This was the question that fascinated anthropologists. At this point we can go back to our friends the Berserkers. They firmly believed that the youths who became 'warriors in bearskins' did so because of a special force known as *wut* or *furor*. They believed this force to be sacred and they attributed it to religious origins. What emerged came forth from the spiritual realm.

Primitive groups changed boys into men by giving them special sacred knowledge about the spirit world, known as *sacra*. The *sacra* were so powerful that they could actually transform a person. For the ancients, sacred knowledge included the secret skills involved in hunting and fighting. All that was vital for manhood had its origins in the spirit world. Coupled with the *sacra* were the continuous ordeals, such as isolation, hunting wild beasts for the first time and hand-to-hand combat. Once the man emerged, he returned to his village to be incorporated into society as an adult.

Researchers who were dismissive of religion had to rethink their position. What was entirely remarkable about primitive rites of passage was the ability of the group to transform a boy into a man in an extremely brief period of time, something that now takes a modern society almost ten years to accomplish. This remarkable feat could only be attributed to a remarkable force – the force of the *sacra* and the sacred realm.

DISCUSS

1   Do you think modern societies should have rites of passage into adulthood? If so, what do you think they might be like?
2   In the absence of official rites, what events are used by society to make you feel you have become an adult?
3   In primitive societies, ordeals and challenges were used to transform children into adults. What events or experiences make you feel like you have become an adult?

into

the

deep

PRIMITIVE RITES OF PASSAGE FOR FEMALES

Women of the Krobo tribe

The Krobo tribe in Africa mark the passage of girls into womanhood by performing a series of rituals known as *Dipo*. The rites begin with a ritual that severs all ties with childhood and then begins a three-week period of seclusion, during which they learn the ways of womanhood. They ritually separate themselves from childhood by discarding their old clothes and wearing special garments that are more befitting of womanhood. They learn the finer points of personal grooming, female conduct, food preparation and the secretive art of dance and seduction.

During their initiation, the girls are tutored by specially appointed guardians. When the tutoring is over and the girls have shaved their heads, they are brought to a sacred grove for other rituals. Once these rituals are over, the initiate is lifted onto the back of a guardian mother, who takes her home at great speed.

Once they have finished their rites of passage, the initiates are brought back to their village where they are adorned with beads and headdresses. Each girl wears an elaborate headdress called a *cheia*. It is made from hoops of corn wrapped in blackened cord and can take up to six hours to make. Tied around their necks and hips are beads that have been handed down to each family. In an 'Outdooring' ceremony, the girls publicly demonstrate their dancing skills for the rest of the tribe, but especially for prospective suitors who have gathered to admire their grace and beauty.

In primitive societies, girls who have become women have been given detailed instruction on what it means to be a woman and the appropriate acceptable behaviour. In these societies, once the rites are over, the newly initiated woman is free to get married and have children.

DISCUSS

1   What do you think are the qualities of a woman in any society? If you were involved in drawing up rites of passage into womanhood, what advice would you give to a young girl?

2   What do you think are the advantages of rites of passage into womanhood? What might be the disadvantages?

A POET'S JOURNEY

> I wish the continent of my soul
> just once, would surface out of sea.

(Lorcan Brennan, 'Rumour of Angels')

I remember being a teenager. I was playing football, meeting friends, being sociable like anyone else. I was even in a band. It was called '747'. On the outside everything seemed fine but inside was a different story. I don't know exactly what age things started to feel different but certainly at the onset of teenage years great surges of anxiety began to well up. At times I could be full of joy but then it could so easily turn to despair. As a young man I had no real way of dealing with these emotions. I remember going up into woods and hills and spending long periods of time there. This would calm me down – I loved the woods, the quiet, the mystery of it all.

I think at that age I was also beginning to look out at the adult world around me and I just didn't know where I was going to fit in. There was a real anxiety

into
the
deep

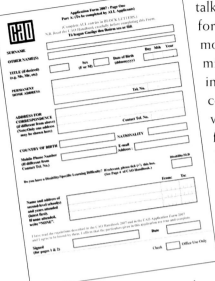

and worry about that. Then there was the talk of what trade I would do. The CAO form was looming, but I was up on mountains, going on walks for miles and miles, getting lost. I knew I'd never get up in the morning for any trade or CAO course. But it seemed all around there were expectations there to just somehow fit in. By some magic I was supposed to know how Lorcan the adult would fit in to the adult world when I really hadn't a clue who Lorcan the adult was or would be.

Looking back now I can see the young poet coming to the surface.

But in school I was hardly going to stand up and say, 'Hey, I think I'm a poet!' I felt I'd be kicked out the door. So I was going around trying to hide this whole part of myself, which was head wrecking.

I remember starting to read biographies to see how other people had gone through this. I remember reading about how Bono from U2 used to get these nose bleeds as a young man. Then he started doing gigs. His first few were terrible, but the nose bleeds stopped. That stuck with me. I was beginning to realise that I would have to allow the new parts of myself to become public in the same way that a singer might start to sing. I felt I had this secret. I was creative, writing privately, becoming very intuitive; words were becoming a very credible way for me to identify my feelings. I can say that now, thirty years on, but imagine saying that to a bunch of young friends in Carnew in 1980!

I really believe that to get a safe passage into adulthood you need a significant adult to lead you through. Friends are great and should be important supports but for me talking with a trusted adult was all important. We had this school retreat and the priest giving it was just brilliant. He was talking about Thin Lizzy and the Boomtown Rats (Bob Geldof's previous incarnation). He was talking about world religions and about how every single person searches for meaning in their lives. He told us to listen to what was going on inside. I remember thinking to myself that I could really respond to that. I looked around and everyone else was as transfixed as me. I wasn't alone anymore! We were all struggling and searching but nobody ever had the guts to say it.

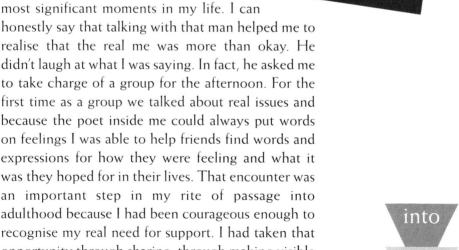

Boomtown Rats

He told us that the feelings of isolation, meaninglessness and loss were all tools to use to get to the stuff inside. I spent a half an hour talking to him and it was one of the most significant moments in my life. I can honestly say that talking with that man helped me to realise that the real me was more than okay. He didn't laugh at what I was saying. In fact, he asked me to take charge of a group for the afternoon. For the first time as a group we talked about real issues and because the poet inside me could always put words on feelings I was able to help friends find words and expressions for how they were feeling and what it was they hoped for in their lives. That encounter was an important step in my rite of passage into adulthood because I had been courageous enough to recognise my real need for support. I had taken that opportunity through sharing, through making visible who I was and I had been supported and accepted by a trusting adult.

The next weeks can only be described as *rains on a parched land*. I was full of confidence – a new 'me' was

into

the

deep

beginning to emerge. The private 'me' was allowing new parts to go public. I started writing poems, even reading them in public and publishing them. No one killed me; no groups jumped from behind a wall and beat me up. I was arriving in the world in a new way with a growing sense of self-acceptance and self-appreciation. My friendships were deepening and I was becoming more connected. The most important thing that happened to me was that I began to like myself. I had always suspected the poet inside but rejected that part of me in case the world would reject it. Everything was coming together. The priest I had talked with later explained to me that this was really a spiritual journey; I was learning new skills in the important practice of becoming me.

At forty-four years I am still making my journey in different ways into and through adulthood and I have found, through my lived experience and from engaging with wiser people and world traditions, that it is in giving we receive.

Ultimately, we find who we really are through finding and expressing our gifts, through giving our lives reflectively and deliberately away.

> ❛ It's necessary to stop. To look about.
> See the distance, the height attained, the
> journey in the bag. Rest easily assured
> life has its meaning. ❜

(from 'Retrospect')

into

the

deep

Lorcan Brennan has published three collections of poetry, Aisling, Rumour of Angels *and* Little Hermits and Other Poems. *His work entails raising awareness of the need for honestly addressing emotional, physical and spiritual issues impacting on our lives through finding specific creative ways towards better self-care.*

Chapter Three

PATTERNS OF INITIATION

PATTERNS OF INITIATION IN TEENAGE CULTURE

In primitive societies, the elders of the group facilitated the youth to die to childhood and spiritual ignorance in order to discover their true purpose in life as adults, whether that be in the role of shaman, doctor, hunter, fighter or the dreaded Berserker.

But what happens to young people in a modern culture where there are no official rites of initiation? In other words, how do they enter adulthood in the absence of such rites? Is it possible that, in the absence of official rites of passage, teenagers might create their own? Might there be bits and pieces of ancient rites of initiation embedded in your own culture? Is it possible that teenagers have included fragments of initiation rites into their lives without knowing it?

In this chapter, we will investigate one particular aspect of teenage culture: alcohol. Many commentators suggest that if the adult world doesn't officially tell teenagers when they are adults, then teenagers create their own rites into adulthood.

One new and dangerous phenomenon in Irish teenage culture is the Post-Leaving Cert celebrations in sunny and foreign locations, now viewed as a new rite of passage. One student commented:

> The Leaving Cert is a transition into the adult world. I am sitting my Leaving Cert next year and already we are saying it is only nine months to freedom and already we are looking forward to our summer holiday. The fact is, if you want people to behave responsibly, you must give them responsibility.

(Siobhan Maguire, *The Sunday Times*, 21/8/2005)

DISCUSS

1   It's up to adults to show teenagers how to become adults. The student above believes that if adults give teenagers responsibility, they will behave responsibly. Do you agree with this position? Give reasons for your answer.

2   In the above article, alcohol is referred to as part of a ritual that acts as a rite of passage into adulthood. Why do you think teenagers use alcohol to mark their transition into adulthood? Do you think it's a good ritual? Why?/Why not?

3   Can you identify other rituals that are used to mark the transition into adulthood by teenagers?

HOW INITIATION MIGHT MANIFEST ITSELF IN CULTURE

If initiation does manifest itself in teenage culture, then it will obviously mirror, though in a fragmented form, the different aspects of initiation rites. They are as follows:

- Isolation
- Confusion/chaos
- Darkness
- Challenges/ordeals/risk-taking
- Initiation into a group

Rites of passage have always involved darkness, confusion, chaos and risk. Yet when properly understood, the rituals facilitated the emergence of an adult into society. In modern societies, rites of

passage created by teenagers often never get past the chaos, darkness and confusion.

'GROWING UP A DRUNK GIRL'

Koren Zailckas wrote a bestselling autobiographical account of her experiences of being a drunk girl. It's called *Smashed: Growing Up a Drunk Girl*. According to Koren, 'smashed' is a prophetic term for being drunk, because that is exactly what drink does to your body, personality and entire world. Koren's world slowly began to implode the more she and her friend Natalie drank.

In the following extract, Koren reflects on a class she just had in school about ritual studies/rites of passage. She sees parallels between these initiation ceremonies and her own culture and life.

Koren Zailckas

 We've been studying rituals in social studies class because our teacher Mr Booth thinks it will shed some light on our forthcoming graduation ceremony. Mr Booth says most initiation ceremonies take place in three parts. First the initiate withdraws. Usually, she's sent away from her family and her village, which represents her old life as a child. Next, she lives a life of solitude and confusion in which she has to fend for herself. Then after time passes, she is allowed to go home and rejoin her community as a full adult, where she is presented with what he calls the *sacra*, meaning something sacred that symbolises her transformation. Mr Booth says our diplomas, in a way, are our *sacra*. But I'm not so sure.

When I think about what Mr Booth says about initiations, I think

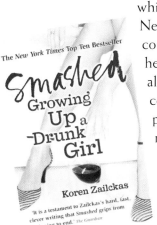

into

the

deep

drinking might have begun for me long before Natalie handed me a bottle this afternoon. It might have been a rite I embarked on two years ago, when I first started withdrawing from my family, shutting myself in my bedroom in the hours before dinner, cutting pictures from magazines or doing nothing, lettering signs to tape on the door that read DO NOT DISTURB. Like the girl who lives alone in the woods, haven't I felt lost since I began to withdraw? My CD changer plays only songs about dejection, 'Creep' and 'Loser' and 'Losing My Religion'. Even my outfits look confused: fishnet thigh-highs under baby-doll dresses or shapeless jeans paired with my dad's flannel shirts, which I amputate at the sleeves. My closet looks like the place where girlhood comes to battle boyhood, virginity comes to battle sexuality, youth comes to battle womanhood. Mornings that I dress in the mirror, I can't decide which virtue, or gender, or level of maturity is winning.

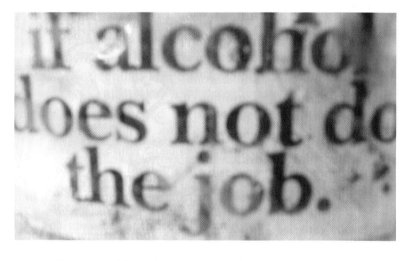

In a way, I have been waiting for something sacred to present itself … It only makes sense for the *sacra* to be the bottle. Natalie awarded it to me, and I awarded it to Laurel, and it marks our new status as drinkers.

(pp. 21–22)

DISCUSS

1 Why do you think Koren drew parallels between rites of separation in primitive cultures and her own desire for isolation and separation?

2 Does the above account present more evidence that teenagers are creating their own rites of passage using alcohol?

INITIATION THROUGH ALCOHOL

Koren's autobiography gives us an insight into how alcohol acts as a fragmented form of initiation. In primitive cultures, ordeals and challenges were set before the young to see if they could prove they were adults. It would appear that in the absence of such official rites, alcohol has become a rite of initiation of sorts.

It's common to hear young men boast of how they drank ten pints the night before and then 'puked all over the place'. Strangely, this can often be greeted with nods of approval and yelps of delight from peers. Quite often, adults tell young people that getting drunk is stupid and dangerous, and in fairness most teenagers are intelligent enough to know this themselves. Very few teenagers would actually consider drinking themselves unconscious and then vomiting over themselves or others a true and noble virtue.

ASIDE

'Teenagers are especially mean to each other to conform to certain things such as alcohol and sex and even worse things. They tend to use the subtle bullying tactic of retelling stories to each other of their weekend nights out, and it is not uncommon to hear young students on corridors saying things like: "Ah last weekend was brilliant. I drank a naggin of vodka and couldn't remember anything! It was the most fun I had in ages. You coming out this weekend?" By talking about it in such a relaxed manner, they psychologically influence their peers through bullying without realising it.'

(Female, 16)

into

the

deep

1 What is your opinion of students who recount their weekend adventures to others? Should you follow their example, or are they lacking in some way? Give reasons for your answer.

2 Do you agree that there is a subtle form of bullying going on in the above situation? Explain.

3 Why do students who have a problem with alcohol try to coerce others to drink in a similar fashion? Are they lonely? Can you think of other reasons?

Many teenagers continue to drink excessively, so we now need to look at the deeper causes that might lead to this abuse of alcohol. We'll presume at this stage of your life that you know that drinking too much is pretty senseless. There are many useful statistics and facts that you

can research yourselves. Here we'll concentrate on possible causes that run deeper and may even prove to have something to do with the desire for initiation.

In the following extract, Koren describes her friend Natalie's drinking and her own involvement.

'She just had too much to drink.'

"Are you ok to stand up? If I set you down you're not going to fall, right?"

Greg tries to lower Natalie to the sidewalk, beside the trolley stop. His questions are more or less rhetorical, as Natalie has been reduced to gurgling whenever we speak to her. Her limbs look too heavy to move. When she tries to lift her hands, they only come up an inch or two before they fall back down and roll away from her. Greg says she looks like a rag doll; I think she looks like one of my dog's dilapidated chew toys.

The second Greg lets Natalie's feet touch the concrete, her entire body folds under her. She assumes the position of a chalk outline on *NYPD Blue*: arms outstretched, with her legs wrenched one way and her neck twisted the other. We let her rest like that while we wait. All around her on the sidewalk, ants are building knolls that look like ginger.

"How did she get like this?" I cover my hand with my mouth as I speak because Natalie is emitting a sour smell that makes me think I might throw up, too. "Honestly? She wasn't drunk at your house. How do you think she got this way? Do you think she took pills or something?"

Greg shakes his head. I'm not sure if he means to say no, or if he is trying to clear the bangs from his face. He says, "Naw, she just had too much to drink. Once you get her home she can sleep it off."

I should believe him because his eyes are calm, in a way that suggests he has been through this scenario a million times before. But I don't. I don't see any way this is going to be okay. In my mind, I have a distinct picture of what is going to happen next: I will get

into

the

deep

Natalie back to the room, tuck her into bed, and sometime during the night she will choke on her own vomit and die. That was the one unmistakable thing I learned from our alcohol unit in health class – sometimes, if people get drunk enough, they can drown in their own puke, like Jimi Hendrix. There is even a parody of 'Purple Haze' that goes "Excuse me while I choke and die". I think I am going to have to resuscitate Natalie while my parents sleep, unsuspecting, in the room next door. I don't know how far you're supposed to tip the head back, or how many seconds you're supposed to wait between giving breaths.

(pp. 70–71)

> **DISCUSS**
>
> 1 How do you react to the above extract? Why would Natalie drink herself to such a state of drunkenness?
> 2 How do you think Koren felt? How would you describe their friendship?
> 3 Drinking excessive amounts of alcohol can lead to death, unless you can manage to get your stomach pumped. Needless to say, this is extremely risky. Why do some teenagers do that? Is it because of the risk? Is it a form of death wish?

We will now examine young people's reasons for heavy drinking in light of what we know about initiation and the dynamics involved.

into
the
deep

THE MASK AND THE QUEST FOR SELF-ERASURE

Koren believes that one of the reasons behind teenage drinking is the fact that often teenagers want to camouflage that part of themselves that they feel somehow ashamed of. They want to erase or transform a part of themselves but are not sure how to do that. As in rites of initiation, there's a need to mask the inner self in the hope that in time something will be transformed.

 Externally, I'm not perfect, but I'm healthy. In fourteen years, I've never once fallen down a stairs or caught my hand in a car door. I've never had stitches. I've never so much as twisted an ankle. It's my insides that I need to hide. Privately, I feel disfigured. I am ashamed of my gnarled soul, which is something no surgeon can correct. Were my inner workings exposed, I feel certain they would make children stare, and adults avert their eyes. Like Lucy, I, too, want a mask, the type Dylan Thomas talks about: "to shield the glistening brain and the blunt examiners."

(p. 42)

> **DISCUSS** Why do you think teenagers want to erase or hide what's on the inside? In what way might this point to a desire for inner change or transformation?

THE DEATH DRIVE

 Initiation and death correspond word for word and thing for thing.

Koren explains how at times she got so drunk that her eyes rolled back in her head, and her friends said, smiling, 'She's gone to a better place'. This is dead drunk.

into

the

deep

At sixteen I'm 5'2" and 105 pounds with a ski parka on, which means it would take one hour of downing eight to ten drinks to kill me. Claire told the doctors I'd been drinking for an hour and a half. I'd had half a thermos of vodka, plus immeasurable sips of rum and Kahlua, straight from the bottles. As the doctor told my father, a few more drinks and I'd have fell [sic] into a coma or died right there on the deck.

No matter how many ways I go over the story, I'll never know if some part of me sought that kind of close call. A good bit of it was inexperience; it was not waiting for all those gulps of liquor to absorb into my system, but just expecting to feel them right away. But I also wonder if that night wasn't the first glimmer of a budding death drive.

(p. 96)

into the deep

DISCUSS

Some youths joyride and get killed. Why do you think the 'death drive', what Freud called the instinct we all have to return to the perfect stillness we felt before birth, exists amongst some teenagers? What other forms does the 'death drive' take? From what aspect of primitive rites might the 'death-drive' be derived?

THE CHALLENGE/ORDEAL — JOURNEY INTO DARKNESS

 That night at the dock, I proved I was the weedy one. And because I couldn't handle my liquor, because that weakness endangered everyone else's drinking with the threat of getting caught, I was temporarily cast aside.

Sometimes drink becomes a challenge to be overcome and, in effect, an initiation. If you can't keep up with everyone else's drinking, then you can't belong to the group. There's a strange logic that unless you can drink eight drinks, you're weak.

Challenges and ordeals were central to primitive initiation practices because it was difficult to leave one identity and personality and emerge into another one. It was through ordeals and chaos that the new identity emerged. Drinking, for Koren, became an ordeal, a very physical and real one, after she left hospital.

 I am hangover free due to the large bags of saline pumped through my forearm's thin veins. Still, I climb the stairs back to my room and sleep for the rest of the day. It's like slipping back into the hole of the blackout – in sleep, I can forget again.

Tomorrow, I'll go for the second day of the young writer's conference, telling the tweed-jacketed director only that I've been sick. In a low-lit corner classroom, I'll try to write a poem I decide to call "Lush", but I won't be able to come up with more than a first few words, scarred by cross outs.

I know the whole ordeal needs to be written about. But two days afterward, I am still far too close to the night to see it clearly …Years will pass before I can see the night of my stomach-pumping to scale. I will need the perspective of six more years before I understand what I am looking at.

(p. 100)

into

the

deep

1 How do ordeals act as rites of initiation for teenagers? Can you explain how stomach-pumping and drug-taking can act as initiations of a sort into adulthood?

2 Ordeals can sometimes express themselves in the form of risk-taking, because if you get it wrong it's going to be some ordeal. What kind of risks do teenagers take and what can be the consequences? Why do you think teenagers take risks? Are they trying to prove themselves and, by doing so, somehow initiate themselves into adulthood?

ASIDE

Teenagers and Risk

It would appear that teenagers take more risks than children and adults and consequently end up in more trouble. There are many possible reasons for this behaviour. Teenagers may take risks as a way of

fitting in: 'I'll look cool'. Another reason, however, centres around a part of the brain known as the frontal cortex. This part of the adult brain assesses danger and decides something is too risky. This part of the brain is only developing in the adolescent, and hence the difficulty assessing danger. Furthermore, when we take risks and succeed, the brain secretes a hormone called dopamine, which gives us a feeling of pleasure. The teenage brain doesn't secrete dopamine to the same extent as the adult brain and one theory suggests that teenagers therefore have to take greater risks to get the same feeling.

into
the
deep

Based on the material presented to you in the last chapter on ancient rites of passage and the extracts from Koren's book, what elements of initiation can you find in other aspects of culture i.e. fashion, music, make-up, film, sport, leisure, entertainment? Can you identify songs or films that seem to have elements of initiation in them?

You might break into groups and base your discussion on some of the following:

- Separation – Do teenagers separate themselves from the adult group? How is this expressed?
- Isolation – 'Do Not Disturb'. Do teenagers want to be left alone? Why?
- Confusion/chaos/death – Are teenagers confused about their identity? Does life seem chaotic at times? Does it appear that a part of their identity is dying?
- Transition/transformation – Is there a feeling that things are changing?
- Threshold zone – Do teenagers sometimes feel in a 'twilight zone'?
- Challenges/ordeals – Are there challenges/ordeals that teenagers experience or create that act as passages or initiations?

into
the
deep

Chapter Four

LIMIT EXPERIENCES AND
THE THEORY OF RITUAL

Between a Rock and a Hard Place

On Saturday, 26 April 2003, Aron Ralston, a twenty-seven-year-old outdoorsman and adventurer, set off for a day's hike through a remote part of Utah. He was very much into hiking on his own for days in remote regions. Eight miles from his truck, in the middle of a deep and narrow canyon, he was climbing down off a wedged boulder when suddenly the rock came loose. Before he could get out of the way, the falling stone pinned his right hand and wrist against the canyon wall. After forty-five minutes of frantically trying to move the boulder, Aron realised it wouldn't budge. He was stuck. In his backpack, Aron had some climbing equipment, a rope and a multi-tool, but no jacket, and only insignificant amounts of water and food. It wasn't much – certainly not enough to last until help could arrive. He had to get himself out.

Zion National Park, Utah

At first, Aron used the tool's knife to try to chip away at the boulder, but after ten hours he had made only a tiny dent. He then rigged up a pulley system to heave the boulder up off his trapped arm, but the rock was too heavy. On Sunday, his hand already dead, Aron considered cutting off his arm. The knife was sharp enough to pierce the flesh but wasn't sharp enough to saw through the bones. He concluded that a serious attempt to sever his arm would be a slow act of suicide. As he eliminated his options one by one, Aron faced the full horror of his predicament. No one knew where he was; no one was coming to rescue him. This was bad.

Soon his water supply was gone and Aron was forced to drink his own urine to stay hydrated, but even that grotesque supply disappeared. By the end of the fourth day, he had given up and began to accept death and its immediate inevitability. Convinced he wouldn't survive, he scratched his own epitaph onto the walls of his rock tomb – 'RIP ARON OCT 75 APR 03'.

As you can imagine, Aron had a lot of time to think while entombed in the canyon. He decided to leave a message on his camcorder for his friends and family:

> In retrospect, I've learned a lot. One of the things I'm learning here is that I didn't enjoy the people's company that I was with enough, or as much as I could have. A lot of really good people have spent a lot of time with me. Very often I would tend to ignore or diminish their presence in seeking the essence of the experience. All that's to say, I'm figuring some things out.
>
> My rambling explanation eases the guilt I feel for my selfishness. Bringing to mind those memories has lifted my spirit and even made me smile despite my present circumstances. That I spent so much of my time leaving my friends behind for solo trips, or even for some alone time when I was with them, reveals a self-centredness that displeases me. The memories evoking the most gratitude for my life are of times with my family and friends. I am beginning to

Limit Experiences and
the Theory of Ritual

understand the priceless nature of their company, and it depresses me to realise that wasn't always the focus of our time together. "

DISCUSS

1 Why do you think Aron began to think about his life in such a deep manner? Why did he think about the quality of his relationships?
2 Can you identify other experiences that might force people to examine their lives? What kind of questions might such experiences provoke?

At 10.32 on the morning of 1 May, the first day of summer, something dramatic happened. Aron started to poke at the carcass that was his hand with his knife. He slit the decaying flesh and a strange hissing sound was released. The smell was noxious. It suddenly dawned on him that his body was beginning to slowly decay and the death process that had begun in his hand would soon seep into his entire system. In a panic he thrashed around trying to yank himself free.

Aron Ralston

" I thrash myself forward and back, side to side, up and down, down and up. I scream out in pure hate, shrieking as I batter my body to and fro against the canyon walls, losing every bit of composure that I've struggled so intensely to maintain. Then I feel my arm bend unnaturally in the

into the deep

Limit Experiences and the Theory of Ritual

unbudging grip of chockstone. An epiphany strikes me with the magnificent glory of a holy intervention and instantly brings my seizure to a halt. If I torque my arm far enough, I can break my forearm bones.

Aron then dropped all of his weight to the canyon floor repeatedly until both bones in his forearm snapped. Once the bones were out of the way, he proceeded to cut through the sinews, muscle, arteries and flesh until his arm was finally free.

It is 11:32 am, Thursday, May 1, 2003. For the second time in my life, I am being born. This time I am being delivered from the canyon's pink womb, where I have been incubating. This time I am a grown adult, and I understand the significance and power of this birth as none of us can when it happens the first time. The value of my family, my friends, and my passions well up a heaving rush of energy that is like the burst I get approaching a hard-earned summit, multiplied by ten thousand. Pulling tight the remaining connective tissues of my arm, I rock the knife against the wall, and the final thin strand of flesh tears loose; tensile force rips the skin apart more than the blade cuts it.

BETWEEN A ROCK AND A HARD PLACE

ARON RALSTON

A crystalline moment shatters, and the world is a different place. Where there was confinement, now there is release. Recoiling from my sudden liberation, my left arm flings down the canyon, opening my shoulders to the south, and I fall back against the northern wall of the canyon, my mind surfing on euphoria. As I stare at the wall where not twelve hours ago I etched "RIP ARON OCT 75 APR 03," a voice shouts in my head:

"I AM FREE!"

into

the

deep

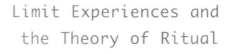

DISCUSS

1 In your opinion, what eventually gave Aron the strength to break his own arm, hack through his own flesh and break free?
2 Would you have done the same? Do you think there was another way out?
3 What do you think he learned about himself from the experience?
4 Why does he say that he was now a grown adult? In what way might his ordeal have been a rite of passage for him into adulthood?

LIMIT EXPERIENCES

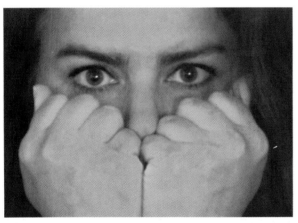

The story of Aron Ralston impacts us on many levels. There's the sense of awe at the sheer endurance involved and the incredible will to survive, so strong that it allowed Aron to self-amputate. Such experiences, which push a person to the very limits of their being, are called limit experiences. Needless to say, they are very powerful.

Limit experiences force us to the edge of our own self-understanding? What would you do if you found yourself trapped in a canyon with diminishing food and water supplies? Well, ultimately you don't know until you're there. Perhaps you might think of another way to escape or you might just give in under the weight of exhaustion and let nature take its course. But the fascinating thing about limit experiences is that they teach us a lot about ourselves. We learn what we are made up of; we learn how much more there is to us; we learn that we are not who we think we are. In limit experiences, we discover who we truly are; we discover the boundaries of our own identity.

into

the

deep

IMPULSE OR INSTINCT

In 2001, a group of students were undertaking a lifeguard course along the banks of the River Liffey in Dublin. Suddenly, they were jarred by the sound of a car plunging into the river. All the students were training to be lifeguards, to save another person's life, but all were paralysed by the dramatic situation unfolding before them. All except one student, who immediately plunged into the waters and swam to the car. He managed to pull a woman to safety. Hailed as a hero by the local press, he later said that he didn't really think about the situation at all. He just jumped in. But plenty others didn't.

DISCUSS

What did the above experience tell the student about himself?

LIMIT EXPERIENCES AND SPORT

Susan Sing was a member of the US world rowing team. She has written about limit situations in sport, those times when you reach the boundary or edge of your own ability to compete and then somehow you find that extra bit and win. She remembers as a teenager running the Berwick Marathon. She started off well and soon switched to automatic pilot. Later, with the finishing line in sight, she remembers hitting the pavement hard. She was down and out and second place was slipping from her grasp.

into

the

deep

Limit Experiences and
the Theory of Ritual

> I lay there a few seconds and I remember my inner world screaming at my body – Get up! Get up! And in my stupor of exhaustion, fever and sweat surrounded by snowflakes and grey skies – like today – I heard footsteps. I knew I had to get up, officials were running to my aid, my friends and even strangers were yelling, "Don't touch her! Don't disqualify her! She can do it!" I got to my hands and knees and I looked down at the asphalt of Market Street hill; thirty years later I can still feel its cold, flat, road-smooth texture beneath my fingers and palms, as I pushed up off of it like a swimmer launching from a platform. All I remember was hearing the breathing and the footsteps behind me. But they stayed behind me and I didn't lose second place.

DISCUSS

Do you know of anyone who has been in a limit situation in sport, or have you been in such a situation yourself? Where does the athlete get the extra bit that's needed to succeed?

LIMIT EXPERIENCES AND THE THIRD PLACE

According to Sing, people are fascinated by limit situations in sport. It's why stadiums are filled every weekend. When Aron Ralston was stuck in the canyon, he was forced to discover something new about himself that saved his life and he was never the same again. The same thing happens in sport, as athletes are continuously forced to the edge of their being. Sing explains it thus:

into

the

deep

> I am not a theologian or psychologist, but I have spent the better part of my life guiding athletes to this precipice, this teetering edge of performance, bringing people to that place, that moment where they seek to go. Why? I believe they do it, we do it,

to see what we're made of – meaning to see if there is anything more, anything other than flesh and sweat and blood. We do it to see if there is a soul looking at us in the extreme fumes of exhaustion. **"**

Sing says elsewhere that many modern athletes draw from the vast fountain of wisdom that is ancient Greek philosophy. The ancient Greeks had much to say about sport and it was from them that the idea of Olympians originated. Their theory was called *arête*. Basically it states, as Sing mentions above, that the athlete goes to a third place in the extreme elements of sport. While the athlete must focus mind and body, according to *arête* they must also draw on spirit or soul.

This theory is very relevant to Aron's experience in the canyon. You may remember that moment when he realised how to get free – by breaking his arm. Ralston described that moment thus: 'An

Athletes trained in this Olympia facility in its ancient heyday

epiphany strikes me with the magnificent glory of a holy intervention.' Later during a TV interview, he recalled how that moment was an intense religious experience for him. An epiphany is a revelation of spirit or soul, and Ralston believed that his salvation came from his own soul.

There is little doubt but that something quite amazing happens at limit situations or those edge places where we go beyond what we know about ourselves. It is also apparent that going to the edge and beyond is tied up with an experience of spirit. Are you interested in going beyond the limits of your own known universe? Are you interested in finding out more about who you really can be? If you are, then read on as we delve back into archaic wisdom. The really good news is that to reach a limit situation, you don't have to collapse in a race or find the nearest boulder and somehow trap your arm under it. You could, but why bother if there's an easier way?

into
the
deep

Limit Experiences and
the Theory of Ritual

BOREDOM VS. LIMIT/THRESHOLD EXPERIENCES: THE THEORY OF RITUAL

This assignment is quite easy. All you are required to do is get bored. So just stop doing everything in class and start staring at the windows and walls and ceiling. You'd better do it in silence, as some talk can be interesting. Just look around you and become really bored. Look at your shoes for a while. Look at someone else's shoes. Just be bored for a few minutes and then discuss the following questions:

* How much of the average day would you find yourself bored?

* What do you usually do when you're bored?

* Where are you usually bored?

* What do you do to stop yourself being bored?

* What kind of experiences save you from boredom? Describe the opposite of being bored.

into
the
deep

Boredom is the exact opposite of limit experiences. It's stale and grey, it yawns and snoozes. Boredom is torturously slow, it's lukewarm and faintly sweet. It's nothingness, and some people will go to extremes to beat it.

THE THEORY BIT

According to the theory of ritual, the in-between place is all-important because of what happens there. The theorists call it the threshold. Look around your classroom. On the occasion that you may be bored, you look at the door longingly, wishing for the bell to ring and the door to swing open. Look at the

doorway now, because the next time you go through it for a split second you'll find yourself in the threshold zone, that foot of space between the classroom and corridor that is nowhere – a place between two places. You long for that threshold because it means out – freedom.

into
the
deep

Threshold experiences change us, which is what makes them so fascinating and attractive. Aron's threshold experience of being seriously stuck changed him: he appreciated friends, relationships and family more than ever before. The threshold experience of the athlete, that limit place where they become winners, is also transformative.

Threshold experiences can be summarised as follows:

* They are not boring but are in fact at the opposite end of life experience.
* They transform us – energise us – change takes place.
* They allow us to reflect on life.
* They change our perspective on things – the world seems different.
* They bring us in touch with our own soul or spirit.

In the next chapter, we will delve more into the nature of ritual and threshold experiences. In particular, we will investigate the spiritual dimension of those experiences.

ASSIGNMENT

1 Give examples in class of rituals that you have experienced that you felt were transformative and energised you.

2 Give examples of religious rituals that you felt brought you in touch with your own spirituality and maybe even changed your perspective on things.

into

the

deep

Limit Experiences and
the Theory of Ritual

Chapter Five

OPTIMAL EXPERIENCES

In this chapter we will start to examine the implications of rituals for your life. We want to push you to the edge of who you are or who you think you are. Maybe you don't want to go there ... maybe you're happy with the way things are. You can make up your own mind.

Often in life people feel that they are stuck in a rut – life is going nowhere ... it's stale, boring. Relationships are unfulfilling and everything seems lifeless and meaningless. Life is just dull and you couldn't be bothered.

DISCUSS

Describe what it's like when life becomes dull and meaningless. Did you ever feel that life was unfulfilling ... that you were stuck in a rut? What was it like? Did you feel that there should be more to life? How do you think you should go about getting yourself out of a rut?

EXTREME SPORTS

A good image of 'the rut' is the couch potato. Life in front of the TV, remote in one hand, snacks in the other – you get the picture. Michael Bane was a couch potato. Then one day he decided to do something about it … and it was a radical idea. He decided to compile a list of thirteen extreme sports … and then do them. First a word about extreme sports.

Denali, the highest peak in North America

Extreme sports can be summarised in one short sentence: the consequences of failure are serious. Failure here means injury or death. Bane did some training and employed the services of some extreme sports gurus. One such guru, Steve Igg, brought Bane on an intensive training session before he attempted to climb the Denali, the highest peak in North America. He forced him to trek through miles and miles of snow, blizzard, rocks and cliffs. Bane was on his last legs and he started moaning about the intense levels of pain, discomfort and exhaustion. Igg stopped in the snow and stared at Bane. In a slow hypnotic voice, he explained to Bane that on the Denali, 'If you make a mistake … you are going to die.'

Later on in this book we will tell you what happened to Bane on the Denali, but for now we need to examine why exactly someone would want to push themselves to such extremes.

'Awareness Has No Frontiers'

In his book *Over the Edge: A Regular Guy's Odyssey into Extreme Sports*, Bane admits from the outset that he was preoccupied with the edge of his own life. He thought he knew himself, but what he knew was so boring that he felt there had to be more to his life and to himself. It was like the centre of his life was the couch and

the TV. It was dull and stale, but he was convinced that out around the edges, the limits that he could force himself to, he would discover the secrets to his existence. He just had to become more aware of who he really was.

He studied the writings of martial artist Bruce Lee, who stated that 'awareness has no frontier; it is giving your whole being, without exclusion'. Bane knew there was something to this statement. He studied further and came across the writings of George Leonard, who wrote the following about the edge: 'Whatever your age, your upbringing, or your education, what you are made of is mostly unused potential. It is your evolutionary destiny to use what is unused, to learn and keep on learning as long as you live ... How to begin the journey? You need only take the first step. When? There's always now.'

Bruce Lee

Becoming aware of who you really are has no frontiers. You may be sitting in a classroom now and you may well have decided who you are and what your capabilities are. Exam results or comments of others may have pigeonholed you into a little box. 'This is who you are ...' That is not the truth. Only you can discover who you are and there is no limit to your ability or your identity.

No matter where you come from, how rich your family, how good your exam results, you are unused potential. No matter what people say about you and no matter what you say about yourself, the full story of who you are and can be is as yet untold.

DISCUSS

Do you think people limit their understanding of who they are? Do you agree that you are unused potential? Why do people limit themselves and others? Give examples of how people put others down and put themselves down? Why does this happen? How destructive is it?

into the deep

MOMENTS OF LIBERATION

Richard Dunne in action
(Photo by Ryan Pierse/Getty Images)

The Irish international soccer player Richard Dunne began his playing career with Manchester City. In those early days he was a rather sloppy and undisciplined character, eating and drinking whatever he felt like. Now and then his lack of fitness and his weight were exposed by the brilliance and speed of some of the best strikers in the Premiership. On Friday the 13th he arrived into City's training ground smelling like a brewery. It was the last straw for manager Kevin Keegan. He wanted him sacked. Fortunately for Dunne, he was tied into a lengthy contract and Keegan was forced to adopt a different strategy. Dunne would be forced to live like a monk.

> He was put on a one-month crash course involving eight-hour days and six-day weeks. More than that, his lifestyle was put under an unforgiving light. Daily, the club put him on a weighing scales and monitored his blood for evidence of alcohol. He could conceal nothing. Four years on, he weighs 15 stone (and falling), is captain of Manchester City and widely seen as a model professional. When manager, Stuart Pearce, offered him the (captain's) armband in pre-season, Dunne felt he had reached a closure of sorts. A point of Liberation.

(Vincent Hogan, *Irish Independent*, 2/9/06)

into the deep

DISCUSS

Dunne was unfit and overweight. Four years later he is the captain of the club and a 'model professional'. He was most definitely unused potential. Why do you think his progress into his unused potential was described as a liberation?

OPTIMAL EXPERIENCES AND THE THEORY OF FLOW

We now need to go back to Bane. He decided to get off the couch, get out of the rut and do something with his life. Here's 'The List' (lucky thirteen!) he made up:

- Windsurf Big Air
- The Kamikaze Downhill Race
- Escape from Alcatraz Triathlon
- Whitewater off a waterfall
- Rock climb
- Cave dive (seriously, seriously dangerous)
- Ice climb
- Skydive
- Skate marathon
- Dive really deep
- Bad Water Death Valley run
- Iditarod bike race
- Denali

We can't go through all the items on this list but let's have a look at the Kamikaze Downhill Race. You might think this is about getting on a bike and cycling downhill. So did Bane. His instructor Karen took him out on the track and he thought he was doing really well, until she pulled him up short and explained that to compete in the race he would have to reach speeds of sixty miles an hour …

"Follow me," she says, then disappears down a steep gravel road. I follow, and by the second switchback I can still see the dust kicked up by her. She is waiting for me by the fourth switchback.

"You are never," she says, without preamble, barely bothering with a smile, "going to get down this mountain if you don't let go of the brakes."

I notice that for the first time my hands have locked into rigid claws, reflexively curved around the brake handles. I tentatively try to loosen a finger, but the muscles in my wrist seem to have seized up.

into

the

deep

"See?" she says, pointing at my claws.

"What happens if I let go and can't stop?" I ask, that being a perfectly valid question in my book.

"Silly Michael", says Karen. "You go off the mountain, and you die."

"Oh."

"It's all in the brakes," Karen is saying. "Don't use 'em."

I nod intelligently. What I'm actually thinking is, *Riiiiight. Bag the brakes. Wait till I hit something solid, maybe a tree to stop ...*

"You ready?" Karen asks. I nod, and we again head down the mountain.

Faith in the machine ... faith in the machine ... We are picking up speed. The bikes fly through the curves. I'm hanging a few feet behind her rear wheel. I ride the biological waves sluicing through my body, adrenaline making time go all mushy and soft around the edges, so slow that I see a piece of gravel, caught by the tires, slowly arc and bounce away, over the edge.

We fly into a long, steep drop, and I rip past her, taking advantage of my weight and gravity. I follow a line chosen by the bike, a bump here, a shift of weight there. I am *here* but not *here*, in the calm centre of a data storm. Sight, sound, smell, the feel of the wind against my face, the terrain through the pedal against the sole of my shoes to my rapidly numbing hands. The same feel of the big wind against a small sail, the curious blending of physical and mental.

into
the
deep

DISCUSS

The above extract explains why people do extreme sports. It's that experience and feeling that people crave. How would you describe the above experience? Would you like it? What is it that you would like/dislike?

One way to describe the buzz of extreme sports is as an intense awareness of the present moment. Bane tracked down something called the theory of flow. He realised that during moments of risk and adrenaline rush, something strange happens to time. We think of time as a past, present and future and quite often we are preoccupied with past or future events. In class, for example, would it be true to say that often your mind is off elsewhere in some past or future event?

Our minds do that a lot but some experiences, such as extreme sports, force us to really live the present moment. Our senses are so stimulated that present, speed, rush, adrenaline … is all that matters.

Dr Csikszentmihalyi (try Dr C for short!) refers to this experience as 'flow'. In *Flow: The Psychology of Optimal Experience* he looks at the psychology behind optimal experiences and he writes: 'When all a person's relevant skills are needed to cope with the challenges of the situation, that person's attention is completely absorbed by the activity. There is no excess psychic energy left over to process any information but what  the activity offers. As a result, one of the most universal and distinctive features of optimal experiences takes place: people become so involved in what they are doing that the activity becomes spontaneous, almost automatic; they stop being aware of themselves as separate from the actions they are performing.'

To summarise, we can state that there are three distinct features of optimal experiences and flow:

- Time gets fuzzy and the **present moment** is all there is. It's an intense experience of now.

- Optimal experiences are called 'optimal' because they are your best possible experiences. This is a person experiencing their **full potential**, their best bits, abilities, challenges and accomplishments. It's the 'Yeah, I can do it' feeling.

- During these experiences, a person doesn't feel separated from reality and the world around them. It's the opposite of boredom and daydreaming. The person is **totally involved and connected** with the world around them and, significantly, with their own bodies.

THE SPIRITUAL DIMENSION

The obvious question is what has all this got to do with religion? People might be tempted to think that religion can be quite boring at times, yet optimal experiences seem far from that. Some who have read Michael Bane's book claim that it is an account not just of a physical and mental journey but of a spiritual one as well. If so, it raises the possibility that religion has something to do with very cool and radical experiences. What do you think?

DISCUSS

From what you've read so far about Michael Bane, extreme sports and the theory of flow, how, in your opinion, could 'The List' be interpreted as a spiritual adventure?

into

the

deep

Optimal Experiences

THE SPIRITUAL JOURNEY AS OPTIMAL EXPERIENCE

 There is no easy way into another world.

(James Slater)

The reason that Bane's journey was described as spiritual was exactly because it contained the elements of flow that we identified above. Spiritual experiences are rooted in the present moment. For example, you may at some time have witnessed a sunrise or sunset, a huge moon in the sky, a thunderstorm, fork lightning or maybe you walked along a beach at midnight with a loved one. Secretly, you may have thought to yourself that in that moment you glimpsed something of the divine. Spirituality is also an expression of your full potential as a human being. It is about being connected to the earth, to those around you and, most importantly, to your own inner self.

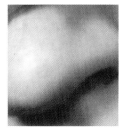

That's all very fine, but it leaves us with a problem. If your school caters for extreme sports (which for insurance reasons it probably doesn't), you can head off during your next class and have an optimal experience, and there, in that optimal moment, you might well witness something of the divine in the world and in yourself. But for those of you who are in schools that don't do deep-sea diving, kamikaze bike runs and escape from Alcatraz swims, you are left sitting in your seats with your heads. You also have a heart, a pair of lungs and two eyeballs. On the front of your face there may well be two nostrils. Strangely enough, according to the most ancient religious and spiritual traditions, that's exactly what you need to experience your own spirituality as optimal experience.

The Challenge

If you are interested in undertaking a spiritual journey and experiencing it as an optimal experience, you need to know that it will be challenging, just as challenging as 'The List' was ... *there is no easy way into another world ...*

into
the
deep

Optimal experiences, the theory of flow and extreme sports give us a very good idea of what the spiritual journey will require. You will have to be able to experience the present moment (far more difficult than you think). You will have to push yourself to the limits of your own self-understanding and potential, and finally you are about to get seriously connected to yourself, others and the world around you.

In primitive rites of passage, secrets of the spiritual world were revealed to those who were about to become adults, and as you are about to become adults, secrets will be revealed to you as well. If you are interested, then it's time to go to the next chapter, where we will begin by taking you along the path of the martial artist.

CHRISTIAN SPIRITUALITY

The word spirituality comes from the word spirit, which in Hebrew (*ruach*) means breath or life force. Christian spirituality is about how our human experience makes known to us God's presence in our lives and how we then respond to that presence in the way we live and the way we pray. In other words, it is about how our human spirit relates to the spirit of God present in our world.

Human beings can come to know God because God has revealed himself to human beings in the past and continues to reveal himself to us today. Throughout history back to biblical times God revealed himself to people in the context of their lived experience. For example, in the Old Testament in the Hebrew people's experience of captivity and liberation; in the New Testament in the experience of Jesus, what he said and what he did; today in the work of people who strive to bring about justice for others and in the wonder and beauty of creation, which is the work of God.

Our spirituality is about how we make sense of the experience of God in our lives. It is in our everyday lives that we experience God and it is in our everyday lives that we choose to respond.

Chapter Six

MEDITATION

Meditation is above all a quest.
(CCC, 2705)

❛ We are all looking for the answer to the undying question: why am I here? For me I found the answer in the least likely place I looked: deep within myself.

Once we understand our true potential and we go through life a day at a time, we recognise that there is nearly nothing that we cannot accomplish and endure, if we but remember from whence we came. ❜

(Richard Pelzer,
A Teenager's Journey: Surviving Adolescence)

❛ Out of his infinite glory, may he give you the power through his Spirit for your hidden self to grow strong. ❜

(Ephesians 3:26)

THE INNER BODY EXPERIENCE

Humanity, since the earliest times, has been in pursuit of the spiritual. Of all the different tribes that have been discovered in the deepest forests, one thing remains constant: almost without exception, they have rituals and rites that acknowledge the presence of some transcendent force in their lives. The quest for the spiritual is ever-present in all places and at all times.

We promised you some secrets about the spiritual quest, and Mr Bane on his bike at sixty mph down the hill, with no brakes, introduced us to it. You might remember from the last chapter that during his optimal experience he said: 'Sight, sound, smell,

the feel of the wind against my face, the terrain through the pedal against the sole of my shoes to my rapidly numbing hands. The same feel of the big wind against a small sail, the curious blending of physical and mental.' It is here, at this moment, that Bane begins to have what can be called a spiritual experience.

What you may not know is that one of the most ancient routes to the spiritual is actually through the body. Hence, for this chapter, all you need are your lungs, eyeballs, heart and nostrils.

Consider the martial artist. The funny thing about martial artists – who, in one well-directed blow, can kill a man – is that peace reigns in their lives; they do not get into fights.

Martial arts is not about violence. The discipline of the martial artist is directed towards an inner spiritual journey. In Japan, martial arts developed in conjunction with Buddhist teachings and, according to Michael Maliszewski in his book *Spiritual Dimensions of the Martial Arts*, 'Espousing such virtues as justice, courage, loyalty, honour, veracity, benevolence, and politeness, the classical warrior was primarily concerned with experiencing a spiritual awakening by achieving the state of *seishi choetsu*, a frame of mind in which one's thoughts transcended life and death' (p. 63).

The key phrase here is 'frame of mind'. The warrior uses techniques and the discipline of martial arts to achieve a particular change of mind and, significantly, he uses his body to do this. According to legend, the Buddhist monks discovered that their disciples found the strict disciplines of the spiritual journey a bit boring, so they developed and utilised the techniques of the martial artist. Now the disciples would continue their inner spiritual journey much more efficiently by learning the techniques of the warrior. The monks discovered that

into
the
deep

one particular aspect of martial arts was vital to the spiritual journey.

In Japan, the modern *budo* system of martial arts was developed as a form of spiritual training and self-defence. The founder, Ueshiba Morihei, still practised the art at eighty years of age. He created it as a method of self-defence based on the principles of non-resistance, which gains control of the attacker's movements so as to neutralise his aggressive momentum. The system emphasises harmony of mind and body. It was impossible for any opponent to overpower him with violence or physical force. For those of you, male or female, who are interested in minimising the effects of ageing, the following is worth noting.

Ueshiba Morihei

Ueshiba prepared for combat by seating himself in prayer, cross-legged, eyes closed and palms downward on his knees. The key to his incredible agility, response, speed and strength was *fudoshin*, or 'immovable mind'. It is the mind, not the physical strength of the body, that lies at the core of martial arts.

into

the

deep

IMMOVABLE MIND – THE FIRST STEP ON THE SPIRITUAL JOURNEY

It is recognised within all spiritual traditions that the attainment of immovable mind is the first step in a person's spiritual journey. The following is an example of a prayer used by a martial artist to ready himself for combat:

> 'I present myself to the Creator
> from the beginning,
> I represent myself to the best of my abilities,
> I ask to receive from the Creator
> in the knowledge of the art
> the things that I do not see
> to engrave in my heart
> until the end.'

(from *Spiritual Dimension of the Martial Arts*)

Once the prayer is said, the martial artist begins his spiritual journey into his mind and body to achieve immovable mind. Immovable mind is totally focused and concentrated, so the warrior is absolutely aware of the threat of his opponent at that present moment. When faced with a deadly opponent, the martial artist cannot be daydreaming about next Sunday's match or thinking about whether he left the gas on at home. He must be totally in the present moment. A distracted mind can literally mean death.

into the deep

DISCUSS

1 Why do you think immovable mind is so powerful?
2 Immovable mind is totally focused and concentrated on the present moment. There can be no thoughts of past or future events. When do you experience immovable mind?

ARRIVING AT THE BEST YOU

We noted in the chapter on rites of passage how primitive tribes believe that the potential within the youth to be an adult comes from within their own spirituality. Your spirituality contains the best you, just as the martial artist prayed before his combat: 'I represent myself to the best of my abilities.'

We will now journey into your own spirituality, using the knowledge we have gained about limit experiences and ritual, the threshold zone, mind–body harmony and the power of the present moment in the immovable mind. It is a journey into *the best you*. You need to think about your potential to be an adult in the world, to be a force of truth, justice, inner strength, a person connected with God, the world around you and your fellow human beings. Remember: 'There is no easy way into another world.'

In trying to find the best you, we reach the first major obstacle … your own head.

An Experiment

You needn't go to the science lab for this experiment. All you need is your own head – and it needs to be awake. Look around the classroom and gently wake up anyone who is asleep. Also, if one or two are daydreaming, wake them up too.

Step One

In order to experience your own spirituality, you need to create a threshold zone in your own head, as it is at thresholds that things happen. The first problem is all those voices in your head. Become aware of your own thinking, the jumble of thoughts that spins around in your head all day. Stop everything in class for five minutes and just listen to the thoughts in your own head.

Step Two

According to research, each one of us processes around 50,000 thoughts a day. That's all the stuff that just pops into your head like … I'm so bored … I've very little credit … feels like a spot is erupting on my chin … I can't stand the look of her … when will

this class be over ... blah blah blah. The Buddhists call this 'Monkey Mind', because your mind jumps around from one thought to the next.

A most interesting thing that researchers have discovered is that 90 per cent of the thoughts in our heads are negative. Most of them are actually based around fear and worry. Now think about your own thoughts again. What percentage of your thinking would you class as negative? Look at the list below.

I'm so bored

I don't have enough money

I look terrible in this

People don't like me

I hate him, he thinks he's it

I wish I had ...

It's not fair

I'll never be able to do that

I'm no good at maths

Step Three

Experiencing your own inner spirituality necessarily means an experience of God. So now we need to tell you something about what God is like (we will cover this area in more detail in a later part of the book). Remember the martial artist's prayer: 'I present myself to the Creator from the beginning ...' It is very significant that the spiritual masters addressed God as the Creator; the reason they did so is very relevant to what's going on in your head.

God is the creator of all that is: you, the universe, everything. Our God is abundant and is the wonderful provider. God is absolute potential. So God doesn't do negative thoughts: Will I create a universe? No, it will never work ... it will never get past

into

the

deep

the committee stages ... how will I get planning permission? Negativity won't get you into God space, so we'll have to try to get rid of those negative thoughts. And because they make up 90 per cent of your thinking, we'll just have to shut down thinking, full stop.

So in step three you have to stop absolutely all thoughts in your head. Don't have any thoughts ... try it. See if it works ...

Most people find the above exercise difficult. For some reason your mind doesn't want to stop thinking. Perhaps it's some remnant of a primitive survival mechanism, from the time when we lived in caves and could be attacked at any stage. So the mind worries, is fearful, and it thinks and thinks and thinks.

[Hint: If you can't stop your mind thinking, try this: relax and then ask yourself, 'What will my next thought be?' You should experience a little mind-gap.]

ASIDE
In one of his books, Carl Jung recalled a conversation he had with a Native American chief who pointed out to him that in his perception, most white people have tense faces, staring eyes and a cruel demeanour. He said, 'They are always seeking something. What are they seeking? The whites always want something. They are always uneasy and restless. We don't know what they want. We think they are mad.'

into
the
deep

Usually during the day we listen to the voices in our heads, watch the home-made movies constantly playing in our minds. Up to now you probably thought that was you – you were your thoughts. Now that you've begun to listen to your own thoughts and even shut them off for a moment or two, you're beginning to realise that there's another deeper and wiser you behind the constant thinking you. Already you're going inside and finding the better you. You've started the journey.

DISCUSS Did you become aware at any stage of the deeper you, the one that can stand back and critique your own mind? What did that feel like? Was it peaceful? Did it feel like a good break? Would you like more of that? Did you like no-mind-time?

A spiritual practice has developed throughout the centuries that allows people to switch off their thoughts in order to access the deeper part of themselves. This practice stops the negative thoughts so that the person can experience the divine within. The practice utilises two secrets that many are ignorant of, secrets known by the likes of Michael Bane and the martial artists: that mind–body harmony is essential and that the present moment is the way to access the inner life. The practice is called meditation.

THE MIND–BODY THRESHOLD

The martial artists knew that using the body was a method of spiritual enlightenment, as did countless others from a variety of spiritual traditions. They also knew about the need for a ritual or threshold to facilitate their meditation. In the next part of this chapter, we will begin using some meditative techniques, but first as a class you need to create a threshold place for yourselves. A threshold space allows you to separate from your old way of doing and thinking. It tells your mind that something new is happening, something is changing, you are changing.

CREATING A THRESHOLD SPACE

A threshold space allows people to behave in a different manner than they would normally behave. Meditation works best in an environment that is free from distractions.

into

the

deep

- If possible, you should use the prayer room in your school for meditation.
- Make sure the space is warm and comfortable, and you may like to have some suitable music playing in the background.
- Candles can create an atmosphere during meditation and can act as a focus for people's attention.
- Oil burners can also add to the atmosphere and are easily available.
- Finally, make sure that people are seated comfortably.

USING THE BODY

In the threshold space that you have created, you now need to follow certain steps. The objective here is to stop your thinking. You may need to practise the steps many times, but as you do so, at home, in church or in the prayer room, you will gradually uncover the deeper self. You will now begin to use your body to focus your mind on the present moment. You will begin to journey into the territory of optimal experiences.

Try the following meditation exercise in a class group or alone:

- *Find a quiet place in the school or at home. Sit in silence or play some quiet, relaxing music. Sit with your back upright and your hands, palms up, resting on your lap. Place your feet firmly on the floor. Your body becomes relaxed, as does your mind. Become aware of the room and the noises around you and then gently close your eyes and become aware of your own posture and breathing. Notice how your breathing is rhythmical and steady. See how your body rises and falls with each in-breath and each out-breath. As*

into

the

deep

you focus on your breathing, accept the thoughts that enter your mind, yet return to your breathing and slowly let your thoughts fade into the background as you journey downwards and inwards with your breath.

- *Journey inwards into the centre of your being ... focusing always on your in-breath and out-breath ... Acknowledge thoughts and gently let them pass away ... Continue on the journey into your inner place of silence and stillness ... Let all worries fade away and allow your mind to enter the peace and emptiness of your inner self ... Let your breathing become slower and deeper ... allow yourself to relax and rest ... enjoy your inner peace ... feel the calm deep within, free from worry or anxiety ... breathe ... deeply and restfully ... Focus now on the calm within you ... Focus on the comfort of your own inner peace ... Stay in this place ... content in its warmth and stillness ...*

- *In your own time, slowly become aware of your surroundings, the noises and the room around you. Count yourself back to opening your eyes, focusing on your feelings of calm and peacefulness.*

THE POWER OF NOW

When Moses went up Mount Sinai, he had an incredible experience, absolutely mind-blowing ... he was one of the first human beings to encounter God. You can imagine yourself in such a situation. You're on your way home from school and you encounter God. What do you say? Moses decided to ask God's name. God replied: 'I am who I am.' Our God is a God of the present moment.

DISCUSS

Identify the times in your life when you are totally in the present moment. What are the events or times when you are totally caught up in what you are doing? Imagine yourself out at clubs or concerts with your friends. Are these present moment events? Why do you like them?

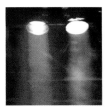

In your discussions, you may have come to realise that, like extreme sports, the best experiences occur when we are totally focused on the present moment. Why? Because if our minds are not focused on the present moment, they wander off into the past or future, and 90 per cent of this will be negative. A constant routine of meditation, which brings you into the present moment, helps you to become more focused.

DISCUSS

1 Many commentators say that our society has become very materialistic, with people buying lots of stuff that they don't need. When you buy stuff, does it help you to be part of the present moment? Do you get a buzz from it?

2 According to one theory, the marketing people have designed the marketplace so that the buyer never arrives. It's called instrumental thinking, whereby what you buy today will be out of fashion soon and you will have to go back to the marketplace with your money. Viewed like this, in what way might buying stuff, materialism, consumerism, threaten our ability to be focused on the present moment?

CHILLING OUT IN GOD'S SPACE

The purpose of meditation is to allow us to enter our deeper inner selves where God can be experienced. We now know that such an experience can only come about in the present moment. After meditation, you will probably feel more peaceful and still within yourself. You have had a break from your own head and its uncontrolled negative thinking. You've had a break from little fears and worries, niggling thoughts about things that might never happen, confrontations and rows with people that may never occur.

So the God we are beginning to encounter is a God of stillness and peace. God is chilled out. God doesn't do worry or unnecessary fear, confrontation or anxiety. Why? Because God created all that is. Inside God resides so much power, potential and abundance that there is nothing to worry about. If at this moment you are upset, worried or fearful, then keep journeying into God's space. It's laid back, chilled. Just relax in God time and enjoy the feeling.

The famous spiritual writer Anthony de Mello wrote about this subject in a book called *Awareness*. He believed that you can only be aware of now, because the past is gone and the future doesn't and never will exist – it's the future! In the next chapter we are going to journey deeper into God space, to see if we can feel something of what the mystics discovered when they went deep into God. Mystics go so deep into God that they can no longer distinguish themselves from God! According to de Mello, mystics from all the religious traditions who have journeyed into God

into
the
deep

have all come back with the same message for humanity: the message that all is well … all is well.

If you are burdened by worry, fears or doubts about your place in the world, then be aware that those thoughts are not originating from your deeper, wiser self. They are originating from the 90 per cent of negative thoughts within you. Experiencing God teaches you one thing – how to chill, relax and be happy. Deep down in your life, in your innermost self, all is well.

> He said to his disciples, "Therefore I tell you, do not worry about your life, what you will eat, or about your body, what you will wear. For life is more than food, and the body more than clothing. Consider the ravens: they neither sow nor reap, they have neither storehouse nor barn, and yet God feeds them. Of how much more value are you than the birds! And can any of you by worrying add a single hour to your span of life? If then you are not able to do so small a thing as that, why do you worry about the rest?"
>
> (Luke 12:22-26)

> Be quiet, go within,
> see I lead you
> out beyond dark ridges
> you were not born for caves
> but sunlight breaking
> drenching everything.
> Be calm, calm beyond belief.
>
> (Lorcan Brennan, 'Little Hermit')

into
the
deep

Chapter Seven

OFF TO THE MONASTERY

MEDITATION: SOME MORE EXPERIMENTS

There are as many and varied methods of meditation as there are spiritual masters. Christians owe it to themselves to develop the desire to meditate regularly, lest they come to resemble the three first kinds of soil in the parable of the sower. But a method is only a guide; the important thing is to advance, with the Holy Spirit, along the one way of prayer: Christ Jesus.

(CCC, 2707)

In this chapter we examine the latest research into meditation. One of the reasons so much research has been done into meditation is because of the positive effects of the practice on people's health and general well-being. Stress is now a big industry and meditation would seem to be an effective way of dealing with this particular modern ailment.

However, the stress industry seems to have taken people's focus off why meditation evolved in the first place. People now use meditation to beat stress and improve their lifestyle but meditation evolved as a process that would allow us to experience our spirituality, to get rid of distractions so as to encounter God. For this reason the practice developed in monasteries.

Later in this chapter we will present you with the results of an experiment. If meditation developed in the monasteries then we thought it would be a good idea to bring some students to a monastery where they would undertake to be led further into their inner selves under the care and tuition of some monks.

DISCUSS

Do you think the problem of stress is confined to adults with jobs, long commutes, mortgages and kids or is your generation also suffering from stress? If so, what are the factors that contribute to it? How do young people deal with stress? What are the healthy ways of dealing with stress?

LOOK BETTER, FEEL BETTER, LIVE LONGER ... AND HAVE BETTER SKIN

There are many people who dismiss religion and all that goes with it as superstition. They claim that it's not relevant and it's all made up. In recent years, however, scientists and researchers have begun to take religious claims more seriously. Jesus, the great teacher advised us to go into our rooms, close the door and be still. He told us to let go of our burdens and be filled with peace and happiness. He told us how to be full of well-being. So does the silence and stillness really help?

In India there are people who have become masters of meditation techniques. They are called *yogis* and belong to the Hindu religious tradition. There was once a great yogi called Trailanga Swami, who, it was claimed, performed many miraculous feats. His spiritual lifestyle often got him in trouble with the authorities

into
the
deep

but they eventually stopped arresting him because he escaped with ease from all prisons and cells. The only known living disciple of Trailanga is a woman called Shankari Mai Jiew. Born in 1826, she received the yogi's teaching from early childhood and lived for forty years in a series of desolate Himalayan caves. She lived to be well over one-hundred years of age and every few years would appear from seclusion for religious festivals. In appearance she 'retained her black hair, sparkling teeth, and amazing energy' (*Autobiography of a Yogi* by Paramahansa Yogananda).

Statue of Shiva performing Yogic meditation

In his book *The Power of Now*, Eckhart Tolle explains the importance of the living moment. He notes the beneficial effects of meditation, and he explains the aging process and its relationship with the effects of time. The outer body, which people put so much time into with gels, gyms, make-up, surgery, makeovers, mirror gazing and hairdryers, will age. The inner self will not, however, and its youthfulness can eventually effect the outward appearance. You can stretch your skin up into your hairline and behind you ears all you like but there will always be one winner: age. Yet the yogis don't age as quickly as we do in the West and it is safe to assume that Shankari Mai Jiew wasn't sneaking off to cosmetic surgery clinics up in the Himalayan mountains.

into
the
deep

During your meditation in the last chapter you experienced your inner body and inner self, which can only be encountered in the present moment. The inner self doesn't do time or aging. The energy and force in your inner self today will be the same at eighty. Time is the enemy of youthful vigour and looks, but the more you become one with your inner, timeless self the less your skin, body and entire system will be ravaged by the effects of time.

OTHER BENEFICIAL EFFECTS OF MEDITATION

Fight or Flight Syndrome

As noted previously, meditation is most significant in the area of stress. When a person is faced with a perceived threat the body prepares for two kinds of action: stand and fight or run away from the danger. This fight or flight response is thought to have helped our ancestors cope with life-threatening situations. When the fight or flight response is activated, adrenaline is released. This turns on the alert button and the person becomes more energetic. There is an increase in heart rate and breathing; blood used for digestion is sent to muscles.

into the deep

However, as humans have evolved it is theorised that the fight or flight response has not developed at the same pace as the brain.

As you go through your normal day, there are mini crises: the way someone looks at you, problems with school work, money issues, etc. For each crisis, your body goes into a mini fight or flight response. Stress-responses hourly, daily and weekly lead to stress and damage health.

In his book *Timeless Healing*, Herbert Benson refers to meditation techniques as the 'relaxation' response to life's mini or major crises. Meditation reverses the ill-effects of the fight or flight response, as outlined in the graph below

Comparison of the Physiologic Changes of the Fight-or-Flight Response and the Relaxation Response

Physiologic State	Fight or Flight Response	Relaxation Response
Metabolism	Increases	Decreases
Blood Pressure	Increases	Decreases
Heart Rate	Increases	Decreases
Rate of Breathing	Increases	Decreases
Blood Flowing to the Muscles of the Arms and Legs	Increases	Decreases
Muscle Tension	Increases	Decreases
Slow Brain Waves	Decrease	Increase

During meditation your system gets to rest. Your heart rate decreases, your muscles relax and your breathing becomes deeper.

Help your Brain

In the school system we presume that more brain activity leads to a big smart brain. Obviously you need to learn and for that your brain needs to be active. However, in research Benson discovered that the brain is a finer tuned instrument after meditation. It seems that the brain really benefits from a break from thinking. Your brain doesn't enjoy constant activity and it's up to you to stop it.

Benson discovered that people who meditate have clearer minds and sharper thoughts. When the brain gets a break it has time to create new ideas. Meditation allows your brain to work in a different way and develop new approaches to problems. Remember, an active brain isn't necessarily a productive brain!

Self-Esteem

According to research, students who practise regular meditation enjoy greater self-esteem. One of the reasons for this is that nothing is more destructive to how we feel about ourselves than the constant negative and worrying thoughts that jump around in our heads. During regular meditation your brain gets a rest from these negative thought patterns and can develop more positive approaches to life.

Meditation allows you to explore your wiser and deeper self. It also allows you to experience God space. So what happens when young people experience and encounter God? Is it even possible to have such experiences?

DISCUSS
Do you agree that meditation can have such beneficial effects on people, from how they look to blood pressure, brain efficiency and self-esteem? Share your answers with the class.

THE MONASTERY

In March 2007 four students spent a weekend in Glenstal Abbey, Co. Limerick. The Abbey is a Benedictine monastery and was founded in 1927. Fifty monks live there and the monastery is directed by an Abbot, who is elected by the other monks for an eight-year term. Glenstal comprises of five-hundred acres of woodland, lakes, walks, a farm and a boarding school.

into
the
deep

The students were greeted by Fr Joseph and were quickly immersed in monastic life. The purpose of their visit was to learn something about meditation and meditative practices, and to sample monastic life.

Here we allow the students to give their own account of what happened during their time in the monastery.

Ciaran

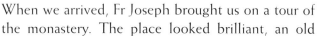

When we arrived, Fr Joseph brought us on a tour of the monastery. The place looked brilliant, an old castle in the middle of woodlands. We went up a steep spiral staircase that led to a tower and when we got out on top we saw for miles around. We saw the whole monastery. Then we went deeper into the castle and into a library that was a very strange shape and allegedly has a secret staircase behind the fireplace.

We planned to go back secretly that night but fell asleep instead.

Personally, monastic life doesn't appeal to me but it's definitely a special place to pray or have quiet time to reflect. It's remarkable because they stick to

into the deep

the same schedule all the time and get up very early. The best part for me was the time spent down in the icon chapel, underneath the main altar of the chapel. We were brought down there in the morning but soon it was completely black until we saw the lights of the little inner chapel. It was definitely a special, intimate and peaceful spot.

Una

I think one of the interesting things was the monks themselves. I really didn't expect them to be so liberal. They are just ordinary people and get to travel around the world. Their lives might seem strange but they don't have to worry about mortgages or money or other things. They don't lead stressful lives, which I think is rare these days. The monastery was also very modern, which was surprising. It was really peaceful over there and loads of people go and stay in the guesthouse to escape from their busy, stressful lives. The great thing is you get time to relax and just have time for yourself. If you had a big decision to make you could go there and think it over without any distractions.

I liked it because I got some quiet time for myself. I don't think I've ever had so much time to think

into the deep

before without any TV, internet or radio to distract me. At first I was dying for any noise at all because it was so quiet there, but by the second day I was used to the silence and liked having no distractions.

There is definitely something special about Glenstal and I think it is because everyone is so happy there. I enjoyed the meditation and especially the one where you completely relax and only concentrate on the present. It makes you appreciate everything more. The monks talked a lot about living in the present, which I now think is very important. They believe that if you live every day as it comes you can be truly content with yourself and not always be thinking and stressing over the future.

I thought the icon chapel was amazing. The healing icon of Jesus was most intriguing. Its eyes were so black that it seemed as though you were looking into his soul or something. It's impossible to describe his face in words. We did a meditation  down there and you feel as if you are being watched over by someone, not in a creepy way but nice and caring or something. It's as if someone is there for you if you have a problem. If I was living there I'd definitely visit the icon chapel every week.

,

into
the
deep

Sue

'I loved my stay in the monastery because it was so calm and peaceful. I completely forgot all the stresses I brought over there with me and thought about the here and now. Meditation at first was funny and embarrassing but after a while I liked it because I just had some peace and quiet all to myself. I know now how it can allow you to reflect because you can focus on one thing, giving it all your concentration. It would be great for decision making.

But I experienced something deeper in the icon chapel. In fact I think I may have been experiencing something spiritual maybe because of all the icons there. Meditation anywhere else can be just relaxing but there seemed to be a special connection with God there. I have tried mediation since but found it hard. I'd like to work on it. I plan to set up a place for meditation in my garden where I can go and reflect. I think it would be good to create a special place to associate with meditation.'

Pat

'What struck me was how much of a different world it was over there. I found the meditation difficult. I could meditate, but only for about 30 seconds, so I'd say that's hardly meditation! In fact, I couldn't even close my eyes to do the meditation with the monk. That's how bad I am. So the meditation didn't go great, but the place itself was cool.

into
the
deep

The monks seem to be very happy – too happy for what they have to give up. One monk, who is now dead, decided to become a hermit over there and went into his room and stayed there for about eight years. I reckoned they had to have a bar somewhere to be in such good form all the time but they only get a few jars on a Saturday night.

The icon chapel was cool – the icons are so old and you're surrounded by history. The healing icon with the dark eyes – there's something special about that one. Sometimes ordinary life seems a bit stale, the drinking and going out. I think deep down everyone believes they are unique but you can't be when you're with everyone else. But down there in the darkness and cool lights everyone felt on a different level – you were different because you were doing something nobody else is really doing. **,**

DISCUSS

1 Meditation was first discovered in monasteries as a way into the soul as opposed to just being a way of dealing with stress. Do you think the students encountered something deeper during their meditative experiences? Give reasons for your answer.

2 If the goal of meditation is to have an encounter with God in what way might the surroundings in the monastery help people to have such experiences? Could you create such surroundings yourself? What is required?

3 Would you meditate just to deal with stress or would you prefer to feel you were in the presence of something else? Give reasons for your answer.

into

the

deep

THE ICON CHAPEL

The four students were all struck by the spiritual atmosphere in the icon chapel. On their trip they got the chance to speak to three students from Glenstal Abbey about their experience of the icon chapel. This is their account.

‘ Every Tuesday night, a group of six or seven boys at the school go to the icon chapel, at about 10pm. Fr Fintan's prayer in the chapel consists, quite simply, of a short scripture reading, read by one of the boys, followed by a reflection period of about fifteen minutes before Fintan closes prayer with his thoughts; boys are free to stay as long as they want. Fintan's final thoughts consist of anything from his interpretation of the scriptures to reflections on recent events or advice on certain things.

The icon chapel is essentially a cave. It is a small, narrow, room (about ten metres by five) located underneath the church. Lining the walls of the room are various 'icons', which are, essentially, marvellous depictions of scenes throughout the history of Catholicism: portraits of Jesus, Mary etc. During prayer we sit on cushions on the floor, candles are lit in the centre of the chapel and after the scripture reading, incense is burned. The chapel is warm and comfortable.

into
the
deep

A very diverse group of boys attend, ranging from sport-stars to swots, rock-stars to wasters. Amongst the group, people have various reasons for going to icon chapel prayer on a Tuesday night – which is by no means compulsory. The most common reason is that people use the quiet time down there to think and reflect on things, like decisions they might have to make. As teenagers, we don't find much time for thinking in the chaotic Leaving Cert. atmosphere, and the preoccupations of sport, relationships etc. The time spent down there is invaluable. It allows you to detach yourself from all of these day-to-day worries and think clearly, in a quiet, calm and spiritual atmosphere. It is certainly useful and definitely helps in making the morally right decisions that are required of us most weeks – and weekends!

Furthermore, icon chapel prayer is also about, well, prayer! It is very different from Mass in so far as, firstly, you have chosen to be there. Also, it is quite an individual occasion, where you can pray specifically and feel as if you are being listened to; it is certainly true to say that you feel closer to God in the icon chapel during prayer. It is a place where you find yourself in a cocoon of your own thoughts. In a world where many decisions have to be made at a youthful age, the icon chapel is an ideal place to gather and reflect on your thoughts and the issues in your life.

To encounter God, or at least a presence, on a weekly basis and truly believe that your prayers are being listened to is a wonderfully cleansing experience. In terms of both prayer and reflection, icon chapel prayer is both calming and rewarding. To get properly in touch with your spiritual side and encounter your faith on a weekly basis is an ultimately satisfying experience.

Rory O'Donovan, Paul Collier, Hugh McCarthy

CHRISTIAN MEDITATION: AN EXPERIENCE OF ENCOUNTER

Meditation is a prayerful quest engaging thought, imagination, emotion and desire. Its goal is to make our own in faith the subject considered, by confronting it with the reality of our own life.

(CCC, 2723)

Christian meditation is a spiritual practice and discipline which, by creating an inner space of calm, facilitates an encounter with Christ. It is not geared towards looking for anything, as in prayers of petition or intercession, but instead, simply an encounter and experience of the presence of Christ. Those who practice Christian meditation are led to become more like Christ in their own lives. They are more likely to serve as Christ served, forgive as he forgave and bring healing to their own lives and those around them. In the Catholic tradition mediation serves to help us deepen our faith in the love which Christ has for us. It is ultimately an encounter with Christ and leads a person 'to union with him' (CCC, 2708).

Within the Catholic tradition there has developed another expression of Christian meditation called *Lectio Divina* or 'divine reading'. It is a careful study of the scriptures where the person's whole attention is engaged without distraction. The mind seeks to consider the scriptures more deeply, seeking to know the hidden truth within. Today *Lectio Divina* is an example of meditation that is particularly suitable for beginners. It is how we come to pay attention to God's word in the scriptures. As a contemporary form of prayer it can be understood as sacred reading.

Chapter Eight

PRAYER

Prayer is the raising up of one's mind and heart to God or the requesting of good things from God.

(CCC, 2559)

Many people treat prayer like a first-aid kit – every home, school and group should have one. This prayer-kit must be fully stocked – Hail Marys and Our Fathers would be essential items, as well as plenty of extras – peace prayers and prayers for the sick and so on.

This prayer-kit is often labelled 'For emergency use only'. So what sort of emergencies would send us running for this kit? Serious illness, financial troubles, difficult examinations, family tragedies – all are examples of occasions in life during which we dip into this prayer kit in search of comfort and meaning. Yet quite often, when the tragedy has passed or the examination has been sat, we put the prayer kit away again – until the next emergency.

There is nothing wrong with this kind of prayer – it is good to turn to God in times of hardship. After all, God understands our anxieties and sufferings. So while this kind of first-aid prayer is important, it would be better if it were not the only kind of prayer. Prayer can be a form of communication with God; it can be a way of being thankful for all that we have received from

God. Prayer can also alert us to what is important about our religion and the implications it has for our lives.

THE CHRISTIAN UNDERSTANDING OF PRAYER

The Christian understanding of prayer is that it is human beings' 'vital and personal relationship with the loving and true God' (CCC, 2558). All relationships require communication if they are to flourish. We communicate in a variety of ways with the members of our family and our friends and we know that our relationships would be starved without that communication. Likewise Christianity believes that without prayer our relationship with God will perish. St Francis de Sales said, 'Everyone of us needs half an hour of prayer each day, except when we are busy – then we need an hour'. In the Old Testament we see the relationship between God and God's people expressed in prayer. The psalms are the

Children singing and playing music, illustration of Psalm 150 (Laudate Dominum). Panel decorating the cantoria (singers' gallery), Museo dell'Opera del Duomo, Florence, Italy

masterpiece of prayer in the Old Testament. They were written by King David and many other authors over a number of years and are still used in both Christian and Jewish Liturgical prayer. 'Whether hymns or prayers of lamentation or thanksgiving, whether individual or communal, whether royal chants, songs of pilgrimage or wisdom meditation, the Psalms are a mirror of God's wonderful deeds in the history of his people, as well as reflections of the human experiences of the Psalmist' (CCC, 2588).

into the deep

Jesus learned to pray from Mary and Joseph in his home in Nazareth. His early prayer would most certainly have been influenced by the psalms, the prayers of his people. Later he prayed in the synagogue and in the temple in Jerusalem. The gospels tell of the many times Jesus prayed as an adult. He prayed at all of the most important times in his life, before his baptism in the Jordan, at his call of the twelve apostles, before his agony in the Garden of Gethsemane and on the cross. Often he went away by himself to pray, 'Very early the next morning, long before daylight, Jesus got up and left the house. He went out of town to a lonely place where he prayed' (Mark 1:35). 'After saying goodbye to the people he went away to a hill to pray' (Mark 6: 46).

Jesus also taught his disciples to pray. When they said to him, 'Lord teach us to pray', he responded by teaching them the Our Father. He also taught them about prayer. He taught that whatever they asked God for in faith they would receive. He also invited them to pray to the Father in his name.

DIFFERENT KINDS OF PRAYER

Sometimes we think of prayer only as a way of petitioning or asking. Seeing that our prayer is primarily our expression of our relationship with God, prayers of praise, thanksgiving, adoration and prayers asking for forgiveness are also important. If we pray for something and if it does not happen we think that God is not listening or that we are not praying properly. However, we must believe that God always knows what is good for us and though our prayer may not be answered in the way in which we would wish it to be God will nevertheless respond in the way that he knows is best for us. Prayer is not magic. Just because we pray we cannot opt out of responsibility for our own lives:

 There was once an old man who had lived a good and pious life, but in his waning years he felt he had nothing to show for it. Finally, he fell to his knees and prayed, crying out: "God, hear me. I've been a good man. I've never asked anything of you before, and I'm grateful for all you have given me. So please grant me just one request: let me win the lottery."

Weeks passed and nothing happened, so again he prayed to win the lottery. Still nothing. After months of fruitless praying, he cried out to the heavens: "God, will you give me a break? All I'm asking is, let me win the lottery!"

Suddenly a voice thundered from the sky, "Will you give me a break? At least buy a ticket!"

(G. Ray Funkhouser)

O Jesus, You who suffer,
grant that today and every day I may be able to see
You in the person of your sick ones and that,
by offering them my care,
I may serve You.

(Mother Teresa)

Oh God, please help me.
I'm so scared,
and so cold,
and so alone.

(from *Go Ask Alice*,
the diary of a young drug addict)

into

the

deep

DISCUSS

1 What are the different kinds of prayer?
2 What do you think the person who wrote the above story wanted us to understand about prayers of petition?

JEWISH UNDERSTANDING OF PRAYER

Jewish prayer is an aid to developing an appropriate attitude towards God. Therefore, Jews actively seek reasons to praise God's creation. There are Jewish prayers to be said when waking up, before enjoying a meal, when witnessing something beautiful in nature and before going to sleep.

שְׁמַ֫ע יִשְׂרָאֵל יהוה אֱלֹהֵינוּ יהוה אֶחָ֑ד וְאָהַבְתָּ אֵת
יהוה אֱלֹהֶיךָ בְּכָל לְבָבְךָ וּבְכָל נַפְשְׁךָ וּבְכָל מְאֹדֶךָ וְהָיוּ
הַדְּבָרִים הָאֵלֶּה אֲשֶׁר אָנֹכִי מְצַוְּךָ הַיּוֹם עַל לְבָבֶךָ וְשִׁנַּנְתָּם
לְבָנֶיךָ וְדִבַּרְתָּ בָּם בְּשִׁבְתְּךָ בְּבֵיתֶךָ וּבְלֶכְתְּךָ בַדֶּרֶךְ
וּבְשָׁכְבְּךָ וּבְקוּמֶךָ וּקְשַׁרְתָּם לְאוֹת עַל יָדֶךָ וְהָיוּ לְטֹטָפֹת
בֵּין עֵינֶיךָ וּכְתַבְתָּם עַל מְזֻזוֹת בֵּיתֶךָ וּבִשְׁעָרֶיךָ
וְהָיָה אִם שָׁמֹעַ תִּשְׁמְעוּ אֶל מִצְוֹתַי אֲשֶׁר אָנֹכִי
מְצַוֶּה אֶתְכֶם הַיּוֹם לְאַהֲבָה אֶת יהוה אֱלֹהֵיכֶם וּלְעָבְדוֹ
בְּכָל לְבַבְכֶם וּבְכָל נַפְשְׁכֶם וְנָתַתִּי מְטַר אַרְצְכֶם בְּעִתּוֹ
יוֹרֶה וּמַלְקוֹשׁ וְאָסַפְתָּ דְגָנֶךָ וְתִירֹשְׁךָ וְיִצְהָרֶךָ וְנָתַתִּי
עֵשֶׂב בְּשָׂדְךָ לִבְהֶמְתֶּךָ וְאָכַלְתָּ וְשָׂבָעְתָּ הִשָּׁמְרוּ לָכֶם
פֶּן יִפְתֶּה לְבַבְכֶם וְסַרְתֶּם וַעֲבַדְתֶּם אֱלֹהִים אֲחֵרִים
וְהִשְׁתַּחֲוִיתֶם לָהֶם וְחָרָה אַף יהוה בָּכֶם וְעָצַר אֶת
הַשָּׁמַיִם וְלֹא יִהְיֶה מָטָר וְהָאֲדָמָה לֹא תִתֵּן אֶת יְבוּלָהּ
וַאֲבַדְתֶּם מְהֵרָה מֵעַל הָאָרֶץ הַטֹּבָה אֲשֶׁר יהוה נֹתֵן לָכֶם
וְשַׂמְתֶּם אֶת דְּבָרַי אֵלֶּה עַל לְבַבְכֶם וְעַל נַפְשְׁכֶם וּקְשַׁרְתֶּם
אֹתָם לְאוֹת עַל יֶדְכֶם וְהָיוּ לְטוֹטָפֹת בֵּין עֵינֵיכֶם וְלִמַּדְתֶּם
אֹתָם אֶת בְּנֵיכֶם לְדַבֵּר בָּם בְּשִׁבְתְּךָ בְּבֵיתֶךָ וּבְלֶכְתְּךָ
בַדֶּרֶךְ וּבְשָׁכְבְּךָ וּבְקוּמֶךָ וּכְתַבְתָּם עַל מְזוּזוֹת בֵּיתֶךָ
וּבִשְׁעָרֶיךָ לְמַעַן יִרְבּוּ יְמֵיכֶם וִימֵי בְנֵיכֶם עַל הָאֲדָמָה
אֲשֶׁר נִשְׁבַּע יהוה לַאֲבֹתֵיכֶם לָתֵת לָהֶם כִּימֵי הַשָּׁמַיִם
עַל הָאָרֶץ

> The Hebrew text of the first two paragraphs of the Shema

Jewish prayers are usually recited in Hebrew. However, they can be recited in any language, whether it is Yiddish, Aramaic, French, English, Spanish or Russian. Even silence is sometimes said to be an appropriate Jewish prayer language. Jews believe that God understands no matter what language a person employs in prayer.

The most important of all Jewish prayers is a prayer called the Shema. The Shema is a prayer that speaks to the Jewish people, and not to God. Its verses instruct the Israelites (the prayer is from the Torah even before the term 'Jew' was used for the Jewish people) what they have to do. Here is a part of the Shema prayer:

into
the
deep

" Hear, O Israel, the Eternal is our God, the Eternal is One. Blessed be God's Name and glorious kingdom forever and ever. You shall love the Lord your God with all your heart, with all your soul, and with all your might. And these words, which I [God] teach you this day, shall be upon your heart. You shall teach them diligently to your children, speaking of them when you sit in your house, when you walk by the way, when you lie down and when you rise up. And you shall bind them as a sign upon your hand, and they shall be for a reminder before your eyes. And you shall write them on the doorposts of your house and upon your gates. **'**

The purpose of Jewish prayer is to increase awareness of God. For an observant Jew, prayer is an integral part of everyday life. Through their constant praying, they are continually reminded of God's presence and of their relationship with God. The most important part of any Jewish prayer, whether it be a prayer of petition, of thanksgiving, of praise of God or of confession, is the opportunity it provides for introspection – time to look inside and see their role in the universe and their relationship to God.

ISLAMIC UNDERSTANDING OF PRAYER

For Muslims, prayer – salat – is an important quality of a believer that distinguishes them from a non-believer. Salat is one of the Five Pillars of Islam in Sunni Islam and one of the ten Practices of the Religion in Shia Islam. The purpose of salat is primarily to act as an individual's communion with Allah. It enables them to stand in front of Allah, thank and praise him, and ask for him to show them the 'right path'. The daily ritual prayers also serve as a constant reminder to Muslims that they should be grateful for

Muslims performing salat

into the deep

God's blessings. It ensures that every Muslim prioritises Islam over all other concerns, thereby revolving their life around God and submitting to his will. Prayer also serves as a formal method of remembering God.

THE FIVE DAILY PRAYERS

Muslims are commanded to perform salat fives times a day. Once they are over the age of puberty, all Muslims are obliged to say these prayers. Those who are ill or otherwise physically unable to offer their prayers in the traditional form are permitted to offer their prayers while sitting or lying, as they are able. The five prayers are all given certain prescribed times (*waqt*) in which they must be performed, unless there is a compelling reason for not being able to perform them on time.

Some Muslims offer voluntary prayers immediately before and after the prescribed prayers. Sunni Muslims classify these prayers as *sunnah*, while Shi'a Muslims consider them *nafil*.

ANSWERED PRAYERS

One of the most common beliefs that people hold is that they prayed for something and that their prayers were answered. A scientist might claim that it was simply a coincidence that what you prayed for happened. So is there evidence that such claims are true?

When we examine scientific evidence for religious beliefs there are some obvious problems. Most importantly, God, or God's activity, is something that can never be proven. God is a mysterious Being and his ways will always remain beyond the scope of scientific proof.

If a person's prayers are answered they might argue that they need no scientific evidence. However, for those of you who are wondering if any evidence exists that prayer can really work, the following paragraphs will prove interesting.

DISCUSS

1 Do you have any evidence that prayer really works? Tell your story to the class.
2 Why do you think it might be helpful for science to validate religious claims about prayer? Why do you think some people might just believe in the power of prayer?

SCIENTIFIC RESEARCH

One of the main problems with scientific research into prayer is the argument that a person might recover from an illness simply because of a feel-good factor. In other words, it's not the prayer that is working or God's power but just some psychological factor. The person really gets better because they appreciate all the attention. It can be argued that the only way research into prayer can be credible is if the people who are being prayed for are unaware that people are praying for them.

In 1988 Dr R.C. Byrd carried out such an experiment in San Francisco General Hospital. After receiving consent from the hospital's ethics committee he set up two groups from a group of 393 coronary care patients. One group would be prayed for by prayer groups (experiment group) whilst the other group wouldn't (control group). Neither group knew which category they belonged to. The experiment lasted for ten months, during which time a team of medical doctors assessed the patients' progress. The results of his findings (based on Byrne, 1988) are in the table below.

Medical variable	Experiment group %	Control group %
Need for antibiotics	3	16
Edema (fluid in the lungs)	6	18
Mechanical ventilation	0	12
Death	13	17

into
the
deep

Along with the above figures, the incidence of pneumonia was 5 per cent less in the experiment group. The incidence of cardiopulmonary arrest was 6 per cent less. These results may not seem dramatic but compared to percentages and statistics in general medical research they are sensational.

In a later study in 1998 by Sicher, twenty AIDS patients received prayers for ten weeks from local prayer groups. The group showed less severe illnesses, and needed fewer hospital visits and overnight stays. The research also revealed that they had better moods.

Some scientists reject the findings of such studies as simply coincidental. However, there is no scientific research to explain the results of such experiments – they are worthy of note but, as yet, no scientific explanation can be given (source: *Psychology, Religion, and Spirituality* by David Fontana).

DISCUSS

1 Why do you think the patients who received prayers showed signs of better healing and health?

2 Some believe that science will never be able to explain the findings of such studies. Why do you think they hold such a view? Do you agree with such a view? Give reasons for your answer.

3 Can you detect any areas where Byrd's study is open to criticism? For example, could there be other factors that might have affected the improved health statistics of the experiment group?

PROBLEMS WITH A SCIENTIFIC APPROACH

In your discussions above you may have identified some problems with Byrd's experiments. Dr Larry Dossey, in his book *Healing Words: The Power of Prayer and the Practice of Medicine*, identifies some concerns about Byrd's investigations and the ability of scientific experiments to assess how effective prayer is. He notes the following points:

- The people in the prayer groups were only given a first name of the person they prayed for. So if, for example, someone was told to pray for a 'John', how can we be sure which John of which group was actually prayed for, presuming that in a group of 393 patients there would be a few 'Johns'.

- Another problem concerns outside prayer. We must presume that people were praying for the patients other than the experiment prayer group. Yet there is no real way to factor in the effects of the prayers of family, relatives and loved ones.

- In the research there is no evidence that the people who were asked to pray actually did what they were asked to do and as frequently as they were asked to.

> **DISCUSS**
>
> Why might the above objections cast some doubt on Byrd's research?

THE PROBLEM WITH UNANSWERED PRAYERS

The wonder of prayer is revealed beside the well where we come seeking water: there, Christ comes to meet every human being.
(CCC, 2560)

In earlier discussions in class, many people may have shared their own accounts of situations where their prayers to God were answered. However, there are also times when people feel their prayers are unanswered. This can create difficulties for people:

'Did I not pray hard enough?'

'Is God just not listening to me?'

'Maybe it's all just made up. There is no God.'

'There is a God, yeah, but this God just doesn't really care.'

'Why did God not listen to my prayer? Is there something wrong with me?'

'Maybe I should have bargained with God … if granny gets better I'll go to Mass every Sunday for the rest of my life.'

DISCUSS

1   Can you identify with any of the above thoughts or feelings? Why might someone make these comments?

2   Can you think of other comments that could be added to the list?

3   Do you have stories about prayer whereby you felt like the people above? You might share them with the class.

One way to approach unanswered prayers is to examine whether there may have been a problem with the nature of the prayer itself. Consider the following examples:

• You're playing in a match for your school at the weekend. Your team manager calls the team to a meeting to inform them that the best player on the opposing team has a threatening leg injury. A decision is made for the team to go down to the school prayer room to pray that the lad's leg actually worsens. In fact, the team decide to stay an extra ten minutes praying that the centre forward sprains his ankle. You play the match at the weekend and you loose to a goal scored by the lad with the 'bad' leg. Where was God? Why didn't God listen to your prayers?

• You're walking along the corridor in school and you notice a new kid who seems to be on their own. You feel sorry for them and decide to go up to the prayer room to pray for them … 'Please God, send that lonely person someone that will talk to them and make them feel like they belong. Please, please God.' The next day you notice that the person is still on their own. Why, you ask, did God not answer your prayer? Off you go back up to the prayer room … 'Please God …'

into

the

deep

• You decide that life is boring and reckon it would be good to start taking drugs. A dealer gives you some hash and late at night when everyone is asleep you stick your head out the window and have a smoke. Then you wrap everything up and put it in a little hiding place under you bed. Next day your mother is driving you to school. She informs you that she has a day off work and she's going to spend it giving your room a good spring clean … 'Once and for all,' she declares 'I'm going to sort that mess under your bed. Have a great day!' You dash to the prayer room and amidst tears of anguish and dread you beg God not to let your mother find the package. You arrive home and are called into the sitting room for a little chat … You think to yourself … 'The least God could have done was to help me out. That's it, never praying again.'

- You find studying for your exams difficult so you decide that there is a higher power … God … who is more powerful than any exam or examiner. Instead of studying you pray constantly that you will pass. You fail.

DISCUSS

Why might God not answer the above prayers?
What seems to be the problem with the above approaches to prayer?

into

the

deep

ASIDE

In his book *When Bad Things Happen to Good People,* Harold S. Kushner makes the point that a person should never pray that something bad should happen to another person. To illustrate the point he relates the following story:

'The story is told of two shopkeepers who were bitter rivals. Their stores were across the street from each other, and they would spend each day sitting in the doorway, keeping track of each other's business. If one got a customer, he would smile in triumph at his rival. One night, an angel appeared in a dream to one of the shopkeepers and said, "God has sent me to teach you a lesson. He will give you anything you ask for, but I want you to know that, whatever you get, your competitor across the street will get twice as much. Would you be wealthy? You can be very wealthy, but he will be twice as rich. Do you want to live a long and healthy life? You can but his life will be longer and healthier. You can be famous, have children you will be proud of, whatever you desire. But whatever you get he will get twice as much." The man frowned, thought for a moment, and said, "All right, my request is: strike me blind in one eye."'

THE MYSTERIOUS NATURE OF GOD'S ANSWER TO PRAYER

My brother Louis was eight years younger than me. It was too much of an age gap for us ever to be friends or buddies. I had my friends and I had more freedom. I always had better, more grown-up toys. Louis always wanted to play with my toys when we were young but I never let him.

I used to spend a lot of energy trying to get rid of Louis. Now Louis isn't here and I spend all my time wishing he were.

I was eighteen, bigger than most guys and I have handed out beatings. People see me as a hard man.

I'm a boxer. I was good at it but every punch I landed I directed it at myself. They sent me to a counsellor. I expected him to tell me to give up boxing. Instead, he told me to box harder. He told me to annihilate the next guy I fought. And that's the strange thing. I won that fight but it was the last one I fought.

I went back to Joe (my counsellor) and we got on really well. He gradually got my story out of me.

It was New Year's Eve. It was one of those Christmases where the weather was all over the place. The sun shone on Christmas day but then the weather turned. A cold spell came bringing frost, black icy frost. The weatherman said that people were only to undertake necessary journeys.

It was the usual story at Christmastime. Louis wanted to play with my toys. I was a strong lad but Louis was small for his age, slight frame, skinny little guy. He wanted to stay and play but I wouldn't let him … I have repeated that line to myself a million times…he wanted to stay but I wouldn't let him … So he went on that journey … in the black icy frost.

My old man got the phone call. We got into a neighbour's car. At the hospital it wasn't real. There was a Christmas tree in the children's ward. We waited and waited. I think my father knew. He kept reassuring me. Louis' brain had swollen after the collision. My mother was alright. But Louis, small frame, skinny little guy … you see there was nothing there to protect him from the impact. In situations like that nobody has to tell you anything. Their faces betray it all. This was bad.

I remember going to the hospital chapel. I wanted to say something but I couldn't because I'd start to cry. Tough man at eighteen. I glared at the cross. I

into

the

deep

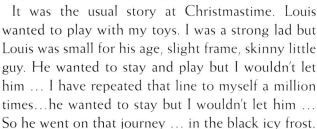

warned God not to let anything happen to the little lad. I didn't plead or bargain. I prayed by threatening God.

We were let in to see Louis as he came in and out of consciousness. I sat up at the top of his bed on the left-hand side. They told me to get rest. I glared at them. I wanted to look into Louis' eyes. To tell him, just once, that I was there.

One evening, it was six o'clock. Louis woke up. I looked at him and I had this toy that he loved playing with. I put it in his hand and squeezed it real tight. To this day I know he understood everything in that one moment. It was enough. I knew Louis for ten years, eighty-three days and twenty hours. But that was our moment.

They buried Louis, and I helped carry and lower the coffin. My father was a boxer and so was my uncle and my cousin. Four boxers lowered his broken little body into a grave and God's rain and our tears blessed his holding place.

After I gave up boxing Joe told me to start making my peace with everyone and myself. I'm thirty-seven years of age now and I have my own kids. One day, not so long ago, I dropped my son off to a party. Like me, he's a sturdy guy. My route took me past the hospital where Louis died and it forced me to make peace with the one person I hadn't. I went back into the chapel ... the place where I had fallen out with God. I spent a long time in front of the cross. It all came back. I had lost my younger brother but I don't know if we'd ever have had a moment like we had in his Christmas hospital bed. My friends rarely speak to their brothers. They've all moved away. I talk to Louis every day.

I looked at the cross and the figure on it. I looked really hard and I made my peace with God, for there on a wooden beam was a small frame ... broken bones ... skinny little guy ...'

(Anonymous)

DISCUSS

1 How does the author feel when he prays to God the first time in the chapel?
2 Does God answer the author's prayer? Give reasons for your answer.
3 From the story, in what way does it appear that God is in some way connected to our suffering?

ON ANSWERED PRAYER

Just as Jesus prays to the Father and gives thanks before receiving his gifts, so he teaches us *filial boldness*: 'Whatever you ask in prayer, believe that you receive it, and you will.' Such is the power of prayer and of faith that does not doubt: 'all things are possible to him who believes.'

(CCC, 2610)

The Christian tradition teaches very strongly that God does listen to our prayers but just not the way we might want. For example, it is natural for people to die and so if God answered all the prayers of those who were dying … no one would ever die.

In the account of Louis' death, God did not intervene and save the boy's life but God was involved. The broken figure of Jesus on the cross suggests that God knows about suffering and desolation. One absolute belief of the Christian tradition is that God is with those who are suffering and broken – through illness, bereavement or any form of tragedy.

into
the
deep

The author above lost his brother but discovered his love for God. He prayed for life, he received love.

DISCUSS

1 When people suffer tragedy or loss, those close to them often pray for them, that they be given strength to cope. Why do you think God answers these prayers?

2 People often pray that those bereaved may be comforted. In what way might God answer these prayers? Are the people who offer up these prayers sometimes part of the answer? Give reasons for your answer.

3 'Prayer, when it is offered in the right way, redeems people from isolation. It assures them that they need not feel alone and abandoned' (Harold S. Kushner). Would you agree or disagree with the above statement? Give reasons for your answer.

'SO YOU SHOULD PRAY LIKE THIS …'

According to Christian tradition Jesus handed on to his disciples a method of praying which is known as 'The Lord's Prayer' or 'The Our Father'. The following is the version of the prayer from Matthew's gospel:

> Our Father in heaven,
> hallowed be your name.
> Your kingdom come.
> Your will be done,
> on earth as it is in heaven.
> Give us this day our daily bread.
> And forgive us our debts,
> as we have also forgiven our debtors.
> And do not bring us to the time of trial,
> but rescue us from the evil one.

into
the
deep

The prayer teaches us the best way to pray and some points are worth noting. Firstly, it recognises that God, our Father in heaven, is the one to whom the prayer is directed. When we pray we should ask for what we need from day to day. The prayer is concerned with the now and not some future or past events. When we pray it is important to keep in mind our relationships with others, especially those with whom we have fallen out. Finally, this form of prayer is known as non-directed prayer. This means that The Lord's Prayer doesn't specify what the person requests. In directed prayer, the person has a specific request, for example, cure from illness. The Lord's Prayer suggests that the best way to pray is when we don't determine what we want God to do for us. Instead, this prayer asks simply that God's will be done in a person's life.

The Lord's Prayer
(in Kiswahili)

into

the

deep

ASIDE

The Spindrift Studies

The Spindrift organisation in Salem, Oregon has for years been conducting studies into the effectiveness of prayer. The studies established that prayer was effective but then set about identifying which type of prayer was most effective. They drew a distinction between directed and non-directed prayer.

Non-directed prayer is an open-ended approach whereby the person has no specific outcome in mind. In their studies they discovered that non-directed prayer was more effective than directed prayer. It would seem that praying is more effective when we're not trying to persuade God what God should do.

into

the

deep

DISCUSS

1   Which form of prayer do you think people use most, directed or non-directed? Why do you think they use that form of prayer?
2   Why do you think the Lord's Prayer encourages us to pray in a non-directed fashion?

Chapter Nine

EUCHARIST AND THE SACRAMENTS

The Eucharist is the 'source and summit of the Christian life. The other sacraments, and indeed all ecclesiastical ministries and works of the apostolate, are bound up with the Eucharist and are orientated towards it.'

(CCC, 1324)

THE DEATH OF MY GRANDDAD

' At the end of fifth year our school chaplain came around to all the classes asking who would like to become a Eucharistic minister. He explained what it involved but also said we could bring the host to anybody we knew who might be sick or dying. It was just in the back of my mind. But I became a Eucharistic minister not realising how soon I would have to use it.

My granddad was a farmer and his land was on the coast and we loved going there as children as the beach was just down a lane. I'd say he was a private man but loved all of us. He was my Mam's dad. His wife died years ago so he was the one we went to visit and stay over with. He was very talented and could have been a very successful businessman but when his wife died he dropped

everything except for the farm just to take care of four daughters.

We loved it there. But then in April last year he took a turn and was confined to his bed. My Mam was worried and the atmosphere in our house changed. We went to stay with our Granddad but he was up in bed the whole time. You only hear about their worsening condition through whispers and the change of mood. Nobody tells you anything directly. One evening my Mam told me to go over to mass that evening with my cousin Dermot. I went out to the yard and he brought me over to the house where the lambs were. A fox or dog had got one and he was bloodied at the neck. Dermot loved showing me gory things; maggots, dead rats, dead calves. I thought he was weird.

At mass it was nice as it was just an evening mass with few there. The evening sun was shining through the stained glass. The priest invited us to pray for our special intentions. So I really did pray for Granddad. I think even Dermot prayed as well. After mass the priest asked us into the sacristy where he gave me the golden pix. He knew I was a Eucharistic minister. He told me to bring the Eucharist back to Granddad. So much happened in that moment. I knew he was dying, that everything would change.

So I went back and was told by Mam to go up to the room with her. I will never forget that because I wasn't a child anymore – I was the one bringing the Eucharist in the little golden pix. There were a few in the room and candles lighting. He was sleeping but Mam gently woke him up. He was very thin but looked at me. His eyes were very watery and he was pale. He barely opened his mouth. I gave him the host and everyone blessed themselves. Later the priest arrived. I was still in the room. He anointed Granddad.

I felt weak after that because I hadn't anything to eat. I left the room but glanced back at the bed knowing I might not ever see Granddad alive again.

into

the

deep

That night the younger people stayed downstairs but the older ones came and went. A farewell procession I suppose. I fell asleep and my Mam woke me early the next morning to tell me he was dead and I could go and see him whenever I wanted.

I had never seen a dead person before so I asked Mam to come with me. I was really nervous even though it was Granddad. At first I just noticed how different the room was, curtains pulled, candles lighting, clean and calm. He was just lying in the bed and from the door he just looked asleep. Up closer he looked different. He looked dead, I suppose. His face was different, especially his lips, all drawn back. His fingers were wrapped around a rosary beads. They looked feminine – white knuckles, purple nails. But after the initial shock I realised he looked very at peace. His eyes looked peaceful and his hair was combed. First time I saw that. If he'd seen himself in a mirror he wouldn't have recognised himself. That sounds stupid but you know what I mean.

The funeral mass was good because the parish priest knew Granddad really well. They went to races. The homily was funny and he told stories

into the deep

about him. But he also explained how the mass was a sacrifice and how Granddad had made many sacrifices in his life to rear his four daughters. The aunts were crying a lot and after communion I just went into my own world. On the front of the altar was a lamb and I thought of the lamb that morning. Death everywhere. But then I looked around the old church. The stained glass windows, candles lighting, friends around and the faint smell of incense coming from the sacristy. For that moment everything seemed ok. '

DISCUSS

1   Why do you think funeral masses are particularly important for people?

2   Do people become Eucharistic ministers in your school? Would you consider it? Why?

3   Do you think a good homily makes a big difference to a mass? Why?

4   What mass do you like going to? What mass was a particular good experience for you? Why? Give reasons for your answer.

EXPERIENCES OF DARKNESS

 On the outside I'm a smiling, successful and attractive sixteen-year old. Everyone thinks I have it sorted out – that everything is fine. I'm in the school drama club and I'm on the school hockey team. But when I look in the mirror at this smiling, successful "student", "daughter" I

into the deep

wish I was her. I'm not. You see there's the surface where everything seems fine. But down below and underneath I've no confidence and have no real idea who the real me is. I exist for other people. I'm "the student", "the daughter", "the girlfriend". I play a role. We go searching in different ways to find who we might be or just to escape from the actor and actress that plays the role. '

(Female, 18)

' What characterises my life is a Saturday morning, well, afternoon. My parents do everything they can to wake me up. They do everything they can to make me study. They do everything they can for me but worry all the time. The teachers in school tell me over and over how I'm wasting my ability and paint

scenarios of the mess my life will be. Everyone wants to pigeonhole me to become this person. I don't understand who they want me to be or even who I am. And there really is no one to talk to – not the lads anyway. I've been asked the question and, yes, I'd love to know who I am. I'd love to wake someday into my own life, my own place with my own people. '

(Male, 17)

DISCUSS

1 Do you think many teenagers feel as described in the extracts above? On the surface everything might seem fine but is there a world underneath where everything is more troubled?

2 Is there a desire in teenagers to become a different person, one you'd be more comfortable living with? Is there a deep yearning for something? Do you want to move on?

into

the

deep

DIVINE BLESSINGS FULLY REVEALED

The lifeguard man doesn't save the people on the beach. He doesn't run to them and jump on them and drag them to higher ground in case the tide comes in. No. He or she will save the drowning people. Have you ever almost drowned and someone saved you? Tell the story now. Or did anyone ever save you from danger? Did you ever save someone?

If you were ever saved it was because you were lost, in danger or on the edge, close to the abyss. Two thousand years ago, Jesus of Nazareth was executed on a cross and there suffocated and bled to death. Yet today approximately one billion people worldwide believe that Jesus was the Son of God and his death saved us all. Many images are used; he freed us, saved us from sin and death, reconciled us to the Father. We've been saved. We might find ourselves in the tomb, so to speak, as the above teenagers have found themselves in darkness but Jesus Christ has raised us all to new life.

The challenge of Christianity is to move on, to find your authentic self, the person God made you to become, the purposeful you, the real you. You have been saved from darkness. As the Letter to the Ephesians explains, we have been blessed with every spiritual blessing in God's love through Jesus Christ: 'Blessed be God the Father of our Lord Jesus Christ, who has blessed us in Christ with every spiritual blessing in the heavenly places ... He destined us before him in love to be his sons through Jesus Christ, according to the purpose of his will, to the praise of his glorious grace which he freely bestowed on us in the beloved' (Ephesians 1:1-3).

We have been blessed with salvation and new life. We have been brought from darkness to light and according to the Catechism of the Catholic Church: 'In the Church's liturgy the divine blessing is fully revealed and communicated'.

(CCC, 1082)

TAKE A STEP ...

OUT OF THE DARK NIGHT ...

... into an old church and it's Christmas Eve. It's freezing outside but it's grand and warm in the chapel where the liturgy is taking place. Everyone you know is there and there are candles lighting everywhere and a big Christmas tree. Incense is burning somewhere and there's singing. It's hard to explain. In fact no words can explain it  but there's something about this ancient Catholic ritual that seems to be in some way comforting and welcoming. There's something good about it, not that it can be explained. And always, have you noticed, just straight after communion, there's no shuffling or agitation. There's this calmness, like everyone has just been fed, not ordinary food, but the food of life, nourishment for your soul, your spiritual self. Go to mass, receive communion, nourish your inmost self, experience your salvation. Leave the darkness behind. Whoever you are ... wake up ... and say thanks to ...

THE ONE WHO SACRIFICED HIMSELF FOR US ...

... on the cross. The old Christians, the ones who were often thrown to the lions, they had to meet in secret, down in the earth sometimes, in catacombs, in the underground graveyards. They broke bread and in that breaking they saw the broken crucified Christ, the battered, bloodied figure who died for us. And they said thanks (in Greek, *Eucharistia*, to give thanks). But ask yourself this question in class now ... if you were God's son would you

into the deep

 Eucharist and the Sacraments   115

become a man and die for your classmates ... to save them? Answer honestly ... so why did Jesus die for us?

We will do our best to explain this though it can't really be explained because in part it's a mystery. The relationship between God and humanity was fractured, broken by sin. The old Jewish priests in the Temple in Jerusalem brought sacrifices into God to be at one with God again ... 'at ... one ... ment' ... atonement. But only Jesus could reconcile us to God, put right the relationship and save us. Only Jesus could achieve atonement. He died on the cross as the ultimate sacrifice to be offered to God to save us, eternally. This was such an important event that Jesus told us to do it again and again and again, to ...

'DO THIS IN MEMORY OF ME ...'

... every time we celebrate the Eucharist. We celebrate a memorial of Christ's sacrifice. He is not sacrificed over and over again each time we celebrate the Eucharist. Instead, we re-present again his sacrifice to the Father. We offer the bread and wine which, by the power of the Holy Spirit, become the body and blood of Christ. Mysteriously, in a way surpassing our understanding, Christ is really present. The Eucharist is a sacrifice because it re-presents the sacrifice made on the cross.

At the heart of the Eucharistic celebration are the bread and wine that, by the words of Christ and the invocation of the Holy Spirit, become Christ's Body and Blood. Faithful to the Lord's command the Church continues to do, in his memory and until his glorious return, what he did on the eve of his passion.

(CCC, 1333)

When we leave the Eucharist we should bring with us something of what we have experienced. Studies show that people who give thanks for what they have are happier because the focus of their attention is on what they have as opposed to what they don't have. Do you focus your attention on what you have or what you don't have? Is your world abundant or scarce? Does society, the media, advertising, marketing drive home what you have or what you don't have? Spend a few moments in class focusing your attention on what you have and thank God for it. If you have difficulty with this exercise, bring in a speaker from a charity that deals with the poor, the abandoned and the lonely. It should focus your attention.

Years ago an SOS came in to a Lifeguard station about a boat that had got into trouble in very heavy seas. The young lifeguard looked out at the angry sea and said, 'We can't go out in this weather. We'll never come back!' The old lifeguard man looked at him and said, 'We have to

into
the
deep

go out. We don't have to come back.' Life is not meant to be about getting, accumulation, in short 'me'. The Eucharist very powerfully tells us that life is about self-sacrifice. It's the choice and path of the hero. The child stays in the cradle and gets. The adult goes out and does. Have you personally or as a class ever focused your attention on those who need your time and help. Have you ever given to another? Studies show it's extremely good for us to self-sacrifice our time and energy for others. Identify a group that you can help. Perhaps collect goods or money for them. Then have a class mass and bring up what you have done during the offertory and perhaps present it to a representative of the charity. It is in moments like this that you leave your childhood and assume truly adult responsibilities.

THE PASSOVER

> They shall take some of the blood and put it on the two doorposts and the lintel of the houses in which they eat it.

(Exodus 12:7)

Jesus celebrated the Last Supper with his disciples in the course of a Passover meal. His actions reinterpreted the Passover when the Hebrews were saved by the blood of the lamb placed on the doorposts of their houses. The Hebrews were saved by the blood of the sacrificed lamb. Now we are saved by the blood of the sacrificed Christ. He is the new lamb and we celebrate a new Passover.

By celebrating the Last Supper with his apostles in the course of the Passover meal, Jesus gave the Jewish Passover its definitive meaning.

(CCC, 1340)

THE TEMPLE

 ... he entered once for all into the Holy Place, not with the blood of goats and calves, but with his own blood, thus obtaining eternal redemption.

(Hebrews 9:12)

King David brought the Ark of the Covenant to Jerusalem. The Ark contained the Ten Commandments. King Solomon built a Temple to house the Ark. It was placed in the Holy of Holies. God dwelt there. Only the High Priest could enter the Holy of Holies on the Day of Atonement to offer sacrifice to God. When Jesus died the veil that separated the Holy of Holies from the world was torn in two. There would be no more sacrifices. Atonement was established. God and humanity were reconciled.

The place where the Ark of the Covenant sat before King Solomon's Temple was destroyed.

THE WORD

Then came the day of Unleavened Bread, on which the Passover lamb had to be sacrificed. So Jesus sent Peter and John saying, 'Go and prepare the Passover meal for us, that we may eat it ...' They went ... and prepared the Passover. And when the hour came, he sat at table, and the apostles with him. And he said to them, 'I have earnestly desired to eat this Passover with you before I suffer; for I tell you I shall not eat it again until it is fulfilled in the kingdom of God' ... And he took bread, and when he had given thanks he broke it and gave it to them, saying, 'This is my body which is given for you. Do this in remembrance of me.' And likewise the cup after supper, saying, 'This cup which is poured out for you is the New Covenant in my blood.'

(CCC, 1169)

into

the

deep

The liturgy of the word contains writings from the prophets of the Old Testament, the gospels and the letters of the apostles. Then follows the homily and Catholics are invited to believe that this is the Word of God. Then we are invited to offer intercessions and prayers for all who are living and in need of God's blessing. In the liturgy of the Eucharist, the offerings of bread and wine are received by the priest.

They will be offered by the priest in the name of Christ in the Eucharistic sacrifice in which they will become his Body and Blood.

(CCC, 1350)

WHAT ARE SACRAMENTS?

ENCOUNTERING MYSTERY

In human life, signs and symbols occupy an important place. As a being at once body and spirit, man expresses and perceives spiritual realities through physical signs and symbols. As a social being, man needs signs and symbols to communicate with others, through language, gestures and actions. The same holds true for his relationship with God.

(CCC, 1146)

In life we encounter experiences which are hard to define and sometimes even understand. Things happen to us that are beyond words. There are moments of awe, such as the birth of a child. It is difficult for parents to put into words how they feel at such moments. When we fall in love we find it difficult too to explain exactly why it is that we have fallen in love with one person as opposed to another. Finally at death, people are often without words when they try to comfort the bereaved.

The above experiences can be called mysterious. We encounter mystery in life when things happen to us that we cannot fully

understand or put words on. Often we use a different way to communicate during those experiences and it is the language of symbol. Lovers exchange gifts as symbols of their love. Places and times become significant for lovers. At death we embrace the bereaved; we represent the deceased's life through symbols of their work, hobbies and family life.

DISCUSS

1 What other experiences in life would you characterise to be mysterious? Share them with the class.
2 What other symbols can you think of that people use at times when they can find no words to describe how they are feeling?

GOD AS MYSTERY

The sacraments are perceptible signs (words and actions) accessible to our human nature. By the action of Christ and the power of the Holy Spirit they make present efficaciously the grace that they signify.

(CCC, 1084)

From the earliest times of our understanding of who God is, God has always been recognised as wholly other, transcendent and mysterious. Yet God became incarnate in his son Jesus Christ. God took on a human and material form and through Jesus fully revealed to us what God is like. According to Christian tradition the material world can reveal the divine and in the sacraments we use water, oil and light among other symbols to reveal God to us. God as mystery is revealed through symbol. We use symbols when we encounter mystery in life.

In the sacraments we use symbols so we can see, feel and touch spiritual realities. What is signified in sacraments at a physical level through symbol, action and word actually occurs at a deeper spiritual level. In baptism when we see the water poured and the words spoken the person is baptised and changed spiritually forever to share a new life with Christ. In confirmation when the bishop anoints, the person receives the Holy Spirit. The

into
the
deep

sacraments then are signs in the form of words and actions that we can see and hear. These signs strengthen faith and they confer the presence and love of God, traditionally known as grace.

SACRAMENTS: ENCOUNTERS WITH GOD

A sacramental celebration is a meeting of God's children with their Father, in Christ and the Holy Spirit; this meeting takes the form of a dialogue, through actions and words.

(CCC, 1153)

When we meet our friends it is easy to see and listen to what they have to say and do. Yet because God is mystery and totally other we encounter God in a different way. We encounter God in the sacraments. The death and resurrection of Jesus Christ is the origin of the Church's existence and is also in a very real way the source of the sacramental life of the Church. Christ acts in the Church through the sacraments and we encounter Christ in the sacraments. We encounter his saving power in baptism. We encounter his presence in the Eucharist.

Christ continues to act in the Church through the sacraments. They are the lifeblood of the Church. Those who celebrate them participate in the death and resurrection of Christ, they can be healed and reconciled through the power of the Holy Spirit and they are called to share in the future in the fullness of God's own life.

DISCUSS

1 From the earliest times Christians have gathered together to celebrate the sacraments. The sacraments enrich community life. Why do you think the sacraments are important in the life of your community?

2 Why do you think some people may have lost sight of the real meaning of the sacraments as encounters with God? Why do people tend to materialise the sacraments and use them as opportunities to display wealth and spend money?

GOD-TALK

Chapter Ten

REVELATION: A CHRISTIAN UNDERSTANDING OF GOD

The desire for God is written in the human heart, because man is created by God and for God; and God never ceases to draw man to himself. Only in God will he find the truth and happiness he never stops searching for: 'The dignity of man rests above all on the fact that he is called to communion with God. This invitation to converse with God is addressed to man as soon as he comes into being. For if man exists it is because God has created him through love, and through love continues to hold him in existence. He cannot live fully according to truth unless he freely acknowledges that love and entrusts himself to his creator.'

(Vatican Council II, GS, 19 § 1. (CCC, 27)

> The underlying belief ... is that God reveals himself to humankind in two ways which are ultimately one: the inner world of our own being – our emotional life of desires and wonder, and our intellectual life of thinking and planning – and the outer world of nature and human history.

(*Youth 2K*, Tuohy & Cairns, p. 6)

> I am the Way, the Truth and the Life.

(John 14:6)

GOD-TALK

IMAGES OF GOD

People talk about God in many and varied ways. In this section we will examine different images of God and the way we talk about God and come to know God. Almost everyone has some

opinion about God; even an atheist has an opinion about God – he or she don't believe God exists. According to some recent surveys up to 90 per cent of Europeans believe in God.

Any conversation about God amongst your peers or with adults will usually reveal many different opinions. Some people believe God is a universal force and can be experienced in nature, events or in other people. This can be understood as an impersonal understanding of God. Others believe that God is personal and that God is someone you can have a relationship with. This is a personal understanding of God.

As Ireland becomes a more multicultural society, you could find yourself in a conversation with someone whose faith holds a completely different understanding of who God is or even how many gods there are. A person who believes that there is only one God belongs to a *monotheistic faith*, while someone who believes that there are many gods belongs to a *polytheistic faith*.

DIVINE REVELATON

God will always remain unknowable to us because of our finite understanding. So how do we ever come to know anything about God? According to the major world religions the answer is *divine revelation*. It is accepted that we need help to come to know and understand God. God has freely chosen to reveal himself to us so as to help us reach an understanding of what God is like. As an individual outside a faith tradition, it would be difficult to come to a deep understanding of what God is like but religious traditions all rely on sacred texts that explain what God is like and how God relates to us. As the Second Vatican Council

Revelation: A Christian
Understanding of God

teaches us: 'By divine revelation God wished to manifest and communicate both himself and the eternal decrees of his will concerning the salvation of humankind. He wished, in other words, "to share with us divine benefits which entirely surpass the powers of the human mind to understand"' (*Dei Verbum*, 6).

ASSIGNMENT

Below are some opinions about God as reported in a book called *Youth 2K*. In class, break into groups and examine the quotes below. Which do you agree with and which do you disagree with? Perhaps you have a completely different opinion. You might like to share it with the group and then report back to the class.

'God's everywhere. God's in good people. God's in people who help you. God's in nature. If you look out the window he's in the trees, he's everywhere.' (Female 17–18)

'Warmth or spirit, not an actual person – more a feeling. I always feel he'll take care of me.' (Female 17–18)

'He is there somewhere but he doesn't do anything.' (Male 17–18)

'I think he's an old man with loads of grey hair and wrinkles because he's been around for a long time, sitting on his big gold chair with loads of people around him dressed in white, kind of a cloud; I think that's the typical image of heaven as well.' (Female 17–18)

'Hopefully, as someone that would be there. That when we die, we'll not just be stuck in a grave and that's the end of us.' (Female 23–24)

As human beings we can never have a completely accurate image of God because our human minds are unable to grasp the mystery that is God. However, as we grow from children to adults, our images of God can become more accurate.

Revelation: A Christian Understanding of God

CHRISTIAN REVELATION

> It pleased God, in his goodness and wisdom, to reveal himself and make known the mystery of his will (see Eph 1:9), which was that people can draw near to the Father, through Christ, the Word made flesh, in the Holy Spirit, and thus become sharers in the divine nature.
>
> *(Dei Verbum, 2)*

Universal revelation refers to a view where God makes himself known to all people and in all times, in nature or human experiences.

The following story tells of an instance of God's revelation through human experience.

> The line was long but moving briskly,
> And in that line, at the very end
> stood a young girl about twelve years of age.
> She waited patiently
> as those in the front of that long line
> received a little rice, some canned foods or a little fruit.
> Slowly but surely
> she was getting closer to the front of that line,
> closer to the food.
> From time to time she would glance across the street.
> She did not notice the growing concern
> on the faces of those distributing the food.
> The food was running out.
> Their anxiety began to show but she did not notice.
> Her attention seemed always to focus on three figures
> under the trees across the street.
> At long last she stepped forward to get her food.
> Btu the only thing left was a lonely banana.
> The workers were almost ashamed to tell her
> that was all that was left.

into
the
deep

Revelation: A Christian
Understanding of God

She did not seem to mind to get that solitary banana.
Quietly she tood the precious fruit and ran across
the street
where three small children waited – perhaps her
sisters and a brother.
Very deliberately she peeled the banana
and very carefully divided the banana into three
equal parts.
Placing the precious food into the eager hands
of those three younger ones –
one for you, one for you, one for you –
she then sat down
and licked the inside of that banana peel.
In that moment, I swear,
I saw the face of God.

The poet Elizabeth Barrett Browning speaks of how we can become aware of God's presence in the world of nature:

Earth's crammed with heaven and every common bush afire with God: But only he who sees, takes off his shoes; The rest sit round it, and pluck blackberries.

There is a more specific form of revelation where God is understood to have revealed himself in a particular time and place or to a particular person. This is known as *particular* or *historical revelation*.

The Christian understanding of divine revelation traces itself back into Jewish history. God has never ceased to take care of us and offer us in love the gift of eternal salvation. The sacred Scriptures offer us a unique insight into the workings of God amongst his people. In the book of Genesis we read how God made himself known first to Abraham and made him into a great nation: 'Now the Lord said to Abram, "Go from your country and your kindred and your father's house to the land that I will show you. I will make you a great nation, and I will bless you, and make your name great"' (Genesis 12:1).

into

the

deep

Revelation: A Christian
Understanding of God

129

God then revealed himself to Moses and made it known that he alone was the only living and true God. Through Moses, God called the people into a covenant relationship so they could be God's own people. During the time that the Hebrew people were slaves in Egypt, God heard their cries for liberation and he responded. God, who first revealed himself to Abraham, Moses and the Prophets, was a true and caring God who responded to the needs of his people. God has revealed himself to be a liberator. Through the events of the Passover, God freed his people from slavery by the blood of the lamb. For Christians, this blood spilt would point to the fullest revelation of God, through his own son, Jesus Christ. Still today Jews believe that God reveals himself in a general way through creation and human experience, yet the Hebrew scriptures remain the most important source of divine revelation.

DISCUSS

1 How has God revealed himself through the ages according to Christian tradition?
2 Why do you think up to 90 per cent of Europeans believe in God?

JESUS CHRIST: THE FULLNESS OF REVELATION

> Long ago God spoke to our ancestors in many and various ways through the prophets, but in these last days he has spoken to us by a son, whom he appointed heir of all things, through whom he also created the worlds. He is the reflection of God's glory and the exact imprint of God's very being ...
>
> (Hebrews 1:1-2)

Throughout the ages, God's people were continuously called into a covenant relationship with God. Yet through sin and failings the people could never live up to the demands of the covenant and so God, in his mercy and love, sent his only son Jesus to

Revelation: A Christian Understanding of God

establish through his death and resurrection an eternal and everlasting covenant. The early Christians understood that Jesus was himself divine and the new Lamb of God. Just as the blood of the lamb had saved the Hebrew people of old during the Exodus, salvation would now be achieved for all through Jesus' blood spilt on the cross.

What is unique about the Christian understanding of divine revelation is that God has been *fully revealed*, once and for all, through his son Jesus Christ, who himself was both God and man. Even though God revealed himself through Abraham, Moses and the Prophets, he has been fully revealed in Jesus Christ. Therefore the only true way we can come to understand what God is like is through the person and teachings of Jesus as found in the New Testament.

10th-century Byzantine illustration of Luke the Evangelist

As noted above, many people have different opinions of what God is like, but the Christian understanding is that we come to truly know what God is like through the person of Jesus. As stated in John's gospel: 'Whoever has seen me has seen the Father. How can you say, "Show us the Father"? Do you not believe that I am in the Father and the Father is in me?' (John 14:9-10).

What Jesus makes clear is that he is the unique and full revelation of God because he himself *is* God. To come to know Jesus is to come to know God the Father.

DISCUSS
1 What is unique about the Christian understanding of divine revelation?
2 According to Christian tradition how can we come to truly know God?

into

the

deep

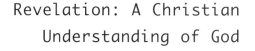

Revelation: A Christian Understanding of God

UNDERSTANDING CHRISTIAN REVELATION

> The Father's self-communication made through his Word in the Holy Spirit, remains present and active in the Church.

(CCC, 79)

Moses with the Tablets by Rembrandt, 1659

Salvation and true freedom were given to us as a gift through Jesus Christ. God wants all to know this and to receive salvation, so from the earliest times the apostles were charged with the mission of preaching this good news. The gospels written during the time of the apostles contain the teachings of Jesus and all saving truth. The message contained in the gospels was first transmitted orally, by word of mouth, in the years immediately after the death of Jesus but eventually were written down by the apostles and those associated with them under the guidance of the Holy Spirit. Thus the message of Jesus and the good news about his death and resurrection were preserved in written form in the gospels.

A student might well ask how we can be sure that the message was handed down faithfully through the ages. Jesus was the ultimate source of teaching authority but passed this on to his apostles, who in turn appointed bishops as their successors. This line of authority remains unbroken today through the teachings of the Church. So the message of the good news has been passed down today and continues to be examined and interpreted by the Church for each new generation. This living transmission is called Tradition and along with the written word of the gospels insures a faithful preservation of the full revelation of God which was Jesus Christ.

into

the

deep

> Sacred Tradition and Sacred Scripture, then, are bound closely together, and communicate with one another. For both of them, flowing out from the same divine well-spring, come together in some fashion to form one thing, and move towards the

Revelation: A Christian Understanding of God

same goal. Each of them makes present and fruitful in the Church the mystery of Christ, who promised to remain with his own "always, to the close of the age".

(CCC, 80)

OTHER RELIGIONS

We have examined how revelation is understood in Christianity and also noted its relationship with the Jewish faith. The Jewish religion does not understand Jesus as the fullness of revelation but looks instead to its sacred texts as the source of divine revelation. The sacred texts of Judaism are known as the Hebrew scriptures, as they were written in Hebrew first during the Exile (587 BCE) and completed around 200 BCE. The Hebrew scriptures are divided into three parts; The Torah (Pentateuch or Law of Moses), The Nev'im (the Prophets) and finally The Kethuvim (the Writings).

In Islam, which is also a monotheistic religion, God is understood to have revealed himself to Abraham and Moses along with the prophets. Jesus, however, is not accepted as being divine but instead is understood within Islam as one other in a line of prophets. They believe that Allah (God) revealed himself for the last time to Mohammad in the sixth century. They believe that this was a complete and ultimate revelation. This ultimate revelation is recorded in the Koran, the sacred text for Muslims. It is the end of a long line of revelation stemming from the prophets.

RELATING TO OTHER RELIGIONS

In Ireland today there are a growing number of different ethnic groups and hence worshipping communities of different faiths. It can sometimes appear confusing that there can be so many different religions but they all point to the human tendency to ask questions and search for meaning. In the last century, explorers and anthropologists discovered many cultures and tribes that had been hidden for generations from modern western society. What was remarkable, however, was the almost universal

into

the

deep

Revelation: A Christian
Understanding of God

phenomenon of some form of religious belief and practice amongst the tribes.

It would appear that humans are aware of a hidden power or even a supreme being to which they attribute not only their own existence and destiny but also moral guidance and meaningful rituals, prayers and practices. Even though the Catholic Church proclaims and believes that Jesus is the way the truth and the life, she rejects nothing that is true and holy in other religions. The Church holds in high regard all those aspects of other religions that lead people to a good and meaningful life whilst promoting justice and liberty for all. In this regard the Church holds Islam in high regard as it acknowledges Jesus as an important figure and worships devoutly the one God.

As noted previously in this chapter, Christian revelation traces its origins back to Jewish history and both Christianity and Judaism share a common spiritual heritage. Therefore Christians should be encouraged to engage in dialogue and discussion with Jews so as to foster greater mutual understanding and appreciation.

The Church believes that all of humanity was created out of love and so must relate to each other in a loving manner. In an age of greater ethnic and cultural diversity the Church's message is timely and relevant:

 There is no basis therefore, either in theory or in practice for any discrimination between individual and individual, or between people and people arising either from human dignity or from the rights which flow from it. Therefore, the church reproves, as foreign to the mind of Christ, any discrimination against people or any harassment of them on the basis of their race, colour, condition in life or religion.

(*Nostra aetate*)

 DISCUSS

1 How does the Catholic Church view other religious traditions?

2 In what way do you think humans from diverse cultures and societies have sensed a hidden power or supreme being in their experiences?

Revelation: A Christian
Understanding of God

Chapter Eleven

IMAGES OF GOD

TIMES OF CONSEQUENCE

Humans have always asked questions: What is the meaning of life? What is right and what is wrong? Why do people suffer? What happens after death? Where do we come from? As we learned in the previous chapter, throughout history and even up to today people have an awareness of a hidden power that lies at heart of our world and our lives. People often recognise this power as a supreme being. There are times in life during which people ask these questions more than usual, times when talking about God seems the appropriate thing to do – we will call these 'times of consequence'.

Many of our everyday activities have no major consequences for our lives. They are not life or death situations, though they may be enjoyable or dead boring. Decisions such as which book to read or which TV programme to watch, whether to stay in or go out with friends, won't make any real difference to your life. During such times, chances are, you won't be thinking or talking about God. But then, a day will come along that has serious consequences for your security, your relationships and possibly even your life.

DISCUSS

1   When do you think people usually talk about God? Give examples.

2   Give examples of situations that have significant consequences for people. Why do people sometimes talk about God in these situations?

DEATH IN THE ANDES

 We may be walking to our deaths, but I would rather walk to meet my death than wait for it to come to me.

(Nando Parrado)

The Andes

In 1972, a rugby team called the Old Christians set off from Uruguay to fly to Chile to take part in a rugby competition. It was October and winter was settling in. Somewhere over the Andes, the plane got into difficulties and eventually crashed over a hundred miles off course into a mountain. It was a day that was to have the most immense consequences for every man and woman on board.

Many were killed. Those who survived would face the most unbearable time abandoned 11,000 feet up a mountain in temperatures of -40 C. They soon learned from the plane's radio that the search for them had been called off. The ice that they could manage to melt barely satisfied their thirst and their food supplies rapidly diminished. They found themselves wasting away as their bodies, through starvation, began to consume their own flesh. These were times of deep consequence, as they witnessed themselves slowly and painfully shrink to skin and bone. There was no food to eat ... that is, except for the dead bodies of their friends and team mates.

Some would survive that frozen unforgiving landscape, others wouldn't. For them, it was time to talk about survival, death, God and the power of love. This is their story.

Dante's Hell

In 2006, Nando Parrado, one of the survivors of the air disaster, wrote *Miracle in the Andes*. He described how the plane had crashed

with incredible force and those who survived had to tend to their own injuries as they lay huddled among the corpses of the dead. Some of the injuries were horrific, and the survivors' coping mechanisms bear testimony to the strength of the human spirit. One man, Enrique Platero, yanked a six-inch steel tube from his stomach, taking with it several inches of his intestines. He pushed

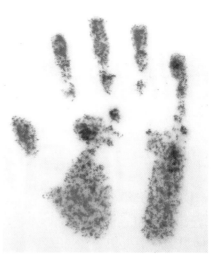

them back in, got bandaged up and immediately tended to those worse off than him. And there were many. Nando himself woke up after two days to discover a hole in his skull. Only the freezing temperatures kept his brain from fatally swelling.

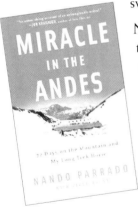

Nando lost his mother in the crash. He tended to this sister for days, but eventually the cold and her injuries took her from him too. For Nando, it was Dante's Hell.

On days of consequence, we talk about God. Those huddled in the fuselage of the mangled plane soon began to debate where God was in all of this, what God was doing in the midst of such tragedy.

DISCUSS

What kinds of discussions do you think the survivors would have had about God? What questions would they have asked?

CHILDHOOD IMAGES OF GOD

Some of the survivors felt that God had saved them from death for a reason and that God would not forsake them now. But

into
the
deep

Nando
Parrado
today

Nando found it hard to follow the prayers of the others when he prayed with them. He too prayed for a miracle, but when he strained his ears there were no sounds of distant helicopters coming to save them. When he thought about their utter desolation and hopelessness, he could only find solace in the love between himself and his father, a man who was unaware that his wife and daughter were dead. The following is an extract from a conversation he had with one of the survivors, Arturo.

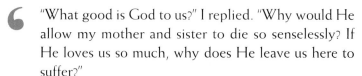

"What good is God to us?" I replied. "Why would He allow my mother and sister to die so senselessly? If He loves us so much, why does He leave us here to suffer?"

"You are angry at the God you were taught to believe in as a child," Arturo answered. "The God who is supposed to watch over you and protect you, who answers your prayers and forgives you your sins … Religions try to capture God, but God is beyond religion. The true God lies beyond our comprehension. We can't understand His will; He can't be explained in a book. He didn't abandon us and He will not save us. He has nothing to do with our being here. God does not change, He simply is. I don't pray to God for forgiveness or favours, I only pray to be closer to Him, and when I pray, I fill my heart with love. When I pray this way, I know that God is love. When I feel that love, I remember that we don't need angels or a heaven, because we are part of God already."

I shook my head. "I have so many doubts," I said. "I feel I have earned the right to doubt."

"Trust your doubts," said Arturo. "If you have the courage to doubt God, and question all the things you have been taught about Him, then you might find God for real. He is close to us, Nando. I feel Him all around us. Open your eyes and you will see Him, too."

(pp. 76–77)

into

the

deep

'I thought God was a giant man or maybe a tall man with a long beard. Oh, and he lived in the sky. He wore robes. But he wasn't someone you related to. Now it's someone else you can talk to other than your parents.'

'As a child God was someone I prayed to in order to get dreams and wishes. Now I see him as someone I pray to for myself, problems etc.'

Arturo tells Nando that, for him, God is close and has not abandoned them. He tells Nando to question all he has been taught about God in order to find the real God, who is love. Arturo, it would seem, is suggesting that Nando has a childlike image of God. This image is of a God who minds us and answers our prayers; a God who does what we ask.

Break into groups and discuss the images you had of God when you were children. What did you think God was like? How do children pray to God? How do their prayers change when they grow up? Has your image of God changed? Like Arturo, do you now think that God is mysterious and hard to understand? Do you have doubts? Is it good to have doubts about childlike images of God? What kinds of doubt do young people your age have about God?

DOES GOD WANT US TO SURVIVE?

After their meagre food supplies had long vanished, the survivors became obsessed in their search for food. According to Nando, once the brain realises that the body has begun to break down its own flesh and tissue for fuel, it sends an adrenaline rush through the system, like an incessant alarm-bell ringing, tormenting the mind.

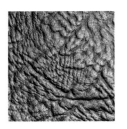

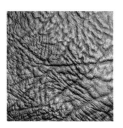

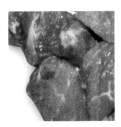

They ate the leather in the plane seats and anything resembling food. There was nothing on the mountain to eat, nothing except the one thing that their minds would not allow them to consider … the human flesh on the frozen dead: 'There are some lines, I suppose, that the mind is very slow to cross, but when my mind did finally cross that line, it did so with an impulse so primitive it shocked me.'

Soon all the survivors had to face a horrific reality: die through starvation or eat the dead and survive maybe long enough for a search to resume. But they were plagued with thoughts of the consequences of such actions: would God forgive them?

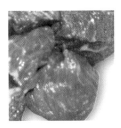

'If you don't eat, you are choosing to die,' Roberto answered. 'Would God forgive that? I believe God wants us to do whatever we can to survive.' They each took some human flesh and chewed the only cold and tasteless nourishment that the mountain could provide.

DISCUSS

1 In your discussions above, you may have mentioned a childhood image of God, where God is there to give us what we pray for. There was a time when we felt we could sit back and wait for the new bicycle to arrive. The survivors wanted God to send them some help, to send rescuers. This was what they prayed for. In the above passage, what is Roberto's understanding of God? Does God answer our prayers? How does God answer those prayers?

2 'God wants us to do whatever we can to survive.' Can you think of examples where God gives people the strength to cope with or survive certain difficult situations? Share them with the class.

into

the

deep

LOVE: A MECHANISM FOR SURVIVAL

One night, Nando had a discussion with Liliana. Nando continued to doubt that God would save them. Liliana told him that there is no way to understand God. All we can do, she explained, is 'love God and love others and trust in God's will'. Nando tried to understand her words but couldn't. He drifted off to sleep, only to be awoken by an unimaginable icy wetness crushing down on his chest. Their plane, the Fairchild, had been hit by an avalanche, and Liliana, who had moments earlier spoken such kind words, had been crushed to death. Nando was driven to confront the horrors of his situation.

> Who could survive such a litany of horrors as we had been forced to endure? What had we done to deserve such misery? What was the meaning of our suffering? Did our lives have any value? What kind of God could be so cruel? These questions plagued me every moment, but somehow I understood that thoughts like these were dangerous. They led to nothing but an impotent rage that quickly soured into apathy. In this place, apathy meant death, so I fought off the thoughts by conjuring thoughts of my family at home. I pictured my sister Graciela with her new baby boy. I wanted so badly to be an uncle to him. I still had the red baby shoes my mother bought for him in Mendoza, and I imagined slipping them onto his little feet, kissing his head, whispering to him, *"Soy tu tio, Nando"*.

(pp. 128–129)

into

the

deep

DISCUSS

1 'What kind of God could be so cruel?' Why do people sometimes think that God is cruel? Can you understand this view? Do you think God can be cruel? Give reasons for your answer.

2 Liliana told Nando to think about love. Based on the above extract, in what way might her advice have helped him to survive, even though he may have been unaware of it?

ASIDE

'These questions plagued me every moment, but somehow I understood that thoughts like these were dangerous. They led to nothing but an impotent rage that quickly soured into apathy.' In the latter half of the twentieth century, pioneering research was conducted in the area of kinesiology, which is the study of muscles and their movement. Researchers found that particular substances caused muscles to weaken, but Dr John Diamond discovered that hostile or negative thoughts or feelings could also cause muscles to weaken. In tests, people who thought negative thoughts were found to have less muscle strength than those who had positive and loving thoughts. So Nando may have been right. Negative thinking weakens our physical systems. What seems remarkable about the above research is that the body itself seems to 'know' when it is in the presence of negative stimuli. One other test worth mentioning involved participants listening to recorded messages, some of which were true whilst others were deceitful. Subjects who listened to the true messages showed a stronger muscle response than the ones who listened to deceitful messages.

into

the

deep

TURNING TOWARDS GOD

> ❝ I had found my limits… ❞

> ❝ To you, O Lord, I call;
> My rock, do not refuse to hear me,
> for if you are silent to me,
> I shall be like those who go
> down to the pit. ❞
>
> (Psalm 28:1)

After sixty days, their source of human meat began to dwindle and Nando began to realise that they must find their own way back to civilisation. One previous attempt almost ended in disaster but Nando was determined that they should climb their way out of the mountains. It seemed like an impossible task without the proper clothing or climbing equipment, not to mention the fact that they were also emaciated and sick. Nando realised that never before in his life were his decisions and thoughts so full of consequence. One false move on the mountains spelt death. His mind was awash with thoughts of dread and fear.

> ❝ What is it like to freeze to death? I wondered. Is it a painful death or an easy one? Is it fast or slow? It seems like a lonely way to die. How does one die of exhaustion? Do you simply drop in your tracks? It would be horrible to starve to death, but I would rather starve than fall. Please God, don't let me fall. That is my greatest fear – to slide down some steep slope for hundreds of feet, clutching at the snow, knowing I am heading for a cliff and a long, hopeless drop to the rocks a thousand feet below. What would it feel like to fall that far? Would my mind shut itself down to spare me the horror, or would I be lucid until I hit the ground? Please, God, protect me from that kind of death. ❞
>
> (p. 164)

DISCUSS

1 People tend to think about God when they face death. What does this tell us about our understanding of God? Why do people turn to God when they think about death?

2 Nando often rejected or fought with God. He couldn't understand God. Yet now, at the limits of his own life, he turns to God, begging God to save him. What does this tell us about Nando's understanding of God? Is it more than an understanding? Is it a relationship? If so, what kind of a relationship is it?

THE OPPOSITE OF DEATH IS LOVE

> I made every step a step towards love and that saved me.

Nando and a companion set off on their journey. The effort to reach the summit of the mountain that blocked their path to freedom was beyond description. They reached the limits of their own bodies, energy, will and determination. There was absolutely nothing left inside them, and yet they kept going until they reached the summit.

They believed that beyond the mountain lay civilisation. But as Nando scanned the view from the mountain-top, one thing soon became clear: there was nothing ahead of them but more mountains and more snow. He raged at God and the mountains and fell to his knees in defeat.

> In that moment all my dreams, assumptions and expectations of life evaporated into thin Andean air. I had always thought that *life* was the actual thing, the natural thing, and that death was simply the end to living. Now, in this lifeless place, I saw with a terrible clarity that *death* was the constant, death was the base, and life was only a short, fragile dream. I was dead already. I had been born dead, and what I

thought was my life was just a game death let me play as it waited to take me. In my despair, I felt a sharp and sudden longing for the softness of my mother and sister, and the warm, strong embrace of my father. My love for my father swelled in my heart, and I realised that, despite the hopelessness of my situation, the  memory of him filled me with joy. It staggered me: the mountains, for all their power, were not stronger than my attachment to my father. They could not crush my ability to love. I felt a moment of calmness and clarity, and in that clarity of mind I discovered a simple, astounding secret: death has an opposite, but the opposite is not mere living. It is not courage or faith or human will. The opposite of death is *love*. How had I missed that? How does anyone miss that? Love is our only weapon. Only love can turn mere life into a miracle, and draw precious meaning from suffering and fear. For a brief, magical moment, all my fears were lifted, and I knew that I would not let death control me. I would walk through the godforsaken country that separated me from my home with love and hope in my heart. I would walk until I had walked all the life out of me, and when I fell I would die that much closer to my father. These thoughts strengthened me, and with renewed hope I began to search for pathways through the mountains.

(pp.186–187)

into

the

deep

> ... for God did not give us a spirit of cowardice, but rather a spirit of power and of love ...

(2 Timothy 1:7)

DISCUSS

According to Nando, 'Only love can turn mere life into a miracle'. Soon after this episode, Nando met a herdsman further down the mountain. How did love perform a miracle? In what way did love save Nando?

THE STRANGE LANGUAGE OF LOVE

Many years have passed since Nando's experiences in the mountains and he has had time to reflect on his understanding of God. He still says the prayers he learnt as a child but he no longer thinks of God in the same childlike manner, as a wise heavenly Being listening patiently to us on the other end of the line. In fact, he feels he no longer really understands who

God is, but on the mountains he discovered something that would be as close as he would ever come to an understanding of God.

In the mountains, Nando discovered a 'silence, a wholeness, an awe-inspiring simplicity'.

into the deep

> It seemed to reach me through my own feelings of love, and I have often thought that when we feel what we call love, we are really feeling our connection to this awesome presence. I feel this presence still when my mind quiets and I really pay attention. I don't pretend to understand what it is or what it wants from me. I don't want to understand these things. I have no interest in any God who can be understood ... In the mountains it was love that

kept me connected to the world of the living. Courage or cleverness wouldn't have saved me.

GOD IS LOVE

 Whoever does not love, does not know God, for God is love.

(1 John 4:8)

God is love, and so God revealed himself to Nando through the love Nando felt for his family. These insights into Nando's experiences of God through the love he felt for his family echo the Christian understanding of a God who can only be really understood as a force and source of love.

What makes love truly incredible is its transforming power. Love saved not only Nando's life but the lives of all the

In 2006 survivors placed a Uruguayan flag at a burial cairn memorialising the 29 passengers aboard the Fairchild 571 who did not survive the ordeal

others who were stranded on the mountain with him. When Nando and his companion finally reached the rescuers, they took out a map to try to discover where the others were. The helicopter pilot and crew listened to Nando but could not believe his story. They told him that not only was it impossible for him to have climbed over such mountains, but it would probably be impossible for the rescue helicopter to ascend such peaks to reach the others. Nando begged them and swore the location was right. The helicopter began its ascent up the steep mountain side. Suddenly it began to shake violently and the pilot informed them that to go any further would put all their lives at risk. This is a life-threatening mission now, and I won't go any further unless

into the deep

everyone on board volunteers.' Nando looked down at the mountains that he had miraculously climbed and realised he might now crash right back into them. Such luck! He thought of his fellow survivors and volunteered.

On 22 September 1972, the remaining survivors of the Fairchild were rescued. They had constantly prayed to a God who is love to save them, and the power of love and sacrifice and the stubborn refusal of one, Nando Parrado, to give up on love, saved their lives.

 Let us love one another, because love is from God; everyone who loves is born of God and knows God.

(1 John 4:7)

DISCUSS

1 Why do you think people instinctively have a belief in a higher power or surpreme being?
2 How does God reveal himself to us?
3 Why do you think Nando discovered God through the love he had for his family?

into
the
deep

Chapter Twelve

GOD AS MYSTERY

SOWERS AND REAPERS

At the surface level, the saying of Jesus from the gospels – 'As you sow, so shall you reap' – could mean that if you sow peas … you will reap peas; sow carrots and reap … carrots. But considering Jesus died a most unpleasant death for his message, it's unlikely that the above statement was meant as a horticultural lecture for his disciples. There was usually a deeper meaning to his words. He had a unique insight into human nature – no one understands as he does how God in him transforms humanity. So what did he mean?

Every day we sow. When you walk into school in the morning, you start sowing. Some examples:

- Steve comes into school cursing God, humanity, teachers, fellow students and his dog. He hates school and rejects anybody or anything associated with it. He does not co-operate. He is a vortex of rebellion. He gets expelled and never sits his Leaving Cert. He sowed rejection and … the system rejected him.

  Luckily Steve's father owns a pub. He loves working behind the bar and goes into it full time. He has a big welcome for everyone, loves the work and guess what … the work loves him. A consequence: huge profit over the first six months.

- Sue likes going out with boys but is always a bit paranoid that something will go wrong. As she cuddles her boyfriend, she's thinking, 'This is great, but I just know something will go wrong.' Guess what? Something always does. Sue sows the thought that 'something will go wrong' every day of her life … and something always does.

DISCUSS

Can you think of other examples where people reap what they sow? You might think of examples from sport, school, relationships or family life.

SOWERS OF ANGER

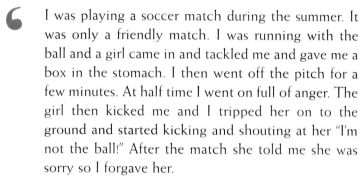

> I was playing a soccer match during the summer. It was only a friendly match. I was running with the ball and a girl came in and tackled me and gave me a box in the stomach. I then went off the pitch for a few minutes. At half time I went on full of anger. The girl then kicked me and I tripped her on to the ground and started kicking and shouting at her "I'm not the ball!" After the match she told me she was sorry so I forgave her.
>
> (Female, 16)

Angry people are a small industry in themselves – there are anger-management courses and classes. Angry people cause a lot of trouble. They sow lots of anger.

DISCUSS

What is it like to live in an angry person's universe? Describe a day in the life of an angry person. What's life like around angry people?

Researchers followed angry people around for a while to discover what motivated their approach to the world. They found that angry people were far more likely to end up in trouble than other people. They were also far more likely to end up in angry situations with other people. It emerged that ordinary people reacted to angry people with … anger. Sadly, angry people ended up walking around in a very angry world, a world full of road rage, arguments and fights. According to the research, other people seemed to know instinctively when someone was an angry person and they related to them with anger. People who were

normally peaceful types became angry when dealing with angry people. It was almost as if angry people were sending out a signal that they lived in an angry world and everyone in it should be angry.

DISCUSS

Why do you think angry people end up living in a very angry world?

CREATING OUR OWN REALITY

Similar research into other types of people revealed equally interesting results: charitable and helpful people had a significantly higher than normal amount of charity shown towards them during their day; generous people lived in very generous worlds. Greedy people rarely, if ever, had any generosity shown to them.

Jesus had a knack of delivering what appeared to be simple one-liners, but they always seemed to point to some deeply insightful truth about human nature ... as you sow, so shall you reap.

In terms of our study here, another fascinating aspect has emerged regarding the reapers' lives. When it comes to God, angry people seem predominantly to believe in an angry God. Likewise, people who are kind and charitable tend to believe that God is kind and charitable. It would appear that whatever kind of world you create for yourself on the inside also becomes the universe that you live in. Create an angry world and you will live in an angry world, and your God will be angry too.

into
the
deep

ASSIGNMENT

List A below describes different personalities. List B describes different images of God. During a class discussion or working in groups, see which image of God would most likely be adopted by each personality.

List A

'I have some spare time so I just do a few hours in the Oxfam shop twice a week.'

'I don't worry too much about the future. I think everything usually works out ok. It'll be grand.'

'Everybody is out to get you, so I reckon it's everyone for themselves. Seriously, look after you your own patch because nobody else will.'

'I was going to smack him one but I let it go. Sure it can happen to anyone. You're as well off forgetting about it.'

'I couldn't be bothered most of the time.'

List B

'Not sure God is too concerned with the world. He's probably there but does his own thing.'

'God doesn't care about us, in my opinion.'

'I don't go to confession much but I have this sense that if I do something, like, yer man upstairs will be ok with it.'

'I think God has a plan for all of us, like a destiny thing. There's something for us all to do.'

'I think God takes an interest in my life. I think God's there for me.'

into

the

deep

LAND OF IMAGES

In the section above, we examined how a person's image of God can be influenced greatly by their own general view of the world. At this stage, it would be good to consider what your own image of God may be, along with recognising other traditional images of God.

You'll notice that we don't speak about images of your principal or of the person who delivers your post. Neither do we do images of butchers or teachers. We don't because we don't need to. You see these people, talk to them and form your own opinions based on a direct experience. On the other hand, we do create images of things that we've no direct experience of. An obvious example is God, but there are many others.

Imagine for a moment that you're a single girl and a friend has approached you with some exciting news. She was visiting some pals last night and met this guy called Bob ... lovely chap. Then in a moment of inspiration she realised that he could be a perfect match for you! Oh the excitement! Giggles all round.

'So what's he like?' you enthuse. She then, at length, gives as accurate an image as possible of Bob. She tells you that he lives in a fabulous house down by the lake, and his family have a boat, and it all just becomes so overwhelmingly romantic that you're beside yourself with anticipation. On Saturday there's a party in his house and yes ... you're invited. Off you go home ... with your head spinning with thoughts ... he sounds gorgeous ... what does he really look like ... how big is the house ... what's his smile like ... his eyes ...

DISCUSS

1 In a scenario such as that described above, what kind of images does a person begin to create in their head?
2 Identify other 'new' situations where people create images in their minds, for example, you are about to meet a long-lost sister from across the world ... visit Old Trafford for the first time ... spend your first day in a new school or college ... go on holiday to a new destination ...

into

the

deep

It is usual for us to create mental images of people that we've heard about but have yet to meet. We do the same with places or houses we are about to visit. You create mental images of your boyfriend's/girlfriend's house and family before you meet them. Then when you meet these people/arrive at these places, you get to compare your image with the reality.

We create images around the unknown. In the situation above, the girl creates images of Bob for as long as he is unknown to her. The real Bob will either live up to expectations – and she'll cuddle up in the boat under the moonlight (just as she had imagined) – or he will not be anything like the imagined Bob and she'll develop a tummy ache and have to go home early!

DISCUSS

'When I think of God I think of clear, blue crystal water and even though God is powerful I think God treats everyone equally.'

'I think God was lonely once and then created us. I think God loves us. God looks after us because we are company.'

'God is there for you when you need help. I really believe that because of something that happened. I am grateful. You need to get to know God so as you won't be afraid on your dying bed. God takes an interest in my life.'

According to Catholic tradition, we will meet God face to face after we die. Until such time, what kinds of images have you created in your head as to what God is like? Above are some responses from other students.

into
the
deep

THE WORLD OF THE MYSTERIOUS

We create images around unknown things, places or people, which we may eventually find out about or meet. But sometimes we hear about people or places that we're never likely to have direct experience of. This is when we begin to enter the realm of mystery, the realm of that which cannot ever be fully understood. This is the realm of God, the realm of the incomprehensible. How we cope with mysteries may tell us something of how we cope with the mystery of God.

Mystery applies to things, events and beings that have been seen or experienced by very few people. For example, in the lexicon of mysterious beings, the Abominable Snowman is a mysterious creature because someone once claimed to have seen it, but most haven't. Mystery belongs to that area of life where we have a snippet of information but not enough to create a whole picture. If we create a whole picture, then it's no longer a mystery.

ASSIGNMENT

In 1856 Paul du Chaillu met an extraordinary mysterious creature while he was in the Congo. He came back and described the creature as a hairy giant: 'He stood about a dozen yards from us, and was a sight I think I shall never forget. Nearly six feet high, with an immense body, huge chest, and great muscular arms, with fiercely glaring large deep grey eyes ... he stood there and beat his breast with his huge fists till it resounded like an immense bass drum.' Du Chaillu had just described a gorilla.

(John A. Keel, *The Complete Guide to Mysterious Beings*)

In the early 1990s three men were walking in a forest just outside Aberdeen, Scotland. As reported, 'one of the party spotted a human-shaped figure running across the track a little way ahead of them. He told his friends, and when they all looked in the same direction they saw a strange, not-quite-human face. A few weeks

into

the

deep

later, the same group were driving in the area when they realised they were being followed by the same tall, dark being. The creature kept pace, even at speeds of 45 miles an hour, but eventually tired and stopped. Again, these men felt a distinct sense of terror and foreboding.' Reportedly, both parties had encountered the Grey Man of Ben MacDhui, a figure that when encountered provokes feelings of terrible fear, panic and dread.

(Matt Lamy, *100 Strangest Unexplained Mysteries*)

Of the above two accounts, which creature would you describe as mysterious? Give reasons for your answer.

HOW DO WE COPE WITH MYSTERY?

In the above two scenarios, it's quite clear that gorillas aren't mysterious creatures. The reason they are not mysterious is because scientists now understand what the creature is and have classified it. However, in 1856, gorillas were mysterious beings simply because scientists said they had no scientific evidence that they existed. It is an aspect of human life that until scientists formulate hard scientific evidence, a phenomenon remains a mystery.

The above has serious implications for our approach to God. Scientists will never be able to present hard scientific evidence or proof that God exists. This is in keeping with the most ancient traditions about God, which state that God is mystery and will always remain beyond human understanding.

Mysteries deal with those aspects of experience that are unknown or unknowable. But there's a very troubling aspect to mystery, which can be illustrated by the following story.

The 'Hugh Troy' Effect

Some years ago in Cornell University in New York State, professors and students were alarmed by the sight of very deep and large animal tracks in the

snow. Aghast, people started surmising as to what created the monstrous marks. Various strange theories were put forward, until a professor declared they were definitely rhinoceros prints. They followed the prints to where they plunged into a deep hole in the frozen lake. Fearing contamination, the campus was forced to stop drinking tap water until hooks were lowered to retrieve the sunken beast.

It later emerged that a young man called Hugh Troy had made the prints using an old wastepaper basket made from a rhinoceros foot. Using ropes, he had carefully mapped out the path of the beast, even to the point of puncturing a hole in the frozen lake. He didn't own up until years later.

The 'Hugh Troy' effect plagues all mysteries – are they just fabrications, made up stories, figments of the imagination or simple hoaxes? So if we're examining a mystery, how do we establish that it's not just an elaborate hoax? There are plenty of people who would say the exact same about our understanding of the mystery of God, that it's all just made up.

ANOMALIES IN THE NATURAL UNIVERSE

We will now take a little journey to look into anomalies in the natural universe. These anomalies introduce elements of serious doubt into our understanding of the world around us. And sometimes, in fact most times, people are not too happy with what they encounter.

VISITOR IN THE NIGHT

In *The Complete Guide to Mysterious Beings*, John A. Keel describes many reported instances of what he terms 'bedroom invaders'. This is a phenomenon whereby someone wakes up in the middle of the night convinced that another presence is in their room. In order to learn more about the occurrences, Keel uncovers some credible witnesses.

In the following extract, Sir Arthur Conan Doyle, the creator of Sherlock Holmes, recounts an experience he had one night.

> I was in my room in Crowborough. I awakened in the night with the clear consciousness that there was someone in the room and that the presence was not of this world. I was lying with my back to the room, acutely awake, but utterly unable to move. It was physically impossible for me to turn and face this visitor. I heard measured steps across the room. I was conscious (without seeing it) that someone was bending over me, and then I heard a voice saying in a loud whisper, "Doyle, I come to tell you that I am sorry". A minute later my disability disappeared, and I was able to turn, but all was black darkness and perfectly still.

(John A. Keel, *The Complete Guide to Mysterious Beings*)

DISCUSS
1 What makes the above account credible?
2 Do you know of people who may have had a similar experience? Do their stories make the above account more credible?

THE MOTHMAN

One of the most famous mysteries of recent times concerns a series of sightings in West Virginia in the US. Though the events occurred over forty years ago and remain 'unsolved', there are plenty of written sources for the modern researcher to investigate.

The story begins in a cemetery near Point Pleasant, West Virginia, on a dark night in November 1966. Five gravediggers were filling in a grave when a movement near a clump of trees caught their attention (as movements do in cemeteries on winter nights). According to their testimony, they saw what looked like a 'brown human being' gliding from tree to tree. The sighting lasted for about a minute.

A recent sighting of the Mothman

Three nights later, two young couples were driving through an abandoned World War II ammunitions dump when they saw a weird figure staring at them from the side of the road. 'It was shaped like a man, but bigger,' Roger Scarberry later told journalists. 'Maybe six and a half or seven feet tall. And it had big wings folded against its back.' His wife Linda, obviously shaken, said: 'But it was the eyes that got us. It had two big red eyes, like automobile reflectors.'

Many years later, Mary Hyre, Point Pleasant correspondent for the *Messenger*, told researchers: 'I've heard them repeat their story a hundred times now to reporters from all over, and none of them has ever changed it or added a word.'

On 4 December, five local pilots spotted the creature gliding low over the river. It had an unusually long neck and was moving its head side to side as if looking for something or somebody. A month later, the mother of Linda Scarberry saw the creature outside a restaurant. 'It was brown and had a wingspan of at least ten feet. I thought I could see two legs … like men's legs … hanging down from it.'

The story eventually took a sinister and tragic turn when in December 1967 the Silver Bridge linking Point Pleasant to Ohio

into

the

deep

Site where the Silver Bridge spanned the Ohio River

suddenly collapsed, killing forty-six people. Some believe the 'Mothman', as the creature was nicknamed, was an omen, a sign warning the people of the tragedy that was to unfold and become a major event in the history of Point Pleasant. Others attribute the tragedy to the interference of the mysterious figure itself.

DISCUSS

1   What kinds of images did people use to describe the creature reported above?

2   Why do you think this case is taken so seriously by researchers into the paranormal?

OVERCOMING THE 'HUGH TROY' EFFECT

The realm of mystery is always open to the argument that it is simply made up … that there is always a Hugh Troy lurking somewhere. Yet people who research mysteries from all over the world claim that it is possible to delve into this realm with confidence once certain factors are present. They would always approach a 'mystery' with questions such as:

* Are the witnesses credible?
* Is there more than one witness?
* Are there written sources?
* Is the mystery linked to historical dates and events?

into the deep

Our images of anything will always be incomplete, just as our images of God will always be incomplete. But it is our purpose here to create as complete an image of God as is possible. God is mystery, but like any mystery we can be confident in our investigation if we can find written records, with the testimony of witnesses and a link with key historical dates and events.

EXPLORING GOD IN THE SACRED TEXTS

> 〝 Then Jesus cried aloud: "Whoever believes in me believes not in me but in him who sent me. And whoever sees me sees him who sent me". 〞
>
> (John 12:44-45)

We noted above that it is important to examine written records to discover more about the nature of a mystery. When it comes to exploring the mystery of God, the core written records are the sacred scriptures.

According to Christian tradition, God became human in the person of Jesus of Nazareth. Jesus Christ is the fullest possible revelation of what God is like. Therefore, by learning more about Jesus, we can confidently say that we are learning more about God. To find out more about Jesus, we need to look for written sources, witnesses and historical details of his life and character.

The key written source of evidence about Jesus comes from the New Testament. According to this text, Jesus was born around 6 or 7 BCE, a few years before the death of King Herod. He was brought up by a family of Jewish peasants in Lower Galilee. He began a public ministry when he was around thirty-three or thirty-four years old. In 30 CE, he entered Jerusalem, and on the afternoon of Friday, 7 April, he was executed by crucifixion. He was about thirty-six years old.

Independent historical sources written at the time – by Pliny the Younger, Josephus and Tacitus – attest to the fact that Jesus was

into
the
deep

a historical character. Their accounts state that he lived in Galilee, began a public ministry and was executed by the Romans in Jerusalem.

There were many who witnessed Jesus' ministry, and after his death they gathered to remember him and recount their stories about him. However, around forty years after Jesus died, these primary witnesses began to die, and with them the story of who Jesus was and what he did. It was imperative that the testimonies of these primary witnesses be written down. And so written records were gathered together into one volume of sacred texts called the New Testament.

Tacitus

We will now examine some of the traditional and contemporary images of God that we find in both the Old and New Testaments.

IMAGES OF GOD FROM THE SACRED TEXTS

We ought therefore to recall that God transcends the human distinction between the sexes. He is neither man nor woman; he is God.

(CCC, 239)

In the Book of Genesis, God emerges as the one who created all: the universe, all living things and humankind. Despite the problems that afflict humanity and our world today, when 'God saw everything that he had made, it was very good ...' (Genesis 1:31).

From the earliest records of God's relationship with humanity, it became clear that, though God created all and it was good, suffering and pain were part of the human experience. Yet from the Book of Exodus, it is clear that God hears the cry of the people when they are in difficulty or slavery and God sets about the process of gaining their liberation. The image here is of an all-powerful God, who uses power to save the people. The God of Exodus is a God of liberation.

The Catechism says that man and woman each reflect the power and tenderness of God and this is apparent in the way that God is presented in the Bible. In Isaiah 42:14, God is compared to a woman in labour and, in Isaiah 49:14-15, God is compared to a woman who cannot forget the child she has borne. The image of God as 'mother' is a very rich one and it suggests a God who nurtures and cares for us as a mother would for a child. In the New Testament, God is referred to as 'father'. Jesus refers to God as 'Abba', a term that suggests intimacy. The image of a God who is lovingly involved in our lives is predominant in much of Jesus' teaching.

DISCUSS

1 What do people associate with power in contemporary society? Is power used as a force for good? How might the image of God as all-powerful being help to show us how power should be used in the world today?
2 How do you respond to the image of God as 'mother'? Why might some people have difficulties with this image?
3 How do you respond to the image of God as 'father'? Why might some people have difficulties with this image?

THE MIND-BLOWING IMPLICATIONS

When we examine the images of God in the Old and New Testaments, some things emerge more clearly about this mysterious being. God is intimately interested in your life and your welfare. God heard the cries of those in slavery in the Book of Exodus and freed them. In order to free them, God did incredible things, sent impressive plagues, stopped an army in its tracks and parted the seas. There may have been a bit of

embellishment in the telling of the story, but one thing is clear: God listens to those who ask for help and God is limitless in responding. God liberates those who ask for help.

ASIDE

'In the beginning God created the heavens and the earth ...'

When God creates, it happens on a major scale. God doesn't just do model aircraft or interior design makeovers. God creates universes. God creates life. God is a major player and God's power is limitless. God is abundant beyond our wildest dreams.

The Milky Way

God is also purposeful. God operates with purpose. God created a universe for us to live in. God created life and everything that exists. God liberates and nurtures like a mother or father.

into

the

deep

ASIDE

What does God sound like?

When they build a Ferrari they want it to go fast. But they also want it to look nice, which it usually does. A lot of effort goes into the sound of the engine. It has to sound more powerful and awesome than rival cars. So when the Ferrari 355 went into production, those lucky enough to be able to buy one claimed that both inside and out, at full throttle, it 'sounded like God'. Music critics claim that the blind singer Andre Bocelli has 'the voice of God'. So, as an experiment, get a Ferrari 355 and drive it through a long tunnel whilst listening to Andre Bocelli. Put the windows down and then listen carefully. What does it sound like? Report back to the class.

A Personal Response …

It was September. Our child was due in December but was born fourteen weeks premature. There were complications and our dream was slowly turning into a nightmare. Charlie was put on life support for three weeks but did not respond to treatment. The inevitable came and we were forced to face up to the fact that the machine would have to be switched off. I was hopeless and completely devoid of any fight. I couldn't pray. But the nurse took me aside two hours before the machine was to be switched off. She told me not to lose hope. The hospital would have to switch off the machine, but it was Charlie's life. Charlie would decide when to die. Now I had hope and I realised for the first time that there was a greater power than any machine. It was the power of life and love. I

into
the
deep

knelt down on the hard floor beside Charlie and I gave him to God. I really did. I told God we could do no more.

At 4.30 they switched the machine off and we stood there in a place without words or sound or even feeling. We stood and we waited. And Charlie, right at this moment, as I write this, is playing for the under-14s football team. They'll probably lose, they usually do.

Nothing matters to me anymore the way it did. I didn't just give my child to God that day, I gave myself too, and I learned that there is a power greater than any power we can ever know about. I have seen it at work with my own two eyes and I live in it each day as I say thank you, over and over again.

DISCUSS What kind of image of God does this mother have? Explain your answer.

CREATED IN THE IMAGE OF GOD

Being in the image of God the human individual possesses the dignity of a *person*, who is not just something, but someone.

(CCC, 357)

There is one explosive line in the Book of Genesis which can prove to be hugely significant for those of you who are interested in teasing out its implications for the images of God in your life. The line reads, 'So God created humankind in his image, in the image of God he created them; male and female he created them' (Genesis 1:27). What this means is that we are like God. We are created in God's image. Now let's revisit the three points made about God above and explore the implications of being like God.

1 I am created in the image of a God with unlimited power to liberate. With that divine spark within me, I can be liberated

and freed from any situation that is bad for me. That power resides in the spiritual fabric of my existence.

2 I am created in the image of a God whose power to create anew is limitless. I can face the world with God's power within me and I can become the person God calls me to be. I can build good relationships with those around me and with God. Then I can work with others to make the world a place of justice, peace and love.

3 I have a purpose. I am here for a reason. There is something that I need to do with my life. I was not born to think negatively about my life. I was not born to 'veg' in front of a TV. I was not born to think 'I can't do it' or 'It can't be done'. The spirit of God's very own abundance and power to succeed lies within me. There is a purpose to my life. I am a force of goodness, creativity and abundance in the world.

To summarise, all of us are connected to a power of infinite possibility, power, love and abundance. There is an indwelling of the power that created the universe, the Spirit of God, in each person sitting in your classroom right now. Not everybody gets this. Look around. Those who are asleep or are daydreaming have lost the message already. Wake up. Wake up to the infinite possibilities that can become manifest in your life.

into
the
deep

IT'S YOUR CHOICE

All who are in God have the indwelling of the Divine within them. As is evident by those who are asleep right now, not everyone will access this divine energy for good. Robert Frost wrote a poem called 'The Road Not Taken', in which he presented the scenario of two roads diverging in a wood. You, right now, are standing in a wood and there are two roads. Which will you choose?

Mawlana Rumi

Read the following two pieces, one a poem from the thirteenth-century poet Rumi, the other an adaptation by Wayne Dyer in *The Power of Intention*.

The question for you: Which piece best describes the, on average, 19,550 days you have left here on this planet? You decide. You live with your decision. Which road will you take?

> You were born with potential.
> You were born with goodness and trust.
> You were born with ideals and dreams.
> You were born with greatness.
> You were born with wings.
> You were not meant for crawling, so don't.
> You have wings.
> Learn to use them and fly.

or

> You were an accident of nature.
> You are subject to the laws of luck and chance.
> You can be pushed around easily.
> Your dreams are meaningless.
> You were meant to live an ordinary life.
> You have no wings.
> So forget about flying and stay on the ground.

into
the
deep

God as Mystery

THE IMPLICATIONS FOR YOUR LIFE

To finish this chapter, you need to think a little bit about how you can integrate the various images of God that you have been presented with here into your own life. In order to help you, you might discuss the following questions in class:

- Why do you think a person might be attracted to a God who can manifest infinite possibilities and potential for goodness and greatness?

- Do young people have dreams? Why might it be important that young people become agents of infinite possibilities in the world? What dreams are needed?

- Do young people need liberation? What kind of things do they need to be freed from? What opinions, images, pressures and strains would they be better off without?

- Do young people want to be left alone to live ordinary lives or do they want to leave their mark on the world? Give reasons for your answer.

- Do young people have ideals and want to be a force for good in the world?

into

the

deep

Chapter Thirteen

GOD IN THE 'BITS AND PIECES'

> ❝ Men build their heavens as they build their circles
> of friends. God is in the bits and pieces of Everyday –
> a kiss here and a laugh again, and sometimes tears,
> a pearl necklace round the neck of poverty. ❞

(Patrick Kavanagh, 'The Great Hunger VI')

In this chapter we will examine two things. Firstly, we will try to build up a final picture of what God is like in terms of the primary written source which is the account of Jesus' life, death and resurrection in the New Testament. Secondly, we will learn how to identify God in our everyday lives, in the 'bits and pieces' of life.

To do this, all you need do is sit back, relax and read the following story chronicling twenty-four hours of a dying man's life. It is the story of Joe Stax.

Twenty-Four Hours to Die

The mortuary attendant opened the heavy freezer door and slid the corpse onto the cold metal slab before removing the small bag of personal items. The bag belonged to another John Doe, another anonymous victim of a violent city, another cold statistic for the governor's office. He took one last look at the pallid and lifeless features. They always looked so peaceful in death, a betrayal of the violence that took the life from them. He ran his eyes down the outstretched figure looking for the assassin's signature. Just two small bullet wounds in the side, two small ruptures in the life of the hapless victim.

The police officer who brought him in asked that they search for any signs of identification. Not on this one. A packet of cigarettes, an empty wallet and a small blood-stained bible. The attendant paused for a moment trying to piece together the last few hours of the lifeless form in his care. A bullet hole, a bible and an empty money belt. This was a first. He slid the corpse into the freezing bay and shut the heavy door. No more to look at here. Another story entombed in silence, cold and darkness …

***

The wail of oncoming sirens jarred Joe's system into flight. It was supposed to have been his last deal before he got out, even though he knew that nobody really gets out. One last deal – the big one. One last pay day and then a flight to nowhere, to be nobody. He grasped his side and felt the warm, damp, sticky fluid that was his blood seeping from his body. He had to move. He had to get to the far side of wherever this was.

Joe Stax was a criminal with a history of incarceration, arrests and outstanding warrants. The criminals of the city have their own emergency services and Joe presented himself to 'Doctor' Figgs with a persuasive wad of cash. Figgs' silence could be purchased. Everything in the city had a price. The good news – the bullet went straight through. No need for immediate surgery. The bad news – it left a nice hole in Joe's side as it exited his soft tissue. Figgs' verdict was delivered in his slow, automated, clinical accent: 'Joe, go to a hospital or you've twenty-four hours to say your goodbyes. Twenty-four hours to die Joe. There's nothing more I can do here.'

Joe wasn't going to a hospital. He wasn't going to present himself with a gunshot wound when the city and her mother were looking for criminals with gunshot wounds. Hospital, cops and another spell inside. Enough was enough. He had twenty-four hours to die.

He couldn't go home and couldn't go to his family, but he felt he needed sanctuary before he could move on. He stumbled to the chapel on twenty-third street where he had been baptised.

Inside, he relished the cold and peace. As always, he felt like he was intruding when he walked in but he felt confident. He had been good to the priests and nuns through the years. Guilt money. A criminal needs to put some treasure in heaven and Joe looked up at the roof that he had generously helped renovate. He slid into the seat and bowed his head. His mind was on fire. His head was screaming about life and about survival. But Joe wasn't listening. He was overriding the primitive wiring in his brain which demanded survival. Blanking out everything he slowly fell into a shallow sleep, slumping forward as if in deep meditative prayer.

Fr Mark was an old priest who wore his fifty years of ministry with an aura of acceptance and love. Joe and Mark were old friends but tonight one would fight to save the other's life.

into
the
deep

God in the 'Bits and Pieces'

Fr Mark took Joe into the sacristy and tried to talk some sense into him. They argued, bickered, but stubbornly Joe refused help.

'Father, you know me and you've known my family. You know how stubborn we all are. Don't change my mind. I have one day to get things right. One day before I meet my maker and your boss. You know my life is a flawed work, Father, but put me right before my breathing ends.'

Fr Mark sighed and shuffled uneasily, but he accepted the word of a Stax. He could not change him now but he would put him right with God. He knelt down on his old arthritic frame and hugged his friend. He traced the cross on his forehead, accepted his contrite testimony and delivered God's own absolution and forgiveness.

Joe listened to the ancient words of absolution, lay silent and then asked his one last request.

'Father, you have studied the sacred texts and even lectured in the university. Please tell me what this God is like. Tell me what I should do in the time I have left to put everything right.'

The old priest furrowed his brow in deep consideration. His grey eyebrows shielded his features as he bowed his head, as if in prayer.

'God loves you Joe,' he said in a slow, rhythmical way, like a sacred chant. You don't have to do anything to deserve his love but I understand your condition. It is not for me to tell you what you should do. Every man and woman must make their choices and stand by them. You, a Stax, should know that. But you want to know what our God is like. God, Joe, is everywhere and in everything. God is in the city, in every street and house and alley. God is in the sounds of the night and of the day.'

He paused as if meaning to go on but stopped short. He turned to a small cupboard and busied himself for a while with pieces of paper. He turned back to Joe and gave him a small leather-bound book. Pages were marked with slips of paper.

'Take this with you to the hospital, Joe.'

Joe smiled and left the sanctuary of the chapel and entered once again the sounds and sights of a city where he would search, and find, perhaps, what he sought.

DISCUSS

1 Why do you think a person might seek to know what God was like only as they approached death? Why not during life?

2 The old priest seems to suggest that God can be found not just in the church but in everyday life? Do you agree with that? Give reasons for your answer.

Joe made it to his late night bar and settled into a quiet corner. He was carrying $10,000 in cash. He hurriedly wrote his will on a piece of paper, bequeathing all to his brother Mike, a brother whom he hadn't seen in over three years. Mike was his only remaining flesh and blood, but atonement would have to be sought. Wrongs were done and they would have to be put right.

He mused on the best course of action to meet with his brother again. How to meet Mike without

bumping into Sarah? How to revisit the past without rupturing it further?

Sarah and Joe had been lovers at one time, but it had become evident to Joe, long before they told him, that Sarah was falling for another man. That man was his brother. Maybe it was guilt that made Mike turn his back on Joe or maybe it was something else ...

Joe opened the small leather-bound book that Fr Mark had given him and read the passage that was circled:

> 'I tell you most solemnly,
> when you were young
> you put on your own belt
> and walked where you liked;
> but when you grow old
> you will stretch out your hands,
> and somebody else will put a belt round you
> and take you where you would rather not go.'

> (John 21:18)

Joe wondered about these strange lines. Where did God want him to go? Was there some place he should go, something he should do? Did God care enough about him, Joe Stax, that he had some plan for him?

Lost in thought and weakened by his wound, Joe didn't see the two figures in black approach from behind.

'Are you Joe Stax? We need to talk to you outside. You have some unfinished business with Pete Ambretti. Mr Stax, you need to come with us now.'

Yeah, Joe knew who Ambretti was. A small-time hood trying to throw his weight around. For a man starting to read the bible, Joe's next move was not in keeping with the book. He still had his .45 tucked into his belt. He deftly slipped it out and pressed the metal hard into the messenger's gut. He grabbed the

into
the
deep

man's belt, pulling him forwards into the barrel of his gun.

'Yeah, I know who Pete Ambretti is. Tell him Joe Stax isn't talkin' to anyone tonight. But tell him I'm a man of my word. Tell him I'll meet him in person in exactly twenty-four hours and I will settle his account. Remember, I am a man of my word.'

A .45 pressed into a man's flesh and pointed upward to his heart and brain creates a very persuasive argument. The man in black turned and walked.

Joe was familiar with this neighbourhood but decided to stay away from the main streets in case Ambretti's people came back. He could take a shortcut to his motel but it would take him down by an old railway line.

Fires burned in barrels and drunks stumbled across used railway lines. Joe kept his head down and walked steadily through this land of the destitute, all too aware that he had $10,000 dollars strapped round his waist. Just as he saw the streetlights ahead a voice cried to him from the darkness.

'Hey man, can you help a blind man, got lost, need someone to take me home.'

Joe wasn't buying it but something about the voice seemed decent and honest. He moved further into to the darkness and close to the wall was an old man, smiling up at him. He moved to get up.

'Gee thanks man, thought I'd be left here all night. Took a wrong turn and I don't feel too safe here.'

'Hey,' Joe protested. 'I'm takin' no one home. I can barely get home myself old man. Sorry. I gotta keep goin'.'

'The good Lord will get you home, man. He gave you two eyes. Sure I can tag along for a while. I'll keep quiet. Promise.'

into
the
deep

God in the 'Bits and Pieces'

Mention of the Lord unstuck Joe's indifference and he took the old man by the arm, picked up his bag and headed out. The bag weighed heavily on Joe's side but he couldn't give it back to the blind man.

'What you got in this bag? Isn't it bad enough being blind without carryin' burdens around as well?'

'Hell, man, that's no burden. There's my books that I need.'

'Books. What's a blind man doin' with books?'

'Only jokin' man. Lighten up. What's up with you?'

'Hey, listen old timer. I said I'll take you outta here. I don't need no lecture. How'd you end up blind in the first place?'

'I used to play with some friends long time ago in a blues group. We called ourselves The Screeching Devils and played some good stuff. Then one night we is drivin' home an' it's raining real bad. Anyways we end up hittin' a wall and my head bounced around a few times like a ping-pong ball. Got some scars and bruises and everything has been black since.'

'So you can still play your music?'

'Oh sure. I used to play the sax but I had to sell it as it was either music or food. You know what I mean man?'

But Joe was lost in his thoughts and as they reached the kerb he let go of the old man's arm as if to bid him goodbye.

'Listen, this is the street. You're on twenty-second and you're facin' north. Nice talkin' to ya but I gotta keep goin'.'

'Sure thing man. Thanks for the company.'

Joe began his slow walk down twenty-second but an uneasy feeling came over him and he couldn't stop thinking about the old man. He turned and as quick as he could, trying to ignore the pain, caught up with the blind man and grabbed him by the arm. The movement startled the old man, who swung his bag at his would-be assailant and just missed Joe's head.

into

the

deep

'Hey hey! It's me. The guy who just brought you outta that place way back.'

'Sorry man, I thought you was a mugger or somethin'. What you doin' back here?'

'Come on with me for a bit. I gotta show you something.'

'You ain't gonna be showin' me nothin'.'

'Yeah, yeah. I know what you mean, but there's a shop I gotta take you too ... somethin' you'll like ...'

Joe took his new friend to a little music store that he frequented with his old man as a kid. It was closed but everything has a price in the city and once the owner opened up he spent the best hour he'd had in a long time watching the old blind man feel and savour each instrument. He and the owner became lost in talking and romanticising about old melodies and long-dead musicians. Joe undid his money belt and insisted the old man take the best saxophone in the shop. As he left, the blind man told Joe that he had just saved his life. He told him about the dreams he had brought back to life for him, about his new income, about money and food. About life. Joe turned his back and headed off into the darkness.

That night in his motel room he opened the small leather-bound book and read Mark 8:22-26.

'They came to Bethsaida. Some people brought a blind man to him and begged him to touch him. He

into

the

deep

took the blind man by the hand and led him out of the village; and when he had put saliva on his eyes and laid his hands on him, he asked him, "Can you see anything?" And the man looked up and said, "I can see people, but they look like trees, walking." Then Jesus laid his hands on his eyes again; and he looked intently and his sight was restored, and he saw everything clearly.'

DISCUSS

1 Why do you think Joe Stax is searching for God?
2 Why do you think he helped the blind man?

Before he died Joe wanted to make peace with his brother, Mike. The next morning found him deep in the heart of the city outside the antiquarian bookshop run by Mike. He didn't notice the black Cadillac which was shadowing his every movement.

Inside, little could be seen except for stacks and stacks of books. It bore out the reality of the cheap logo on the front of the shop: 'Stax and Stacks of Books.' The shop was long and narrow, divided into sections. Joe stopped along the way, browsing, pausing, putting off the inevitable.

At the end was a small counter and hunched low over papers was the familiar figure of his brother, Mike. He was older, greyer and had put on a few pounds. When he saw Joe's face his first reaction was a faint smile, an instinctive expression of brotherly affection. Then a darkness flashed across his eyes and, stammering a little, he said hello and mumbled something inaudible to Joe.

A dying man doesn't have much time so he cut to the chase and explained how he needed to sort things out between them. He explained about how Mike was the only family he had and, no matter what went on before, Mike was his flesh and blood. Mike told him to sit down, and worry and fear registered on his face at Joe's pale features, the sweat on his brow and his heavy limp. Joe explained how he bore

into
the
deep

God in the 'Bits and Pieces'   179

no ill feelings towards his brother and Sarah, about how he could never keep down a relationship anyway.

'Look Joe,' Mike began. 'I haven't seen you in three years and now you come back into our lives looking for some reconciliation. I don't know what to think, Joe. This is a lot … and …' as he lowered his eyes, 'anyway Sarah will be here in ten minutes. I think it's best if you're not here. Ya know what I mean, Joe? Go get a cup of coffee and come back. It will be better. We can talk. Joe, this is just all happenin' so fast.'

Joe went back out on the streets but didn't quite feel like coffee. Across the road was the museum of modern art. This was the exact same building his mother brought him to many years before, a time when she harboured hopes for his artistic talents.

The museum was bright and airy, a contrast to the dark cramped conditions of Mike's place. Joe made his way to the American artists and once he found them he sat down opposite 'Gas' by Edward Hopper. It was Joe's favourite piece, not least because of the uncanny resemblance of the gas attendant to his father, James Stax. Joe thought back to his brother and another reason that brought him to his doorstep. It was the small New Testament. That morning he read 'The Prodigal Son' from Luke 15. It was a story about forgiveness. It was what he was trying to accomplish with his brother but, like the son, his brother was staying away from that moment of reconciliation.

Joe shifted his weight and began to feel, for the first time, the life ebbing slowly out of him. He gazed up at the canvas. He wondered, like the prodigal son, like the gas attendant, if somebody was waiting for him. For Joe, the gas attendant was his God, perhaps an automotive God waiting to serve the cars and folks that happened to come along. The attendant was waiting in the light outside his service station that, at a glance, resembled some type of

God in the 'Bits and Pieces'

shrine or church with its small white steeple. There was God waiting for people to come out of that heavy black darkness into his light. For a long time Joe peered into that heavy black darkness to the right of the picture. The light was welcoming, less threatening.

'Gas' (1940) by Edward Hopper

And here was Joe waiting for his brother to come out of his own heavy darkness of shame and guilt. He gazed at the red pumps and all the while the blood red of Joe's own life was making its way through bandages and clothing. Joe Stax was dying.

DISCUSS

1 It would appear that when a person is dying they begin to prioritise their actions. Why do you think it was important for Joe to attempt a reconciliation with his brother?

2 The imagery of light and darkness is strong in the Christian tradition. How do you think God can overcome darkness in a person's life?

When he went back to the shop his brother took him at once by the arm and sat him down. He questioned him about his condition, but Joe just asked him over and over were things good between them now? Eventually, Mike told him that everything was fine and said that they should see more of each other and that Joe should come out to their place in Queen's some Sunday and see the kids. Mike was a new man now, full of talk and life, unburdened for the first time in over three years of shame and guilt. Joe wanted to stay here in the neighborhood where he

into

the

deep

grew up but he knew it was time to get back to the church and Fr Mark. At the doorway they clasped hands and Mike told him he'd see him soon.

Joe sat in the back of the taxi cab and took out the small book. Weakening fast, he wanted to get to the bottom of his quest, to see what God was like. He opened on the prodigal son and flicked two pages back. There was a piece on providence and trust. Joe needed to read this now as his system was beginning to panic. Searing shots of pain coursed through his body warning him of death, alerting him to his plight ... 'That is why I am telling you not to worry about your life or what you are to eat, nor about your body and how you are to clothe it ...' He read and reread the lines and now Joe needed to move to some higher place inside himself where he could find peace or else it would all end right here. If miracles do occur sometimes they are small events tied into the bits and pieces of everyday life.

He looked back down at the book and continued on ... 'Sell your possessions and give alms. Make purses for yourselves that do not wear out, an unfailing treasure in heaven, where no thief comes near and no moth destroys. For where your treasure is, there your heart will be also.'

Instead of driving to the church Joe asked to be let off at the exact place where he got swung at by the old blind man. Joe entered the dark railway embankment and made his way along the line. His movements were deliberate now. Slowly, as he walked, he unbuttoned his blood-soaked shirt and began to open each pouch on his money belt. One

woman was sitting feeding her small child from a dirty bottle.

'Please mister, give us some money, gimme five bucks to feed my kid. Come on mister, please.'

Joe handed her two thousand dollars and her eventual whoops of delight strengthened his stride.

An old couple who huddled near a make-shift fire received another two thousand and a young girl asleep, probably run away from home, another thousand. He wanted to rid himself of the belt, his past, but its tight fabric was holding the life in him. He turned off the railway and headed left to the church. All the time the black Cadillac kept a close watch.

Fr Mark quickly brought Joe into the sacristy where the previous evening he began his quest. The priest gave him a drink and would only entertain a conversation if Joe promised to go to a hospital.

'I promise I'll take care of myself,' was his only reply.

They settled into their two chairs and Fr Mark asked him if he had discovered what God is like. As Joe spoke the priest's features softened and he nodded as the wounded man began to speak.

'I'm not sure what I found Father. I didn't see any apparitions, no voices spoke from the clouds, but when I left here last night I turned my back on something or some part of me.' He sipped some water, paused and continued.

'I met a blind man, walked with him and talked with him, and he told me I saved his life. I put music back in his lungs and a vision back in his old heart. I met my brother, whom I hadn't seen for three years, and I forgave him his wrong and he's all happy now and wants me to meet his family and be with him on Sunday. You know Father, I lost my money in an abandoned railway station and the deserted and forgotten ones of this city found it. After a life of greed and crime I hope in my last day I gave life just as my own life spilled itself out. But I didn't meet

into

the

deep

God anywhere except in some old tunes and a picture in a gallery, in bits and pieces of my life. Now tell me, what is God really like?'

The old priest stood up and turned towards the hapless victim dripping crimson blood on the sacristy floor.

'Joe, God is in the bits and pieces of everyone's life. God is in the fragments of our days, in small miracles of kindness given and received. He's in music and pictures.' He bent down on one knee and looked into eyes that were becoming grey and more lifeless with each passing moment.

With what strength the old priest had he grabbed Joe by his shoulders and eye-balled him with a stern old priest's stare.

'I told you you'd find God in the city and you found him in the old blind man and your brother and the poor and destitute. But most of all you found him inside yourself. What you did since I last saw you is exactly what God is like. Look no further Joe, because you've found God in the wreckage of your shattered life. Now get outta here and get yourself fixed.'

Joe had no fight in him now. He rose from his chair, threw his arm around the old priest and said, 'I'm goin' to a hospital.'

Outside the night was calm and breezy. Three blocks and he was at St Mary's. But the screeches of the Cadillac's tires were an omen of bad things to come.

into
the
deep

God in the 'Bits and Pieces'

Maybe on another night Joe Stax would have died, not from his wound, but from Pete Ambretti's accountancy practices. Joe had forgotten his appointment, forgotten his word, but Pete was in a good mood that night and took the bloodied money belt and left him with his life. There was just enough left to settle his account. Pete put him in the back of the Cadillac and drove him to St Mary's, brought him in himself, took his gun and his bible and scolded him at length in front of the nurses about how lousy he was with a hunting rifle and that he was never bringing him hunting again.

Joe lay back on the stretcher and watched the lights on the ceiling pass by overhead as they rushed him down to emergency. He would never have walked the three blocks, would never have lived if Pete Ambretti had not been guided by God's very own hands to follow Joe through the streets of the city to settle his account. And that's the strange and mysterious way that God works. Pete Ambretti settled his account with Joe Stax and saved his life just at the very edge of eternity.

Back in a sacristy, three blocks from St Mary's, an old priest wipes away the tears from his face as he prays for another man's life. Fr Mark reads and smiles and bows his old grey head:

> 'I am the resurrection.
> If any one believes in me, even though he dies
> he will live,
> And whoever lives in me
> Will never die.
> Do you believe this?'
>
> (John 11:25-26)

Joe didn't die that night and his was not the body on the mortuary slab. Pete could have given Joe's money to the destitute but decided instead to gamble the lot of it. He lost it, and more, and, unwilling to pay his debt, attempted to send his fellow player into the

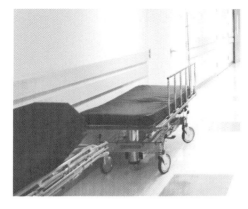

sweet arms of Jesus. But Pete was shot and dumped not far from where Joe gave his money to the abandoned. Pete lay there with Joe's empty money belt and Joe's bloodied bible.

DISCUSS

1 What image of God is presented in the above story? Why might this image of God appeal to people?

2 Joe himself became an image of God. What qualities do you see in people that act for you as an image of God?

ASSIGNMENT

Joe finds God in the bits and pieces of his life. Are there any songs or pictures, films or stories in your own culture that you see God in? Identify them and perhaps bring them in and share them with the class the next day. Try to discover what it is exactly about the different examples that reveal to you something about the nature of God.

into

the

deep

A
LIVING
FAITH

– DOING

JUSTICE

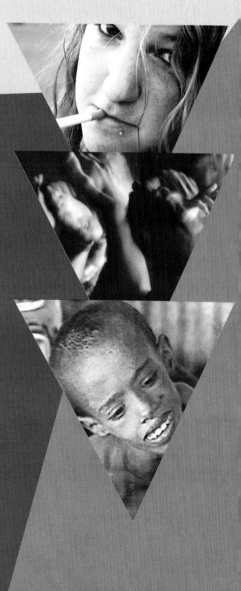

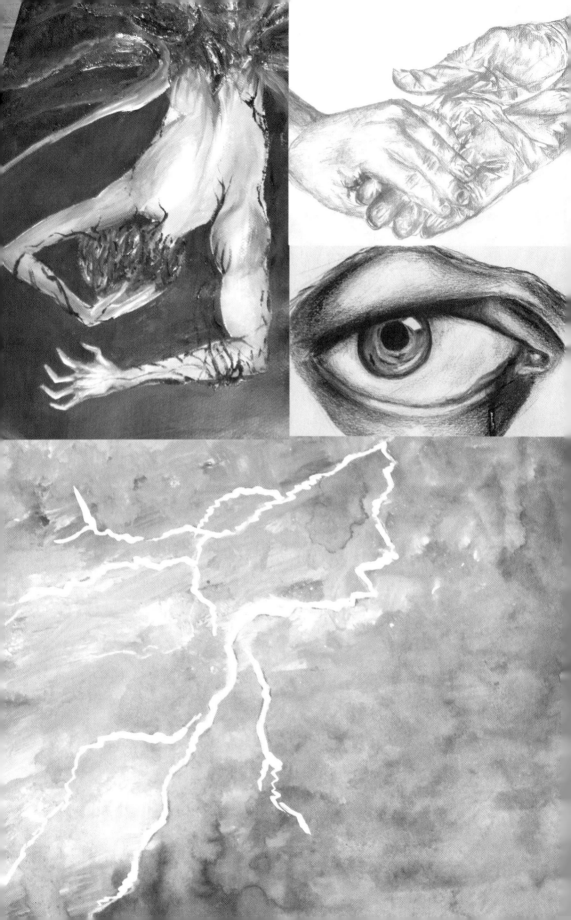

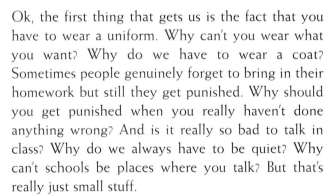

Chapter Fourteen

SOCIAL ANALYSIS

IT'S ABOUT JUSTICE

A sense of justice demands that people be treated fairly and equally. Teenagers seem to have an inbuilt sense of injustice, a sense of when they themselves or others are being treated unfairly. Later, we will look at examples of injustice in the broader world, but our sense of injustice begins and is most appropriate in whatever situation we happen to be in. Usually, injustice is most relevant to our immediate situation. When one group of teenagers was asked to identify the sources of injustice in their lives, this is what they had to say.

On School ...

Ok, the first thing that gets us is the fact that you have to wear a uniform. Why can't you wear what you want? Why do we have to wear a coat? Sometimes people genuinely forget to bring in their homework but still they get punished. Why should you get punished when you really haven't done anything wrong? And is it really so bad to talk in class? Why do we always have to be quiet? Why can't schools be places where you talk? But that's really just small stuff.

The worst is the pressure of the points system, the CAO. This is wrong and especially for students who aren't bothered with academics. I know some people who are really smart at stuff but never do well in their exams because they're not interested in the system. They'll get very few points, yet somebody with absolutely no personality will become a doctor and will have to break the news to you that you're

dying of cancer. They'll be as subtle and as compassionate as a rock flying through a window. Because they were good at physics they can be a doctor. Explain that! School's obsession with the CAO is not right. Why should anybody be judged by the amount of maths, physics or geography they know? It's stupid. I want to be a civil engineer but I have to learn Irish poetry? Why? I will never, ever build a bridge through Irish. '

DISCUSS

Do you think the education system is unjust? Give reasons for your answer. Can you think of a better system?

On family ...

' I hate having older siblings because you're always compared to them, even if it's just in a subtle way. There definitely is a pressure on you to "do well" in life, which means make money basically. They [parents] try to steer you into this career even through you've no interest in it. They just want to be able to tell their friends, "Oh, Jack is doing dentistry." So go ask Jack, "Hey Jack, are you interested in teeth?" And Jack says, "Huh?" I think a lot of parents just want to live their lives through their kids because they didn't do well enough. Well

into the deep

tough, leave us alone to do our own thing. Encouragement is different to pressure. I don't think parents realise this.

Then they have this real confusion over how to handle us. We're old enough to stay at home and babysit our younger brothers and sisters but not old enough to stay at home on our own. Go figure that one! We're old enough to work but not old enough to go out. Or you're not old enough to work but then they won't give you any money. And privacy. Could I please have some privacy? My bedroom is my sanctuary. Could people please stay out of it? Please. I'm not three. I need my own place. Finally, what's their problem with us hanging around in groups? Why can't we hang around with who we want to?

DISCUSS

Parents might not give you enough responsibility, but are there legitimate reasons for that? Are some young people unable to deal with responsibility? Explain your answer.

On friends ...

There's this problem of being able just to be yourself. Everybody is part of some group and you kinda have to go along with what's happening in the group. So if there's drinking or smoking happening, then you have to do it. There's this expectation to be like the others, even though everybody has a notion that they're individual. Most people start drinking because of peer pressure.

With girls then, there's this whole bitching thing. It's rampant and you can never feel really safe. Everyone is jealous or threatened by anybody who

into the deep

looks good or is just doing well. There's this secret desire to pull everyone down to your level. If a girl looks real good it becomes, "She thinks she's it, God's gift". If she is popular with boys, it's just because "she's easy".

DISCUSS

Do you agree that teenagers can be the cause of injustice in their own lives? Can you think of other examples when teenagers are just not good to themselves and are treating one another unfairly? Share them with the class.

DIFFERENT UNDERSTANDINGS OF JUSTICE

Justice can be defined under four headings:

Right relationships: Our lives are constituted by a web of relationships: family, friends, work and school. These relationships should work in such a manner that all involved are treated fairly and equally. For example, parents should treat their son or daughter fairly and, likewise, the son or daughter should return fair treatment. If responsibility is given, it should not be misused. Alternatively, there are times when responsibility should be given but it's not. An employer should treat you right and you should treat the employer right. For example, you should be adequately paid but you should likewise do the appropriate amount of work for that pay. In class, can you give other examples of how injustices can emerge from the web of relationships that you are involved in?

Retribution: Retribution sounds nasty and sometimes it is. For example, being imprisoned for ten years is tough, but it didn't happen for a parking fine. If a person gets imprisoned for ten years, it means they are being punished for some serious wrong committed against society. Usually, justice as retribution is a prohibitive measure to prevent people from doing wrong against others. If you commit a crime, you get punished. In your school situation, a code of conduct gives precise measures that will be taken if you do wrong in the school community. In class, give examples of retributive justice in the school system. Is it necessary and is it always fair?

Fair play: Justice in any system is a protective measure to make sure that everybody in the system is treated fairly. At home, if the son is allowed to go out when he's sixteen and the daughter is only allowed to start going out when she's seventeen, the daughter may protest that this is not fair play (the older brother will most probably snigger at this). In school, if a teacher appears to have a favourite student, who doesn't get punished to the same extent as others, this may seem like a lack of fair play. When the team is being picked by a parent of one of the players, fair play may come into question if a son or daughter is constantly being chosen, even though they seem to be underachieving. In class, give other examples of justice as fair play.

Human rights and equality: In a society, there are certain human rights that every person should be granted in equal measure. Everyone should be given access to health care and education. People should feel that their safety is protected. Everyone has the right to life. They should be allowed vote and own property. Can you give examples in class of instances where an individual's human rights are denied them?

JUSTICE IN THE CLASSROOM

The following is an extract from a true story about an American teenager who suffered horrific injuries after a car accident. After battling to survive, little did she think that her greatest battle would have to be fought in the classroom.

Speeding down the highway, the driver noticed the exit too late. He tried to make it anyway. The car ripped out nine metal guardrails and flipped over

three times before it came to stop on its roof. Someone pulled Donna from the car, and she crawled over to check on her friends. There was blood everywhere. As she pulled her hair back from her eyes so she could see better, her hand slipped underneath her scalp. The blood was coming from her. Practically the entire top of Donna's head had been cut off, held on by just a few inches of scalp. When the police cruiser arrived to rush Donna to a nearby hospital, an officer sat with her, holding her scalp in place. Donna asked him if she was going to die. He told her he didn't know …

Mom and Dad were not prepared for what they saw at the hospital. The doctors had to wait until our parents arrived to stitch up Donna's head. They didn't expect her to survive the night.

At 7:00 a.m., my parents returned home. Terri was still sleeping. Mom went straight to her bedroom and Dad went into the kitchen and sat at the table. He had a white plastic garbage bag between his legs and was opening it up when I sat down at the table with him. I asked him how Donna was and he told me that the doctors didn't think she was going to make it. As I struggled to think about that, he started pulling her clothes out of the bag. They were soaked with blood and blonde hair....

Donna was in the hospital for two weeks. Many of her friends went to see her, especially Claudia, who was there a lot. Mom and Dad never liked Claudia – maybe because she seemed 'fast', maybe because she

into
the
deep

spoke her mind; I don't really know. They just didn't like her being around.

Donna came home with the entire top half of her head shaved. She had hundreds of stitches, some of which came across her forehead and between her left eye and eyebrow. For a while she wore a gauze cap. Eventually she had our hairdresser neighbour cut the rest of her hair. It had been so soaked and matted with blood that she couldn't get it out. The hairdresser was such a kind person. She found Donna a human-hair wig that perfectly matched her hair.

Donna celebrated her sixteenth birthday and went back to school. I don't know where rotten people come from, and I don't know why they exist, but they do. There was a very loud-mouthed, self-centred girl in some of Donna's classes who took great pleasure in tormenting my sister. She would sit behind her and tug slightly on Donna's wig. She'd say very quietly, 'Hey, Wiggy, let's see your scars.' Then she'd laugh.

Donna never said anything to anybody about her tormentor until the day she finally told Claudia. Claudia was in most of Donna's classes, and from then on she kept a close eye on my sister. Whenever that girl got close to Donna, Claudia would try to be there. There was something about Claudia that was intimidating, even to the worst kids in school. No one messed with her. Unfortunately, though, Claudia wasn't always around, and the teasing and name-calling continued.

One Friday night, Claudia called and asked Donna to come spend the night at her house. My parents didn't want Donna to go – not just because they didn't like Claudia, but because they had become so protective of Donna. In the end, they knew they had to let her go, even though they probably spent the whole night worrying.

Claudia had something special waiting for my sister. She knew how awful Donna felt about her hair, so Claudia had shaved off her own beautiful long brown hair. The next day, she took Donna wig

shopping for identical blond and brown wigs. When they went to school that Monday, Claudia was ready for the teasers. In a vocabulary not allowed inside school walls, she set them straight so that anyone ready to tease my sister knew they would have to mess with Claudia. It didn't take long for the message to get through.

Donna and Claudia wore their wigs for over a year, until they felt their hair had grown out enough to take them off. Only when Donna was ready did they go to school without them. By then, she had developed a stronger self-confidence and acceptance.

My sister graduated from high school. She is married and has two great kids. Twenty-eight years later, she is still friends with Claudia.

(Carol Gallivan, *Chicken Soup for the Teenage Soul II*)

into
the
deep

DISCUSS

1 Does the above story appear to you to be an account of an injustice? Why?

2 What type of an injustice is involved here? Has it to do with right relationships, fair play, retribution, or equality and human rights? Give reasons for your answer.

It is probably clear from your discussions that Donna was a victim of injustice in her school. Were there steps that could have been taken to prevent such an occurrence? Consider the following questions before expressing your opinion:

- Why was the driver speeding down the highway in the first place?

- Why do you think Donna's parents did not like the one girl, Claudia, who could best protect her?

- Why did the girl who tormented Donna victimise someone who looked different? In school, is there a particular way you should look?

- Should there have been a system in place within the school to deal with Donna's tormentor and protect Donna from such treatment?

- Why weren't Donna's parents alerted to the situation?

SOCIAL ANALYSIS

Social analysis is a highly significant tool that's needed when trying to deal with unjust situations. It involves trying to find out what exactly are the reasons for an injustice. Let's consider the assignment you have just undertaken. Here, you were actually implementing a social analysis because you were trying to establish the causes of the injustice and the possible solutions.

into the deep

Donna was despicably bullied, but maybe Claudia's intervention, though it worked, was not the most appropriate response to such a situation. It is not a student's responsibility to take on bullies: the school should have had a procedure for dealing with bullying. The bullying was able to continue because of a failure in a system – the school's policy on bullying. The crucial question to be asked is

why adults weren't alerted. If they had been and if appropriate action had been taken, Claudia would not have felt it necessary to take such drastic measures.

Social analysis looks at structures that perpetuate injustices. In the story of Donna, there was a problem with the school protection policy. Crucially, for that injustice never to occur again, changes would have to take place within the school structure and in how it communicates its anti-bullying procedure to the students. Questions would also need to be asked about the amount of faith and trust the students have in the system.

In summary, injustices can only be adequately dealt with by examining the underlying reasons and structures that cause the injustice in the first place. Injustice can only be properly treated when we apply a proper social analysis.

DISCUSS

1   Given the insights that we gained from our social analysis, how should Claudia, Donna and her sister have dealt with the injustice?

2   Can you identify any structures in your own lives that may be the cause of an injustice? What can you do about them? You may like to refer to the following examples.

   -   Political: 'Politicians don't do enough for young people. They allow the drinks industry to exploit us; they complain that we drink too much but they don't exactly make it hard to get drink. But the more we drink the more money goes in tax, so it's just hypocrisy. And why are drugs so freely available in every town and village in Ireland? Why don't they do something about that?'

   -   Economic: 'We're definitely used as a source of cheap labour for businesses and there are loads of people not even getting the minimum wage. And we're exploited by mobile phone companies for sure.'

   -   Social: 'In society, there's this whole downer on teenagers. The media are the worst. They

love bad stories about our drinking and sexual habits. It's unhealthy. They're obsessed with what we get up to. Grow up! Like here's an example. Last month we raised a whole load of money for charity but when we rang the local paper to come up and take pictures they wouldn't. Same week though, big spread on how loads of teenagers got drunk at the weekend. And the adults didn't?'

-   Cultural: 'Girls have this massive thing about being thin ... excuse the pun! But seriously, we're supposed to look a certain way and we didn't invent it. It's just part of the fashion culture that we have to look like this. And then boys buy into it.'

THE POWER OF LIFE AND DEATH

In 1985, a young nurse called Claire Bertschinger was stationed at a feeding centre in Ethiopia during a particularly devastating famine. Those who turned up at the feeding centre were dressed in the barest of rags and the air was heavy with the smell of vomit, excrement and human sweat. Adults and children screamed, begging for help. Flies buzzed everywhere, crawling

over everything and everybody, spreading infection. Amidst this scene from hell, Claire had to decide who to admit into the feeding centre. At first there were a hundred or so, but soon the numbers swelled into well over one thousand. The local volunteers couldn't select who to admit, because some were their relatives and friends. The following is an extract from Claire's book *Moving Mountains*.

 The pressure was unbearable. As I walked up and down between the rows, I was careful never to stop in case someone thrust a baby into my arms, but even so parents tugged at my clothes, calling, "Mama, mama. Come, come, come", pleading with me to take their child. If I had taken one, I would have had to take them all, and that wasn't possible. I couldn't take just the children of those who were the strongest and could shout out. That wouldn't have been fair. To be fair, I would have to pick the right ones. And the right ones weren't necessarily the most malnourished or closest to death, because we knew those would be dead within the next twenty-four to forty-eight hours anyway. We didn't have sufficient food for more than a fraction of the sick children, let alone the starving adults. We had to do the best we could with the little we had. This meant I had to select those who had the best chance of survival if they were helped now but who would die without emergency feeding.

But how do you select only fifty or sixty from over 1,200 children who are starving or sick in one way or another? All of them either screaming or lying too still, their flesh hanging off their bones, with pus pouring from infected scabies lesions. Flies crawled over infected eyes that were gummed shut. Many of the children were permanently blind from vitamin A deficiency, their bellies grotesquely swollen from

into
the
deep

malnutrition. Often their heads were shaved, with just a tuft of hair left. I was told that according to local belief, if they died, God could grab it and pull them up to heaven.

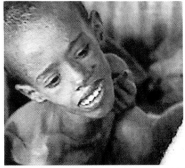

The selection procedure took a long couple of hours under the baking sun. By putting my hand around each child's arm, I could feel how malnourished they were. Not difficult when they were all so dreadfully thin, their dry papery skin covering just bone – no muscle to speak of, no fat. With a nod of my head, they were either in or out. I picked the ones who I estimated fell between the 60 per cent and 75 per cent weight-for-height ratio, those who I could see still had a spark of life in them, who would have the best chance of responding to our feeding. I inked a cross on arms or foreheads to show which ones I'd selected. I knew that if I simply touched them, parents desperate for their child's life to be saved would swap their own child with the chosen few as they walked into the centre. We'd seen it happen before. I had to force myself to turn away from the despair of the parents and children I passed over. This selection process was the fairest we could achieve, but hell – what a job, what a decision.

I couldn't understand how everyone remained so orderly. Although people tugged at me, no one really got out of line. Perhaps what I took for a sense of dignity was simply resignation and hopelessness. It was terrible to see people brought so low. I felt they expected so much of me. And what did I have to give? To most of them, nothing. They must have thought I was playing God, but I certainly didn't feel like a god. I felt guilty and ashamed that I could save so few and was sending most of them to certain death. I felt like a Nazi condemning innocent people to the death camps. I've lived with that ever since.

into

the

deep

1 Do you think Claire was justified in her selection procedure? Give reasons for your answer.
2 Why do you think so many people were reduced to such appalling conditions?
3 What do you think might be the solution to such a situation? Is there anything you can do about such situations at present or in the future?

ASSIGNMENT   Applying a Social Analysis

In her book *Moving Mountains*, Claire Bertschinger gave a further account of being moved to another feeding centre. As you read the following text, try to identify the underlying structures which, along with the drought, gave rise to the famine in Ethiopia.

It was July 1984. I was one of two nurses who had been posted by the International Committee of the Red Cross (ICRC) to the remote town of Mekele in the Tigray province of northern Ethiopia. Our job was to run a supplementary feeding station for children under the age of five, chosen from among the tens of thousands of displaced people who had descended on the town. The conflict between the Marxist government troops and the rebels in Tigray and Eritrea had driven countless civilians from their homes, forcing them to trek for miles to towns rumoured to have feeding centres, in the hope of finding food and shelter. In addition, overgrazing, deforestation and poor agricultural practices had combined with three years of drought to parch the land, and many more starving families had had no choice but to leave their homes in search of food. It was a disaster of epic proportions.

into
the
deep

Chapter Fifteen

JUSTICE

– AT THE HEART OF IT ALL

'Justice toward men disposes one to respect the rights of each
and to establish in human relationships the harmony that
promotes equity with regard to persons and to the
common good.'

(CCC, 1807)

Within the Christian tradition the person and message of Jesus
Christ is viewed as a blueprint for living. Jesus came to give us
life, and life to the full. He came to promote peace, justice and
equality for all. His message, preserved in the gospels, contains a
wisdom that, if embraced, leads to a fairer and more just society
for all.

Jesus changed completely people's images and understandings of
who God was and what God looked like: for example, he ate with
sinners, prostitutes and tax collectors; he allowed women into his

close circle of friends; he
let the Samaritan woman
give him a drink. Jesus
made it clear that outcasts
were included, that God
loves all. Being just and
promoting justice is a
contemporary expression
of Jesus' life and message.
Jesus came for the lonely,
the broken-hearted, the
damaged.

All the major religious
traditions promote justice
as a proper and true way to

Mary anoints
Jesus in
Bethany in
this icon.
Martha serves
the meal in
the
background.

Qur'anic manuscript

live human life with others. In the Jewish Hebrew scriptures God is revealed as one who is just and calls upon all to work towards a society that reveals God's justice and peace. In the story of the Exodus God intervened in the lives of the Hebrews to free them from the injustice of slavery. In the other great monotheistic faith of Islam, Muslims believe that living and acting justly is the path that leads to Allah's mercy, favour and pardon. In the five pillars of Islam, *Zakat* (almsgiving), the third pillar, is viewed as a way of justly redistributing wealth to those less well off. In Hinduism a central teaching called *dharma* means righteousness, law or duty. Dharma includes the full range of one's social and moral obligations leading to harmony and peace. Finally, Buddhists follow a Noble Eightfold Path which leads to ethical living in harmony with all beings.

We will now look at ways in which we ignore or respond to the call to do justice.

into

the

deep

Justice
– At the Heart of it All

TAKING A STAND

In 2004, a small group of students from Mount Sackville school in Dublin decided to become involved in a charity called 'Focus on Romania'. They heard that the Romanian prime minister was visiting Dublin. They were invited to a hotel reception for him. The prime minister, sensing a good photo opportunity, was glad to welcome the students into his group. But he was in for a shock. The teenagers weren't willing to let the opportunity slip by them; they circled around him and demanded that he close dilapidated and inhumane orphanages in Romania. Adults looked on bemused. Trapped, the prime minister agreed. This was an example of teenagers taking a stand against an injustice.

As it transpired, the Romanian officials closed down the worst orphanages and built a centre of excellence to take care of orphans, as well as group homes to act as a pilot project for the rest of the country. So it's not just about taking a stand, it's also about making a difference.

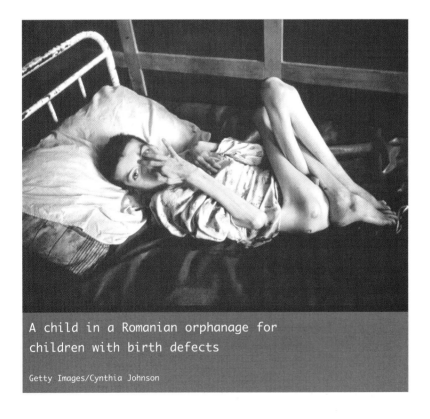

A child in a Romanian orphanage for children with birth defects

Getty Images/Cynthia Johnson

into

the

deep

DISCUSS

1 Many hold the belief that teenagers in particular are more willing to take a stand against injustices than adults. Why do you think that is?

2 One argument suggests that teenagers are more idealistic about what they can change in the world, while adults have become cynical about their ability to change the world. Will your generation remain idealistic or will you become cynical? Give reasons for your answer.

3 In fifty years or so, many of the adults you know will have died and your generation will be in charge of the world. How important is it that your generation remains active in the fight against injustice? What are the most important priorities for your generation? What are the local and global issues that need to be tackled?

SPIRITUAL ENERGY

Why is it that some people take a stand and do something, while others do nothing? Did you ever notice amongst your friends that some take a stand against a wrongdoing while others remain silent? How many bullies go unchallenged? How often have you heard someone's character being lacerated while you remained silent? How did you feel? Were you ever in the situation where you knew what the right thing to do was, but just didn't do it? Would you like to be able to take a stand? If so, you need to dig deep into a spiritual energy that's inside you.

When Pope Benedict was appointed, he got down to the work at hand. His first public teaching was on the subject of creating a more just society. He said the Church must not remain on the sidelines of the fight for justice. He stated, 'She has to play her part through rational argument and she has to reawaken the spiritual energy without which justice, which always demands sacrifice, cannot prevail and prosper' (*Deus caritas est*, 28a).

But the Pope is not alone in his recognition that the fight against injustice is a spiritual one that requires a spiritual energy. Let's take a look at the film *Fight Club*.

into

the

deep

Justice
– At the Heart of it All

FIGHT CLUB: 'THE GREAT WAR OF THE SPIRIT'

> ❛ The more people sell you the idea of spiritual peace through what you drive and how you look and how you live, the less connected you become. ❜
>
> *(Fight Club)*

The film *Fight Club* is based on the novel of the same name by Chuck Palahniuk. The film stars Brad Pitt and Edward Norton and is centred around an illegal fight club, where young professional men engage in hand-to-hand bare-knuckle fighting. It's not that they don't like one another ... not at all. They fight, not against one another, but against an unjust system that has lied to them, a corporate culture that has

Brad Pitt in Fight Club

deceived and seduced American youth with lies. They fight against the injustice of deceit.

Corporate and big-business America promised a better lifestyle, fashion and status. It promised happiness. You can look good in your clothes, house and car, but does that deliver real deep-down happiness? According to the book and the film, it doesn't.

into

the

deep

Justice

— At the Heart of it All

DISCUSS

Corporate America represents the adult world. *Fight Club* suggests that the adult world is selling youth short. It promises wealth but not spiritual peace. Do you think the adult world sells you short? What does it tell you will give you peace and happiness? Does it sell you wealth, status and property as the ultimate dream? Do you agree with that or do you feel it's a lie? Is it an injustice against your future?

Fight Club depicts a revolt against the lies that have been told to American youth. The lie is that while corporate wealth and greed can give you any material thing you wish for, it cannot give you access to the spiritual. It cannot give you truth. It cannot give you peace or happiness. The crime and injustice it commits is that it robs the youth of the most precious commodity: access to their spirituality. Without this, there can be no happiness. As the central character, Tyler, states:

> You have a class of young strong men and women, and they want to give their lives to something. Advertising has these people chasing cars and clothes they don't need. Generations have been working in jobs they hate, just so they can buy what they really don't need. We don't have a great war in our generation, or a great depression, but we do, we have a great war of the spirit. We have a great revolution against the culture. The great depression is our lives. We have a spiritual depression.

(Fight Club)

into

the

deep

Justice
— At the Heart of it All

1 Why are people listening to the advertising companies and buying stuff they don't need? Did you ever buy something because you thought it would make you happy but it didn't? How did you feel? Are the advertising companies a part of a structural injustice against youth?

2 What are the signs that your generation is undergoing a 'spiritual depression'? Does your generation need a 'great war of the spirit'? Who would fight it? How would it be fought? What would it be fought against?

THE PROPHETS TAKE A STAND

 I am the Lord your God, who brought you out of the land of Egypt, out of the house of slavery.

(The Book of Exodus)

The fight against injustice is a spiritual one. As far back as the data takes us, people within the Judaeo-Christian tradition have been taking a stand against injustice. Predominantly, these people were called prophets and they courageously took a stand against the perceived injustices of their day.

Justice plays a central theme in the Bible because God is revealed as a divine force against injustice. God freed the Hebrews from slavery, as recounted in the Book of Exodus, and that liberating action and intervention in human history sets the tone for God's activity with humanity. God hears the cry of the poor, the abandoned and enslaved, and God responds.

In like fashion, the prophets of the Old Testament took action. Amos challenged corrupt judges who distorted the justice system. He encouraged all to 'hate evil and love good, and establish justice ...' (Amos 5:15). Micah and Isaiah challenged those who made laws that oppressed and denied people their rights (Isaiah 10:1-2, Micah 6:8).

into

the

deep

DO WIMPS GET CRUCIFIED?

If you've ever been to a rock concert, you will know that before the main act comes the supporting act. Supporting acts introduce, set the tone and give us a flavour of what's to come. So around two millennia ago, when a wild man called John began to preach about the one who was to come, there was a sense that the one who was to come would have a wildness about him. They were not to be disappointed.

St John the Baptist in the Wilderness, c.1625 (oil on canvas) by Guido Reni

John the Baptist, the 'voice in the wilderness', prepared the way for Jesus of Nazareth. John the Baptist hit the Galilee scene with a bang, and so did Jesus. John the Baptist spoke the truth and challenged deceit and wrongdoing. When John preached, he did so under the shadow of a blade that would eventually shut him up. He was beheaded for attacking the establishment of King Herod.

The one that John heralded would suffer a similar fate for challenging the injustices of his day. There is a perception that Jesus was in some way weak and

into
the
deep

210

Justice
— At the Heart of it All

pitiful. But Jesus had a radical new vision for the earth and its people.

Like teenagers, Jesus was passionate about justice, but his was a justice that worked. There was an old way of thinking that taught that if someone took your eye out, you should take their eye out too. Or, if someone took your tooth, you should take one of theirs (why you'd want one, you can figure yourselves).

The problem with the old retributive system of justice was that it just didn't work. If you retaliate by taking the other guy's eye out, doubtless he'll be back to take what's left, and you likewise. Result … two blind men. It doesn't make sense.

Jesus is best understood as a truth speaker, a prophet. He noticed that the prevailing wisdom at the time was to love your neighbours and hate your enemies. Prophetically he taught that that system wouldn't work. Instead, we should love our enemies and pray for those who persecute us (Matthew 5:44). He also taught that those who fight for justice will bring great happiness and satisfaction into their own lives.

So was Jesus right? Is justice best served by praying for your enemies? Do those who fight for justice lead happier and more fulfilled lives? Deep within your spirituality, a voice cries in the wilderness of injustice and confusion. It cries out to you to do something. The fight against injustice is a spiritual battle. You're invited to take a stand.

AN INCREDIBLE STORY OF SURVIVAL

Sometimes from the midst of horror, a story emerges that transforms our understanding of the human spirit and its ability to survive almost anything. Immaculée Ilibagiza grew up in Rwanda in a secure and loving home, surrounded by supportive friends and neighbours. But in 1994 her idyllic world was ripped apart by a ferocious genocide, which resulted in one of the most horrific killing sprees witnessed in modern history. The Hutu majority, spurred on by an incomprehensible viciousness, killed almost a million of their fellow country men and women in the space of three months.

Immaculée was separated from her family and sought shelter in a local pastor's house. He himself was a Hutu and he took a great risk by taking in Immaculée and five other women. Unable to be seen, they had no choice but to huddle together in a bathroom four feet long and three feet wide for a total of ninety-one days. Even the pastor's own children could not find out that they were there. For ninety-one days they were cramped, hungry and forced to remain in absolute silence. These conditions may seem extreme but the following extract from Immaculée's book, *Left to Tell*, outlines just how precarious their position was when the Hutus came looking for them.

The summit of Mount Sabyinyo marks the borders of Rwanda, the Democratic Republic of the Congo, and Uganda

Photograph by David Pluth

 Hundreds of people surrounded the house, many of whom were dressed like devils, wearing skirts of tree bark and shirts of dried banana leaves, and some even had goat horns strapped to their heads. Despite their demonic costumes, their faces were easily recognisable, and there was murder in their eyes.

They whooped and hollered. They jumped about, waving spears, machetes and knifes in the air. They chanted a chilling song of genocide while doing a dance of death: "Kill them, kill them, kill them all; kill them big and kill them small! Kill the old and kill

Justice
– At the Heart of it All

the young ... a baby snake is still a snake, kill it, too, let none escape! Kill them, kill them, kill them all!"

It wasn't soldiers who were chanting, nor was it the trained militiamen who had been tormenting us for days. No, these were my neighbours, people I'd grown up and gone to school with – some had even been to our house for dinner.

Government leaders in Rwanda were urging Hutus to do everything possible to kill any Tutsis they knew, even neighbours and friends. All factories and places of work were closed down to give the Hutus time to kill the Tutsis. Radio stations broadcast messages encouraging the slaughter all day long: 'If you're working in your field and spot a Tutsi woman in the bushes breast-feeding her baby, don't

waste a golden opportunity; pick up your gun, shoot her, and return to work, knowing that you did your duty. But don't forget to kill the baby – the child of a snake is a snake, so kill it too!'

The mob went through the pastor's house looking for the women and shouted how they would rip them apart when they found them. The pastor managed to keep them out of the bathroom where the women were hiding, but he told the women that the mob would return and that they would find them.

For the Tutsis in Rwanda, their predicament was incomprehensible. Immaculée wrote: 'The world had seen the same thing happen many times before. After it happened in Nazi Germany, all the big, powerful countries swore, "Never again!" But here we were, six harmless females huddled in darkness, marked for execution because we were born Tutsi. How had history managed to repeat itself? How had this evil managed to surface once again?'

into

the

deep

DISCUSS

1 Genocide is an injustice which is carried out on a large scale. After the atrocities of Nazi Germany, the world presumed that similar events couldn't happen again. Why do you think the Hutus could have embarked on such a calculated rampage of murdering men, women and children, people who were their very own neighbours?

2 Immaculée asks how it could happen that the powerful nations would allow the genocide to take place. Why do you think the international community allowed the genocide to happen without trying to do more to intervene and stop the unimaginable slaughter?

Immaculée had always been a religious person, and so in the darkness of their hiding place she turned to God. She believed that God had answered her prayers to be saved, as the Hutu gangs somehow could not find their hiding place, even though they returned repeatedly, being suspicious of the pastor. She knew that as a Christian she should forgive the Hutus, but one night she was forced to re-examine her ability to forgive.

> One night I heard screaming not far from the house, and then a baby crying. The killers must have slain the mother and left her infant to die in the road. The child wailed all night; by morning, its cries were feeble and sporadic, and by nightfall, it was silent. I heard dogs snarling nearby and shivered as I thought about how that baby's life had ended. I prayed for God to receive the child's innocent soul, and then asked Him, How can I forgive people who would do such a thing to an infant?

As time wore on, the conditions in the bathroom deteriorated rapidly. Two more women had joined them, but incredibly there was more room because they had all shrunken due to serious weight loss. Immaculée lost almost half her body weight due to the meagre diet that the pastor managed to smuggle through to

them. She explained: 'Our skin was pale, our lips were cracked, and our gums were swollen and sore. To make matters worse, since we hadn't showered or changed clothes since we'd arrived, we were plagued by a vicious infestation of body lice. Sometimes the tiny bugs grew so engorged with our blood that we could see them marching across our faces.' Immaculée never ceased praying during her ordeal and she believes that it was prayer that gave her the strength to continue.

Exhumed skeletons of victims of a 1994 massacre at the Murambi Technical School in Rwanda

But the agonising suffering went on inside Immaculée's mind as she wondered about the fate of her family. She was particularly worried about her brother Damascene, a very progressive young lad who had a master's degree. One day, from outside the tiny window in the bathroom, she heard a story about a group of Hutus who had captured a Tutsi with a master's degree. She was convinced it was Damascene. They talked of how they had taunted the boy, asking him how they could have caught him if he was so smart. One boy wanted to know what made Damascene so smart and so he decided he would look at his brain. So he chopped the boy across the head with his machete and then looked inside his skull.

Throughout the country, the barbarism continued. The radio told the Tutsis to go to the churches for sanctuary, but then they were locked inside and burned. Stacks of bodies lay strewn by the roadsides, while packs of wild dogs fed on the corpses. Rwanda

into

the

deep

Justice
– At the Heart of it All

215

had descended into the most unimaginable depravity, and it was on a huge scale. Hundreds of thousands were being killed.

Memorial of the genocide in Rwanda

All of Immaculée's family were killed in the genocide. But Immaculée's story is an account of how she believed God had somehow managed to save her. Dishevelled and malnourished, the day eventually came when they had to leave their shelter. The group had to head to the roads but they were soon tracked down by a group of Hutus who couldn't believe there were still Tutsis left alive. As they walked, the Hutus encircled them and began to slice the air with their machetes. Immaculée began to pray: "'Dear God," I prayed, walking as fast as I could and holding my father's rosary tightly in my hand. "Only You can save me. You promised to take care of me, God – well, I really need taking care of right now. There are devils and vultures at my back, Lord … please protect me. Take the evil from the hearts of these men, and blind their hatred with Your holy love."' The group continued to walk and when they looked up the Hutus were gone. It is an event that Immaculée believes was a miracle.

into

the

deep

Justice
– At the Heart of it All

FORGIVENESS: A RESPONSE TO INJUSTICE

 You have heard that it was said: "You shall love your neighbour and hate your enemy." But I say to you, Love your enemies and pray for those who persecute you.

(Matthew 5:43)

Eventually Immaculée and her group made it to safety and, after the genocide finished, she returned to her old home, found the bodies of her family and gave them a proper burial. She knew, however, that there was one thing that she needed to do. She needed to meet the person responsible for the deaths of her loved ones.

She arrived late one afternoon to the prison in Kibuye. The guard, Semana, knew the prisoner responsible and he brought Immaculée to him. His name was Felicien, a successful Hutu businessman. Once she was given the name, she realised that his was the voice in the house that had shouted looking for her. Immaculée had come face to face with the man who had killed her family and hunted her down like an animal.

> **DISCUSS**
> 1 If you were in the same situation as Immaculée, what would you do?
> 2 What would be the consequences of your actions in fighting the injustice? How would it help?

Immaculée waited for Felicien to enter the guard's office. When he saw Immaculée, the colour drained from his face and he stared down at the floor. Semana screamed at him to explain why he butchered Immaculée's mother and brother. Felicien hunched lower, too embarrassed to face her.

 Felicien was sobbing. I could feel his shame. He looked up at me for only a moment, but our eyes met. I reached out, touched his hands lightly, and quietly said what I'd come to say.

"I forgive you."

My heart eased immediately, and I saw the tension release in Felicien's shoulders before Semana pushed him out the door and into the courtyard. When he returned he was furious.

"What was that about, Immaculée? That was the man who murdered your family. I brought him to you to question … to spit on if you wanted to. But you forgave him! How could you do that? Why did you forgive him?"

DISCUSS

1 Why do you think Immaculée responded to her family's assassin with forgiveness?
2 In what way might forgiveness prevent another repeat of ethnic cleansing in Rwanda?

HOW WILL WE RESPOND?

In the next chapter, we will examine ways that we can respond to injustice. But the most important thing is that we, as a global community, work to stop the cycle of injustice. Immaculée gives us her own opinion:

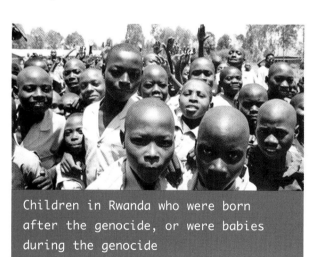

Children in Rwanda who were born after the genocide, or were babies during the genocide

into
the
deep

Justice
– At the Heart of it All

> As for the land of my birth, I know that Rwanda can heal herself if she learns the lessons of forgiveness. Tens of thousands who were jailed for killing during the genocide are starting to be released into their old towns and villages, so if there was ever a time for forgiveness, it is now.

THE CHURCH'S MISSION ON SOCIAL JUSTICE

It can be tempting to view the Church as a body that is really only concerned with spiritual matters and has little interest in the real affairs of people. But this is not how the Church views herself. God became human in the person of Jesus Christ who was intensely involved in the affairs of those around him; bringing healing, forgiveness and constantly challenging injustices in society. So too, the Church as minister of salvation, 'is not in the abstract nor in a merely spiritual dimension, but in the context of the history and of the world in which man lives' (*Compendium of the Social Doctrine of the Church*, 60).

The Church is a recipient of the divine wisdom preached in the person of Jesus Christ and written in the gospels. It is a message primarily concerned with freedom and salvation. Where men and women are, the gospel must find a place. Therefore as society

progresses the Church must address the range of issues that affect our place in the world; issues that can sometimes be destructive to freedom and true happiness. The Church teaches the demands of justice in society as is set out in divine wisdom and the gospel message.

As the Church contributes to social justice in the modern world she addresses a range of issues in her teachings, from the rights of workers to the role of governments in their running the economies of the world. The Church is intensely aware of how the distribution of wealth and riches in the world can often lead to an unfair and unjust creation of absolute poverty, especially in developing economies. The Church concerns herself primarily with the proclamation of the mystery of salvation in the person of Jesus Christ. It is only on this basis that the Church concerns herself with everything else: 'the human rights of the individual, and in particular of the working class, the family and education, the duties of the State, the ordering of national and international society, economic life, culture, war and peace, and respect for life from the moment of conception until death' (*Centesimus annus*, 54).

Justice
– At the Heart of it All

Chapter Sixteen
JUSTICE IN ACTION

SO WHAT CAN YOU DO?

In the previous chapters we examined injustice in your own lives and in the lives of others. We examined injustices in school, family life and amongst your own friends. We read a disturbing case of bullying in school. We read about feeding camps in Ethiopia and the horrors of genocide in Rwanda. Sometimes when people read about injustice they get angry because of their belief that what happened shouldn't have or what is happening shouldn't be. People also get frustrated because it sometimes seems that there's little we can do to change the situation. Sometimes in the face of injustice we feel powerless. Before we progress we need your class to discuss some important questions.

DISCUSS

1 Do you get angry about injustices in your own world and in the wider world?
2 Do you sometimes get frustrated about your inability to do anything about injustices?
3 Do you want to be able to challenge and tackle injustices in the world?

 Nothing happens until something moves.

(Albert Einstein)

In Chapter 12, we read about Claire Bertschinger. Her situation seemed hopeless, selecting children who might live with proper care. Those who weren't selected would in all probability die.

She was just one person acting against the injustice of famine, poverty and hunger. It is tempting to think that one person can, in reality, do so little. In fact, Claire Bertschinger's single challenge to injustice, her single voice in a feeding camp would eventually have unimaginable global significance.

The BBC reporter Michael Buerk heard about the feeding camp and brought a crew to film Claire's work. They filmed a four-minute segment, brought it back to Britain and aired it on the six o'clock news. In a flat in London a rock star from Dublin was watching and was appalled by what he saw. He immediately rang Midge Ure from the band Ultavox with a simple message: 'We have to do something about this.'

The something which they did was to organise one of the biggest rock concerts in history: Live Aid. It became one of the iconic moments of the twentieth century when musicians from around the world gathered to use their gifts to bring global attention to the situation in Ethiopia. Live Aid raised £50 million for Africa, inspired by the events in Ethiopia.

One voice working in an anonymous feeding camp in Ethiopia led to one of the greatest acts of global charity ever witnessed.

During Immaculée Ilibagiza's 91-day ordeal in the bathroom she frequently repeated a piece of scripture to herself from the eleventh chapter of Mark's gospel. It was a verse that also inspired Claire Bertschinger and featured in the title of her book, *Moving Mountains*. The verse reads:

> Have faith in God. Truly I tell you, if you say to this mountain, "Be taken up and thrown into the sea," and if you do not doubt in your heart, but believe that what you say will come to pass, it will be done for you. So I tell you, whatever you ask for in prayer, believe that you have received it, and it will be yours.

(Mark 11:23-24)

There is a profound spiritual message in the above scripture passage. It is natural for us to feel inadequate in the face of huge obstacles and great injustices but a Christian response to injustice

tells us most definitely to get involved and believe we can make a difference.

If one person, Claire Bertschinger, hadn't made her own single stand against the injustice of famine in Ethiopia, Live Aid wouldn't have happened; if one person, Michael Buerk, hadn't taken a film crew out, Live Aid wouldn't have happened; and if one musician, Bob Geldof, hadn't picked up the phone to Midge Ure, Live Aid wouldn't have happened. Live Aid didn't remove injustice from the world or even Africa but it made a difference. Individual people took a stand against injustice. They raised their one single voice and something happened. People who would have died lived.

Claire Bertschinger with Bob Geldof

As you read this text, you too are one single voice who in your life will either take a stand against injustices or not. It is important for you to realise that there will be implications for the decisions you make. You may only be a single person, you may only have a single voice, but the consequences of what you say and do will be significant. What will you do?

into

the

deep

DISCUSS

As a class group, what are the ways that you can identify of becoming more involved in justice issues?

Ten Minutes from Death

During the Live Aid concert a particularly poignant moment came when a video was beamed across the world featuring a young Ethiopian girl ravaged by hunger. Her eyes were sunken and lifeless and her lips parched. She was cradled in the arms of a nun.

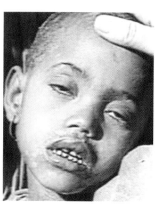

The nun later admitted that the girl was ten minutes from death. Her image was shown while the haunting song 'Drive' by the group the Cars was played. It was an image that stunned the crowd into silence.

In 2005, twenty years after Live Aid, another rock concert, Live 8, was organised by Bob Geldof. During the concert, this footage was shown again, freezing the girl's image on the huge screen behind the stage. Geldof addressed the crowd: 'This little girl was given ten minutes to live. But because of the concert we did twenty years ago she has done her exams in agriculture this week. Some of you were here twenty years ago. Some of you weren't even born. I want to show you why we started this long walk to justice. Don't let them tell you it doesn't work.' He then led Birhan Woldu, the little girl from the image, onto the stage. She had travelled 3,700 miles from her village in the mountains of

Birhan Woldu on stage at 'Live 8 London' in Hyde Park on 2 July 2005

into

the

deep

> northern Ethiopia for the show. He said: 'Birhan is a symbol of hope and courage. She is proof we can make a difference.'
>
> Because of the publicity and awareness that the Live Aid project had created, a film crew led by Brian Stewart, a Canadian journalist, filmed the younger Birhan. After the filming was over she showed a flicker of life and was immediately put into the care of nurses. Stewart sponsored her education and he eventually produced a film 'Beyond Tears' about her remarkable tale of survival.

Justice not Charity

After Live Aid, it was clear that one rock concert that provoked so much charity would not solve the problems of poverty and famine in Africa. African countries were saddled with huge debts owed to the World Bank. Only once these debts were erased could Africa emerge as an economic force capable of sustaining itself. The debts owed were the cause of the injustice that plagued an entire continent. What was needed now was more than charity. What was needed was justice. Live 8 didn't raise money but instead it raised awareness. It hoped to gather all the single voices from around the globe, from Tokyo to Toronto, into one powerful message of support for debt relief. While Live 8 was in progress so too was the G8 summit of political leaders with the power to tackle debt relief.

Bono, who was one of the organisers of Live 8, also performed. He began with a rendition of 'Beautiful Day'. He told the audience: 'This is our moment. This is our chance to stand up for what is right. We are not looking for charity, we are looking for justice. Make history by making poverty history.'

DISCUSS

Why do you think Bono believed that justice was a more potent response to poverty than charity? Do you agree or disagree with his stance? Give reasons for your answer.

into

the

deep

On why It's good to get involved ...

Most people get involved in justice or charity work because of their genuine belief that they may be helping someone somewhere. But recent scientific research has come up with startling evidence to suggest that doing good and getting involved with the welfare of others actually has significant health implications for the doer.

Christianity has been long recognised as a source of wisdom and meaning for its followers. The beatitudes in Matthew chapter 5 indicate that those who do good to others will find happiness. Now research is backing up that claim. In their ground-breaking book, *The Healing Power of Doing Good*, Allan Luks and Peggy Payne outline the significant health benefits of helping others. It would appear that when we help others we actually help ourselves

The authors begin by telling the story of a girl who lost her boyfriend in a horrific racing car accident which she herself witnessed. For twenty years she was plagued by nightmares and flashbacks, and fantasies of her own destruction. Almost twenty years later she faced up to her fear and became a volunteer in a hospice for the dying. She decided to overcome her fear of death by facing it head on. The work was extremely demanding and exhausting. When one particular patient died, she herself, alone, washed and prepared the body. It was a moment that became her liberation. Death was no longer something sudden and horrific but something calm, expected and natural. She was cured of her nightmares and

into

the

deep

flashbacks. The story, according to Luks and Payne, outlines how doing good makes you feel good. Their research discovered the following:

* People who participate actively in the welfare of others and who remove others from unjust situations suffer less from the ill effects of stress
* 95 per cent of volunteers claimed that helping on a regular basis gave them an immediate feel-good sensation. They call it 'helpers'-high'
* Volunteers felt an extra surge of energy
* Those who help regularly maintain that their overall health improved which meant less pain, stress, colds and better general well-being
* Helping strangers had more beneficial effects than helping family members
* The effects on health of helping others are similar to the effects of regular exercise.

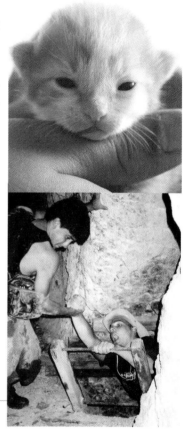

Luks and Payne conclude that, based on scientific research, exercise and nutritional supplements are not enough to improve health and well-being. The research concludes that no matter how much people concentrate on themselves, optimal health and happiness is only achieved by helping others.

into
the
deep

DISCUSS

Why do you think people today seem to be more preoccupied with helping themselves than with helping others?

ON MAKING A DIFFERENCE

The following is an account by one young person of how she became involved in working for justice. Perhaps you will be able to identify with her feelings and imagine for yourself a life that is intentionally aware of injustice.

' It started with the rainforests. I have memories of lying awake at night as a young teenager, fretting over the trees and the animals living in them, the destruction of jungles and the finality of that destruction. I'm not sure when my concern moved from trees to people. Perhaps somewhere in my mid-teens: I didn't think that the world was fair, but the impact of this unfairness was becoming more visible in humanity. Bad things were happening on TV, wars were being fought in places I could only dream about, and there were always, always people with hungry faces.

I went on to study geography at university, and travelled to Ghana to carry out research into fair trade and cocoa farmers during the summer of my second year. What surprised me most about that trip was the perception of such work from the multi-national chocolate companies. They were suspicious,

deeply suspicious of this "fair trade" concept. Who would do such a thing? Why would people pay more than they had to for chocolate? It was that lack of comprehension that dazed me somewhat. Did some people just not understand justice?

That's why I felt so comfortable coming to work for Trócaire, five years later (after a rather circuitous route that took in China, London, a music shop in Belfast and a brief period as a harpist!). Their mandate is not only the alleviation of poverty in the developing world, but education and campaigning on that poverty in Ireland. The two aspects are inseparable, and to work in an organisation that focuses only on overseas poverty without addressing the root causes would be for me like working in a vacuum. Why work with the have-nots and ignore the haves? Injustice is a coin of two sides.

I've been working for Trócaire for four years, in four different countries. What I have seen over that time has been enough to convince me that injustice is an ugly and ever-present aspect of humanity. Injustice is not just the family who struggle to make a living from their small dry plot of land in Pernambuco, Brazil, or the woman who is HIV positive in Salvador and whose boyfriend left her and their children to move in with another woman and more than likely infected her with HIV. It's not just the young man who hasn't seen his mother for fifteen years because to go back to his own village in Burma would put himself and his family at risk; or the mother who walked with her family for fourteen days to get to Thailand to escape the forced labour and the hunger and the fear that became unbearable when the army killed her husband. They are on one side of the injustice coin, but on the other side is the big landowner who

into
the
deep

decides to build a dam on his own land to irrigate his fields, thus stopping the river from reaching the poor community downstream. It's the government that would provide more drugs to treat HIV/AIDS if they didn't have to pay the high prices that the pharmaceutical companies ask for. It's the diplomats who remain mindful of the fact that Burma has reserves of gas and oil and don't criticise the Burmese government for the grave human rights abuses it is carrying out against its own people in case they affect their chances of accessing those resources.

It's not all ugly, of course, because I walk into work every day and see people who are dedicated to overcoming injustice. They speak with passion about Liberia, Zimbabwe, India and Peru, about small farmers, refugees, abused women, orphaned children, and they do so because lives are changing. They are changing because people thousands of miles away agree that injustice is wrong, and they get involved and they weigh down their Trócaire box with coins. Two people walk into an office in the local government buildings in Brazil and demand to know why permission was given to build a dam. They end up fighting for a part of the local government budget to be given for the construction of rainwater catchment tanks for their community, and they win. A woman speaks about how her country is being torn apart by war and fear, and a group of Irish teenagers pool their pocket money to support the young people who are learning how to combat war and fear. There's the beauty in humanity, and it's that beauty that tempers the ugliness. Perhaps injustice is an unavoidable part of the human condition, but that doesn't mean that people are prepared to accept it in themselves and their own communities. As long as they continue to believe that things can be different, we can all still hope.

(Meabh Cormacain, Trócaire)

into

the

deep

DISCUSS

1   In what ways can you identify with Meabh's opening statements about how she was troubled about the unfairness of the world?

2   What do you think prevents her from just giving up in the face of such organised injustices in the world?

3   Are you prepared to accept injustice as a part of life or do you want to do something about it? What can you do both as an individual and as part of a class group?

WHAT IS TRÓCAIRE?

In 1973, the Bishops of Ireland gave Trócaire a strong and clear mandate to 'work for a just world' which is as relevant as ever

today: abroad, to help those in greatest need in developing countries and at home to raise awareness and campaign for structural change on the causes of poverty. 'These duties are no longer a matter of charity but of simple justice', the Bishops said. Since then they have endeavoured to be faithful to this mandate, which highlights the moral outrage of poverty and injustice and calls upon us to be passionate advocates for change.

Vision

Trócaire envisages a just and peaceful world where people's dignity is ensured and rights are respected; where basic needs are met and resources are shared equitably and in a sustainable manner; where people have control over their own lives and those in power act for the common good.

Mission

Inspired by gospel values, Trócaire works for a just and sustainable world for all.

Trócaire gives expression to this mission by:

- Providing long-term support to people who live in extreme poverty in the developing world, enabling them to work their way out of poverty.

- Providing appropriate assistance to people most in need in emergencies and enabling communities prepare for and resist future emergencies.

- Tackling the structural causes of poverty by mobilising people for justice in Ireland and abroad.

They also do this by:

- Working in partnership with civil society organisations in Ireland and abroad.

- Working directly on development education, advocacy and campaigns that emphasise the underlying causes of poverty.

> ❛ There can never be room for a poverty that denies anyone what is needed for a dignified life. ❜
>
> (Pope Benedict XVI, *Deus caritas est*, 20)

A CATHOLIC ORGANISATION

In the following piece Trócaire outlines its own identity and vision:

Values
'Our work is grounded in Catholic social teaching, which stresses the profound sense of the dignity of each person and their inalienable human rights and their responsibilities, regardless of culture, colour, gender or religion. This belief in the unity and diversity of humankind is the basic value we bring to what we do. As we seek to achieve our mission, we endeavour to put the following values into practice both within the organisation and in our programmes and relationships.'

Solidarity

'We recognise that we all belong to one human family, and that living together on this earth brings with it rights and responsibilities for everyone. We will take on our responsibility to share our resources and our skills with those who need them, in a spirit of mutual collaboration.'

Participation

'We will work in partnership with colleagues and partners, involving and consulting with them and listening and responding to their needs based on a foundation of mutual understanding, respect and responsibility.'

Persistence

'We will be steadfast and persistent in the delivery of our work, recognising that discernible impact can take a long time to achieve.'

Courage

'We will be courageous in our struggle for justice, speaking out fearlessly when we campaign for and on behalf of others. We will encourage a climate of risk-taking and innovation that embraces those who think creatively while acting responsibly to deliver our goals.'

Accountability

'We recognise and respect the enormous trust placed in us by our supporters and partners and our collective responsibility to act with the utmost integrity in stewardship of those resources. We will at all times strive to be accountable, transparent and cost-effective in the use of those resources.'

'We work with people that share our vision of a just and peaceful world, regardless of religion or race. We equally recognise that being a Church agency provides us with special opportunities both in Ireland and internationally as all faith communities have a key role to play in educating for justice, fostering dialogue, sharing resources and mobilising people.'

'"We are a rich nation, then, while others are poor. But there is more to it than that. We are a rich nation to some extent because others are poor. Part of our prosperity is due to the fact that people in the developing countries are not getting a fair deal."'

(Pastoral Letter on International Development, 1973)

'Trócaire is full of many people dedicated to working for a just world. It is a place full of an energy and a passion for justice. It is also a challenging place to work. How do you respond every day to issues such as chronic poverty or famine or human rights without wondering are you really making a difference? And we do wonder. But we wonder because that is our job ... to continuously ask questions about the world that we live in and how we, individually and together, can make it a better place for all. Taking that first step to sincerely ask such questions is in itself the beginning of change – a step that each one of us can take whether or not we work for Trócaire.'

Chapter Seventeen

CARE FOR THE EARTH

> ❝ There is scarcely any proper use of material things which cannot thus be directed toward people's sanctification and the praise of God. ❞
>
> (*Sacrosanctum concilium*, 61)

> ❝ God said "Let there be light"; and there was light. God saw that the light was good, and God separated the light from the darkness. God called the light Day, and the darkness he called Night. And there was evening and there was morning, a first day. ❞
>
> (Genesis 1:1-3)

OUR RELATIONSHIP TO THE NATURAL WORLD

> ❝ I saw this documentary once about a woman who spent a year living with a group of apes somewhere in a jungle. She was doing some research. But there was this one ape that used to wander off on his own at night. She began to follow him and realised that every night he

did the same thing: he would go to this waterfall and sit there gazing at it for ages; then he'd wander back to the rest of the apes.

There are times when I'd love to just get up and wander off into a forest or something. I'd love to be alone in a forest at night – just forget about everything and relax in nature. I always think I'd find something there … though I don't know what. **'**

More than anybody else poets have discovered the strange allure of nature: for example, woods at night, sunrises, sunsets, running water, bird song or dew drops on grass have all been sources of inspiration for poets. Something happens to us when we're alone with nature and the earth and one interpretation is that we see a glimpse of the presence of God. It has long been acknowledged in the Christian tradition that God is revealed in the wonder and beauty of nature; in fact God can be revealed in almost any material thing.

The poet Patrick Kavanagh delights in the commonplace beauty of nature. He begins the poem 'Canal Bank Walk' with 'Leafy-with-love', suggesting that the growth of plants and grasses on the banks of the Grand Canal in Dublin have been nurtured by God's love. The 'green' water of the canal is given a sacramental significance as Kavanagh portrays it as baptismal water – 'Pouring redemption for me'. The poet lays himself before God – 'That I do the will of God, wallow in the habitual, the banal'.

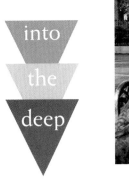

Memorial to Patrick Kavanagh on the banks of the Grand Canal, Dublin

Later in the poem, Kavanagh wishes to be immersed in the world of nature – 'O unworn world enrapture me'; to be enraptured in a web of fabulous grasses, to be clothed in a nature-based garment – 'With a new dress woven from green and blue things'. This poem represents the rebirth of Kavanagh as a poet. He is appreciative of and reverential towards the natural beauty of the Grand Canal and its surroundings.

One of the reasons that we glimpse God in nature is because for that singular moment we are enraptured in the beauty of what lies before us. All other thoughts, worries and stresses disappear and for that moment we are at one with the present, at one with nature, the earth – this living, breathing planet.

DISCUSS

1 In what ways are humans attracted to nature? Did you ever have an experience of nature that was powerful, memorable, awesome? Share it with the class.
2 How do humans relate to nature? Do you think we should be at one with it and care for it? Why?

into
the
deep

Christians believe that nothing exists that does not owe its existence to God. Everything that God created is good. We must therefore respect the goodness of every creature and avoid doing

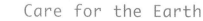

anything that would harm or destroy any of God's creatures. To do so would have disastrous consequences for the environment and for human life.

Everything that God created is interdependent. Everything is different and nothing in itself has all that it needs to survive: neither a sparrow nor an oak tree nor a human being can exist without resources from outside of itself.

The universe and everything in it is incredibly beautiful. This beauty gives us a tiny clue as to the beauty of God. Human beings are the high point of God's creation.

> So God created humankind in his image ... God blessed them and God said to them, "Be fruitful, multiply, and fill the earth and subdue it ..."
>
> (Genesis 1:27-28)

Muslims learn that God created the universe and everything in it and that there is order, balance and proportion between the different elements of creation. In the Qur'an, human beings are described as the vice-regents of Allah on earth. A vice-regent is someone who exercises powers on behalf of a ruler. Human beings are therefore expected to deal with the earth as God would. The religion of Islam has always viewed animals as a special part of God's creation. Muhammad taught: 'A good deed done to a beast is as good as doing good to a human being; while an act of cruelty to a beast is as bad as an act of cruelty to a human being.'

into
the
deep

A PARTICULAR RELIGIOUS VISION ... AND WHY IT'S RELEVANT

As with 'Canal Bank Walk', religious imagery can often be found at the heart of a poetic appreciation of nature. This poetic vision and understanding echoes a profound religious understanding of nature and the created world.

In the opening chapters of the book of Genesis in the Old Testament we find a powerful and poignant description of the created world. God created and God saw that what was created was good. According to Christian faith, God created the earth and the entire universe. In one particular case, a planet evolved that teemed with life – human life. It is our home: planet Earth.

We are told in Genesis that God told us to 'fill the earth and subdue it; have dominion over the fish of the sea and over the birds of the air and over every living thing that moves upon the earth' (Genesis 1:27-28). For centuries the command to have dominion over the earth was viewed as a licence to exploit creation, to rob it continuously of its natural resources without any concern for possible ill effects.

OUR CONTEMPORARY ENVIRONMENTAL CRISIS

 ... man has unhesitatingly devastated wooded plains and valleys, poluted the waters, deformed the earth's habitat, made the air unbreathable ...

(Pope John Paul II's General Audience Address,
17 January 2001)

Climate change is a reality. Today, our world is hotter than it has been in two thousand years. So what is causing this climate change?

- CO2 emissions from traffic
- Deforestation
- Burning trees and litter

- Large power plants that use fossil fuels
- Intensive livestock rearing.

If these activities are not brought under control, the speed of climate change over the next hundred years will be faster than anything known since before the dawn of civilisation.

At the moment, you might be dreaming excitedly of a place in college in Dublin or Cork. Maybe you're thinking of going to study in Trinity College and imagining afternoons watching 'the match' in Croke Park and nights out at The Point. In a few generations, however, these landmarks could be under several meters of water. You could go to Cork, but it might fare no better, as UCC and Pairc Ui Chaoimh may also be the preserve of sub-aqua teams!

into
the
deep

Our attitude to having dominion over the earth and exploiting its resources is having alarming consequences:

- Household waste has increased by 60 per cent in the past decade.
- Of the groundwater in this country, 40 per cent is contaminated with e-coli bacteria.
- Over-fishing is rapidly leading to barren oceans as fish stocks are seriously threatened.
- Over-grazing and large-scale intensification of agriculture has increased in Ireland leading to a loss of both plant and animal diversity.
- Chemical agriculture is causing the erosion of the soil on an unprecedented scale.
- Over 1,200 species of bird are heading over the abyss of extinction.
- Global carbon dioxide emissions have been accelerating at a rate faster than predicted.
- Rainforests redress our carbon emissions but we are extinguishing them at the rate of one acre per second.
- Almost half the world's rivers are drying up and becoming polluted.
- Warmer temperatures are making icecaps melt. Already the ice sheets of Antarctica are breaking up and melting. This in turn enters the seas and raises water levels.
- 'It is estimated that over twenty five percent of all living species will become extinct in the next thirty years' (Sean McDonagh, *The Greening of the Church*).

DISCUSS

1 Do you think the current environmental crisis is affecting your lives at present or is it something for future generations to worry about?
2 Do you think our political leaders are doing enough to address the current environmental crisis? Give reasons for your answer.

into

the

deep

A WAY FORWARD

> ❝ Earth is entrusted to man's use, not abuse. ❞
>
> (Pope John Paul II, 11 November 2000)

> ❝ This is our hope, that the children born today may still have, twenty years hence, a bit of green grass under their feet, a breath of clear air to breathe, a patch of blue water to sail upon, and a whale in the horizon to set them dreaming. ❞
>
> (Jacques Cousteau, *Make Peace Your Target*)

In recent decades religious thinkers have paved a way forward through our ecological crisis by understanding the text of the Book of Genesis from a different perspective. We should not understand ourselves as ones who have a licence to exploit the earth and have dominion over it. Instead we should see ourselves as stewards of this home of ours. Dominion in this sense means that we are indeed in charge of this planet but in such a way that we are responsible for its balance and well-being. This alternative understanding of Genesis can be sensed in Genesis 2:15 where God asked human beings to mind the Garden of Eden: 'And the Lord God took the man and put him in the garden of Eden to till it and keep it.'

TAKING ACTION

> ❝ Action taken now to reduce significantly the build-up of greenhouse gases in the atmosphere will lessen the magnitude and rate of climate change. ❞
>
> (*Joint statement by eleven national science academies to world leaders, 2005*)

It is important to remember that all our food and shelter is made from materials taken from the natural environment. We need wood, stone, and cement to build our homes and schools; oil and gas to fuel almost everything we do. All our food, water and textiles come from nature.

'Only when we consider all of these can we begin to realise just how much we are part of the natural world and how much we depend on the Earth's natural resources' (An Taisce). If we continue damaging our planet and depleting its resources, we will cause suffering to future generations.

In recent years, the issue of climate change has become so huge that people in all walks of life are speaking out and trying to make a difference. You have probably already heard of Greenpeace and you may even know some of its tireless volunteers who fight for a cleaner, better world. But there are other organisations too who are trying to make a difference – Friends of the Earth (www.foe.ie) and Stop Climate Choas (www.stopclimatechaos.ie) to name just two.

Live Earth

'Live Earth' was a twenty-four hour, seven-continent concert series that took place on 7 July 2007, bringing together more than one hundred music artists and two billion people to trigger a global movement to solve the climate crisis. It reached this worldwide audience through an unprecedented global media architecture covering all media platforms – TV, radio, Internet and wireless channels.

Madonna performs at the Live Earth concert in July 2007

Live Earth marked the beginning of a multi-year campaign led by the Alliance for Climate Protection, The Climate Group and other international organisations to drive individuals, corporations and governments to take action to solve

into

the

deep

global warming. Former US Vice President Al Gore is the Chair of the Alliance and Partner of Live Earth.

All Live Earth venues were designed to maintain a minimum environmental impact and showcased the latest state-of-the-art energy efficiency, on-site power generation and sustainable facilities management practices.

Umbrella Action Day Against Climate Change

On 10 June 2007, hundreds of Irish people – young and old – gathered in Sandymount Strand, Dublin to take part in 'Umbrella Action Day Against Climate Change'. This was their chance to show the Government they want Ireland to do its fair share to prevent climate chaos. Choreographer Muirne Bloomer and some dancers led the crowd in an umbrella demonstration to the strains of the Beach Boys' 'Wouldn't it be nice'…

Al Gore

Al Gore

Former US presidential candidate, Al Gore, recently released the film *An Inconvenient Truth*, showing just how compelling climate change can be:

 Al Gore plunges headlong into a serious wake-up call for the planet with a series of lectures about the problem.

Gore's advice is for individuals to take steps to reduce their own inadvertent poisoning of the atmosphere, and to persuade others to do likewise. It's a powerful message, and one that is likely to remain long after the film comes to a conclusion.

(www.foe.co.uk)

into

the

deep

The Big Ask

As I write the final pages of this chapter, thousands of people, including various celebrities such as Jude Law, are gathering in the UK to support The Big Ask (see www.thebigask.com). They remind us that if we don't take action now, we'll see more unusual and extreme weather every year. Millions in the UK and Ireland will be at risk of flooding. Billions worldwide will face droughts and violent storms but the world's poor will be the worst hit. They believe that the UK needs to show leadership in tackling climate change and that a strong Climate Change Law is the best way of doing this.

The law, they say, should 'make the Government cut the amount of carbon dioxide released in the UK by 3 per cent year on year. It's a steady path that will show the world the way while giving us all time to adjust'.

PRACTICAL STEPS YOU CAN TAKE

According to Greenpeace, to prevent climate change we need a 'revolution in energy policy and an evolution in the way we all use energy'. This energy (r)evolution will make the world a cleaner place. This is not just wishful thinking – it is possible and you can play your part by:

- Getting better informed about the issues.
- Learning how you can use energy smarter in your own home and school.
- Encouraging your friends and family to do the same.
- Turning off electrical equipment when it's not in use – don't leave the TV on standby and don't leave your mobile phone charger plugged in.

into

the

deep

- Recycling as much waste as possible.
- Using your green bin fully and correctly.
- Getting involved with organisations that fight for a cleaner environment, such as Greenpeace.

You could also talk to your parents about the following:

- Buying products made from recycled material or packaging that is easily recyclable, e.g. glass rather than plastic bottles.
- Buying energy-efficient products, such as low-energy light bulbs.
- Getting a compost bin for food waste.
- Starting a worm farm in your garden to recycle kitchen scraps and garden waste into fertiliser.
- Growing some of your own food or buying food that is grown locally.
- Using bicycles and public transport instead of cars.

To learn more about how you can play your part in saving the planet, visit www.enfo.ie.

Our environment sustains us and gives us life. We don't have to stop using the earth's resources but we do have to stop wasting them.

> In this newfound harmony with nature and themselves, men and women will once again walk in the garden of creation …

(Pope John Paul II's General Audience Address, 17 January 2001)

into the deep

Care for the Earth

STORY

Chapter Eighteen

STORY

WHAT'S IN A STORY?

The following story was recounted to me about ten years ago by a teacher working in a school in the midlands. She was introducing the students to the topic of story and she told them the following yarn:

> A salesman was driving home late one winter's night along highway 42 outside the town of Jacksonville in America. In the distance, he thought he could make out the shape of a young girl walking along the side of the road. It was cold and beginning to rain, so he pulled over to see if she wanted a lift. She got in and he kept driving. He tried to strike up a conversation

about the weather but got nowhere. She seemed cold, so he offered her an old jacket that was lying in the back seat. When she turned around to get it, he got a distinctly strange smell, musty, like old clothes. After about two or three minutes, she signalled for him to pull over and let her out. He did so and drove off, but he was left with a particularly strange feeling about the whole matter. He was convinced that he had dropped her off at the old Lutheran cemetery. One hundred yards down the road was the Ridgefield gas station, and he made a mental note of this.

The next day, he was driving back down the same road. When he reached the Ridgefield gas station the whole incident from the night before came flooding back to him. He had time to spare, so he turned at the gas station and, sure enough, about one hundred yards up was the old Lutheran cemetery. He felt a bit odd following up on the encounter with the young girl but the strangeness of the event had captivated him. The gate was locked, so he climbed over the old stone wall and began to browse through the headstones. Suddenly, he came up short. Just in front of him was a familiar object: it was his old jacket, strewn over a headstone. He approached and read the inscription: 'Jane Hawking, Died 16 November, 1984. R.I.P.' The driver looked down at his watch and checked the date: 17 November. And the year? 1994.

into
the
deep

,

The teacher left the class to mull over the implications and possibilities of the classic ghost story. The following week, she decided to tell the same story to a different class. She began as before, but when she got to the part about the cemetery, she was interrupted by a group of students who informed her that she was telling the story all wrong. The incident had actually happened to a friend of a friend of theirs only last month. It happened only ten miles away, over at a local disused cemetery. It wasn't a

jacket that was discovered but a jumper, and the girl on whose headstone it was strewn over had drowned. Though the day was sunny and dry, the jumper was dripping wet. The girl in question had failed her Leaving Cert and was found at the bottom of her father's lake. The teacher was informed that it was a 'true' story.

URBAN LEGENDS

The story outlined above is a classic tale, usually referred to as an 'urban legend'. Urban legends are a particularly fascinating type of story because nobody really knows where they originated from or if they ever really happened to anybody. However, the most amazing thing about urban legends is their ability to become part of whatever culture they enter.

THE HIDDEN EDITOR

The above urban legend obviously originated in America. However, over the weekend, the story suddenly happened only ten miles away at a 'local disused cemetery'. Somewhere and somehow, the story metamorphosed over the weekend into a

local event and switched from the category of urban legend to 'true' story.

The amazing thing that occurs with urban legends is that someone decides to edit the story to suit their own locality and circumstances. In the above story the original event occurred in America, with no indication or reason for the girl's death. Yet when the story was retold to the teacher, some serious editorial work had been done.

DISCUSS

1 How do you think urban legends manage to get edited so much? Who does the editing? Are they aware they're doing it? Why do they do it?
2 Can you explain why the 'editor' made the changes in the above example?
3 In your opinion, how did the changes affect the impact of the story?

GRABBING ATTENTION

We could go on analysing the cultural factors at play in the formation and transformation of urban legends, but that would be to do them an injustice. Urban legends, like all stories, need to be told. That's why stories exist.

The purpose of a good story is to get the listener's attention. The above example of the 'Vanishing Hitchhiker' falls into the supernatural/terror category. This category also contains the story of the couple stranded on a desolate road who learn from the radio that a psychotic man has just escaped from the local asylum. The rest is predictable enough. Have you heard it? Can you finish it?

into
the
deep

Another category of urban legend offers a warning about becoming too interested in fear and the effect it can have on a victim. Here is an example.

A journalist wanted to discover just what it was like to be an inmate on death row. He interviewed several but he felt that he could not really appreciate what it was like for them unless he was able to go through the experience for himself. He wanted to feel what it was like to be a dead man walking and to go to the electric chair. So, with the agreement of the prison authorities, he was put in a cell, given a prisoner number and prepared for "execution". His legs and head were shaved and shackled, and he was led to the electric chair. His number was 12136 and the guards were obviously told NOT to execute this "inmate". His editor back in the office, however, thought he would get a better idea of what it was like to be executed if he REALLY thought he was being executed. So, as he reached the chamber, the prison officer called out: "Inmate 34123 for execution." The journalist quickly replied that he was actually 12136 and that this was not for real, to which the prison officer replied: "That's what they all say." At this point, the journalist went berserk, pleading his innocence, etc. They strapped him in to the chair and pulled the hood over his face. Now, they reckoned, he'd be able to write a great article. And so they left him there for a little while to get accustomed to the idea of dying. When they went over and lifted up the hood they found a dead man. He had died of fright.

DISCUSS

1 Do you think the above story really happened? If not, why do you think someone would make up such a story?

2 What are the qualities of urban legends that make them good stories?

3 What do you think might be the purpose of urban legends?

4 How do you think urban legends manage to transform from culture to culture and adapt to the locality in which they are told? For example, if an urban legend originates in America, how can it suddenly have 'happened' in Ireland?

into

the

deep

CAUTIONARY TALES: CHECK THE AUDIENCE

One of the earliest urban legends was 'Little Red Riding Hood'. You'll notice that this story is told to small children, though if you've read it to yourself recently, that's okay ... it's a good story! However, the fairy tale has a definite purpose, which is ... well, what do you think? Why was the fairy tale first told to young children?

'Little Red Riding Hood' wouldn't work with a group of businesspeople or chefs. It's a story for children that is lost on anyone else.

Stories are created and survive for a reason. One classic urban legend tells of a young girl who is left at home one night by her parents for the first time. She point blank refuses to allow her parents hire a babysitter because she has a big dog to mind her. Her parents argue with her but eventually they give in. Alone, she turns on the TV to hear that 'a convict has escaped from the local prison'. She runs off up to bed and keeps the dog under the bed for protection. She wakes several times during the night and she puts her hand under the bed to check on the dog. On each occasion, the dog gives her hand a big lick. The next morning, she awakes to find her dog dead and a note beside her saying: 'Humans can lick too.'

This story has so many variations that it seems to survive because of its cautionary tale to parents, children, babysitters and – needless to say – dogs.

It would seem, therefore, that urban legends exist and survive independent of whether or not they're true. In fact, truth is not really of concern in urban legends at all; they're just good stories.

They serve a purpose that's good enough to guarantee their survival. And this brings us to an important aspect of stories: someone once said that all stories are true – it's just that some of them actually happened. They can contain truths about human life and existence even if the events they describe never actually happened.

DISCUSS

1   Can you give examples of cautionary tales that were told to you as children; for example, concerning picking your nose, straying away from home or the bog hole at the end of the field?
2   What truth is contained in the above urban legends about human existence even if the events never occurred?

CHECK THE CULTURE

Urban legends change as culture changes and they must adapt to suit the culture in which they are told. In relation to the first urban legend that we discussed above, about the 'Vanishing Hitchhiker', you will have noticed that when it was told in Ireland, the details were changed to suit the culture. For example, reference was made to the 'Leaving Cert' and a nuanced hint at the pressures associated with the exams. Reference was also made to the girl's father, with perhaps the unconscious message to parents to lay off the pressure or … you never know what might happen.

One urban legend that never really travelled was the one about a girl with a 'Beehive' hairdo. The story didn't travel because it was time bound to a particular culture, i.e. Irish society in the 1950s. Apparently, girls in those days were putting huge amounts of spray in their hair in order to achieve the beehive shape, and parents suspected they

into the deep

weren't washing it often enough. A story emerged (we wonder from where!) of a girl who didn't wash her hair very often. At school, she was continually scratching her head, until one day her friends insisted she had to go and see a doctor. In her hair, the doctor found a nest of black widow spiders. Not nice. The message? Wash your hair ... regularly.

> Because "Beehive" hairstyles were bound with a particular culture the story didn't survive, but one possible cultural adaptation concerns maggots that grow in the "dreadlocks" of reggae fans. One can imagine a father and mother sitting down one night and trying to decide on a story that will prevent their daughter from dating the reggae boy from down the street ... "you can go out with him Charlene but don't stroke his hair because ..."

(J.H. Brunvand, *Too Good To Be True*)

Stories are bound by their particular cultural setting and their purpose serves the cautionary needs at the time.

WHAT MAKES A GOOD STORY?

Good stories all have certain qualities:

- They address the particular culture in which they are told.
- They usually have a hidden purpose.
- They are tailored to suit a particular audience.
- Details are included that can be edited later.
- They usually have a strong emotional impact, like fear or humour.
- They have the ability to change the behaviour of the listener.
- They have some element of credibility, yet some element of incredibility too.

THE MAKING OF ORAL TRADITION

In order to examine how stories can have a life of their own, try this experiment. Break up into groups in class and 'invent' a story. It may even be a version of a previous story, but you want your story to appear like it's 'true' and original. Tell all your stories to the class. Then leave the class with the task of implanting the story into the rest of the school and even into the locality. See if any of the stories take hold and, if they do, examine the extent of editing that has been done to them.

Caution: Look up the terms 'libellous' and 'slanderous' in the dictionary. Read carefully!

Two terms may be used to describe what you are doing in this experiment. Firstly, your story can be referred to as a narrative; then, as you begin to tell your story in the school or wherever, an oral tradition, i.e. the passing on of a story by word of mouth. Many stories are constructed for oral transmission and, like the stories and urban legends that we have discussed, they can travel over generations and even continents.

DISCUSS

1 What stories can you retell in class that belong to an oral tradition within your own culture? What urban legends have been passed on to you?

2 What other types of story get passed on through an oral tradition within a culture? (Examples may include jokes, but be careful what jokes you tell in class!)

FROM ORAL TO WRITTEN TRADITION

Stories usually start out their lives in an oral form, but sometimes, and for various reasons, they then enter a written form – a written tradition. For example, on your mobile phones at the moment, there may be a collection of jokes that have taken the written form. Before mobile technology and text messaging, jokes were

transmitted in spoken form. Stories, it would seem, will adapt any form in order to survive.

One advantage of stories taking the written form is that they can be more easily spread around and transmitted to a greater number of listeners. Stories transmitted via e-mail can be dispersed with incredible speed.

Yet there's another reason why stories get written down, and that's to try to establish their veracity or truth. Think for a moment of an incident in school where a window gets broken by a ball. After an immediate evacuation of the scene, the school authorities begin an investigation and eventually three suspects are hauled into the principal's office. The three are separated and told to write down exactly what happened.

This is a classic ploy. If the three people are telling the truth, their stories will more or less match, with slight variations; if they are telling lies there will be significant discrepancies. There can only be one truth but there can be multiple lies.

into the deep

THE NEW TESTAMENT SCRIPTURES AS STORIES

'The Word of God, which is the power of God for salvation to everyone who has faith, is set forth and displays its power in a most wonderful way in the writings of the New Testament' which hand on the ultimate truth of God's Revelation.

(CCC, 124)

The Mandylion of Edessa from the private chapel of the pope in the Vatican. Considered to be one of the earliest images of Jesus

The study of urban legends tells us a lot about how stories come to be written. What makes urban legends particularly interesting is that it's very difficult to trace them back to a definite source. Usually they are attributed to 'a friend of a friend', or 'AFOF' in urban legend speak.

Unlike urban legends, the scriptures of the New Testament can be traced back to a definitive source, i.e. the person and preaching of Jesus of Nazareth. Stories emerge from significant events; in the case of urban legends, it's difficult to establish if there was ever a real significant event, or if the story was simply made up in order to fulfil a certain purpose. In the case of the New Testament, there was a real and historical event, yet from that event, stories have emerged which have travelled over centuries and continents.

We know from independent historical records that Jesus was a historical character. We know that he lived in Galilee and was eventually crucified under the reign of Pontius Pilate. After the death of Jesus, those who followed him believed that he had risen from the dead. So they met together to recount stories about the

significant event that was his life, death and resurrection. The followers of Jesus began to create an oral tradition when they passed on these stories orally to others.

DISCUSS

Why do you think the story of Jesus of Nazareth has survived? What makes it so powerful? In what way is it different from other stories that we encounter in our culture?

FROM ORAL TO WRITTEN TRADITION

The followers of Jesus gathered and told their stories orally, but eventually a number of things began to happen that required the stories to be written down:

- The original apostles and followers of Jesus, who were eyewitnesses to his life and deeds, began to die. In order that the stories of Jesus would not die with them, small collections of Jesus' words and deeds began to be created.

- The story of the life, death and resurrection of Jesus began to spread far beyond the confines of Jerusalem and Israel. Obviously, the apostles and followers of Jesus couldn't be everywhere, so it was necessary to write letters and small collections of sayings that could be copied and sent to other regions where small faith communities were emerging.

into

the

deep

- Creating a written record was seen to be a good way of correcting the inconsistencies, discrepancies and false rumours that had begun to threaten the story of Jesus of Nazareth.

What was the purpose of the New Testament scriptures?

All stories serve a purpose. Those who wrote the New Testament scriptures also had a very definite purpose but it wasn't to record all the details of Jesus' life as a biographer would do. Have you ever read biographies of 'B-list' celebrities? They're simply factual accounts of their lives because there's very little else to write about. Nothing of significance has happened in the person's life, yet for some reason they're a celebrity.

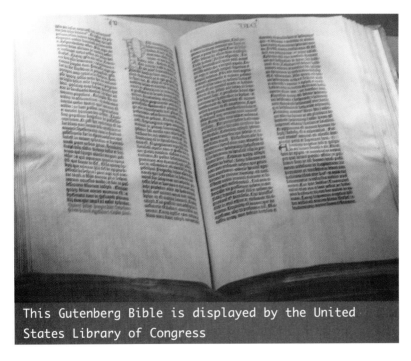

This Gutenberg Bible is displayed by the United States Library of Congress

The New Testament is not a biography that tries to gather all the historical data of Jesus' life. There was no need of a factual account of Jesus' life. He was neither a 'B-' nor a 'C-list' celebrity. Jesus had actually accomplished something with his life, which is probably why 34 per cent of the world's population proclaim to be Christians and fifty million copies of the Bible have been sold.

into

the

deep

So what was it about Jesus? St Paul sums it up as follows:

> For I handed on to you as of first importance what I in turn had received: that Christ died for our sins in accordance with the scriptures, and that he was buried, and that he was raised on the third day in accordance with the scriptures, and that he appeared to Cephas [Peter], then to the twelve ... Last of all, as to one untimely born, he appeared also to me.

(1 Corinthians 15:3-5, 8)

As stated in this quotation, the 'good news' or *kerygma* of the early Christian community was based on the belief that Jesus died and rose from the dead. He overcame sin, death and darkness. He was the Messiah, the one sent by God to save us. But there was more to it. He doesn't remain some distant historical character who achieved something. Those who followed him believed that their lives were transformed by following him and his message. For that very reason, the stories about him are still alive, adapting themselves to each culture and each historical epoch.

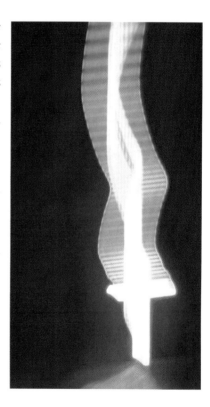

into
the
deep

DISCUSS

What stories from the Bible do you remember? What aspects of the scriptures do you find interesting? Does the Bible have a relevant message for contemporary culture? Give examples in class.

WHAT ABOUT THE CULTURE AND THE AUDIENCE?

The Gospels are the heart of all the Scriptures 'because they are our principal source for the life and teaching of the Incarnate Word, our Saviour'.

(CCC, 125)

When the writers of the four gospels decided to write their own accounts of what happened, they drew upon various sources. The gospels of Matthew, Mark and Luke have much in common because both Matthew and Luke borrowed pieces from Mark, whose gospel was the first to be written. Matthew and Luke also had another unknown source called 'Q'. In addition to this, the early Christian communities would

There is a strong emphasis in Mark's gospel on the sufferings of Christ

have passed on their stories to the evangelists. Because of their similarities, the gospels of Matthew, Mark and Luke are called the synoptic gospels. The gospel of John is quite different from the other three and it uses more symbolic language.

We noticed with urban legends that stories often get edited in order to suit a particular audience or culture. So the story of the 'Vanishing Hitchhiker' had references to the Leaving Cert in it when it was retold in Ireland. Likewise, the authors of the gospels edited their material to suit their own audiences and the particular culture in which they found themselves. For example,

into the deep

Mark wrote his gospel for the Christians who were being persecuted in Rome around 65–75 CE. For that reason, there is a strong emphasis in Mark's gospel on the sufferings of Christ, his death and resurrection. The gospel was tailored for those who themselves were enduring great sufferings: 'As for yourselves, beware; for they will hand you over to councils; and you will be beaten in synagogues; and you will stand before governments and kings because of me, as a testimony to them' (Mark 13:9).

Matthew wrote his gospel in the period from 70 to 85 CE. His gospel was written for Jews who had converted to Christianity and, therefore, it has many references to Jewish culture, customs and beliefs. In chapter 5, Matthew refers to Jewish beliefs about how people should treat one another: 'An eye for an eye and a tooth for a tooth' (Matthew 5:38) and 'You shall love your neighbour and hate your enemy' (5:43). Jesus, however, had a new message about human interaction and it transformed the older way of looking at things. Jesus' message was radical and challenging, and in the next chapter we will examine particular aspects of Jesus' message as it is described in Matthew's gospel.

Women figure predominantly in Luke's gospel

'The penitent Mary Magdalen' by Titian (c.1565)

into the deep

Luke, on the other hand, wrote his gospel for Gentiles or non-Jews in the period 80–95 CE. Gentiles were regarded as in some way second class by their Jewish neighbours, so Luke presents Jesus as a person of compassion who accepted Gentiles and forgave sinners. Women also figure predominantly in Luke's gospel, even though they were also regarded as second-class citizens. So like the other evangelists, when Luke wrote his gospel he had his own particular audience and culture in mind. (See Luke 7:36-59, 10:29-37 and 13:10-17.)

into

the

deep

Story   265

Chapter Nineteen

TRUTH

WHICH STORY IS TRUE?

In the last chapter, we examined the concept of story and we looked at the New Testament scriptures as examples of story. We might be tempted to say that some stories are true because they are based on real events, while others are not true because they are just made up. However, even stories that are not totally based on fact have elements of truth in them. We will now look at the three possible categories into which stories can fall, in terms of how 'true' they are.

THE 'TRUE' STORY

Is there really such a thing as a true story? In class, can anyone stand up and tell a story that the entire class will agree is totally and absolutely true? Try it now and you'll find that it's a harder task than you think. In fact, you might find it's almost impossible.

ASSIGNMENT

Select two people in your class who support rival teams. Then select a match in which both teams played. (If you can, bring in a video of the match and show a piece, especially a controversial incident.) Ask each supporter to give a factual and true account of the match.

DISCUSS

Did both supporters give a different account of the same incident? Why? Is it possible to give a true and factually accurate account of events?

ASIDE

Petr Cech's Head

On Saturday 14 October 2006, Chelsea played Reading in the FA Premiership. Early on in the match, Reading drove the ball speculatively into the Chelsea penalty area. Stephen Hunt pursued it as he was entitled to do, until the Chelsea goalkeeper Petr Cech rushed off his line and dived to smother the ball. The Reading player attempted to veer to his left, but the momentum of the 'keeper took him into

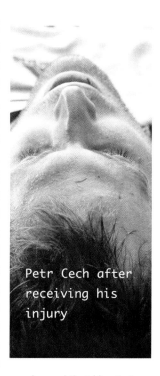

Petr Cech after receiving his injury

Hunt's path. Video evidence showed that Hunt's knee went forcibly into Cech's head. Cech suffered a fractured skull and required surgery. The Chelsea boss, Jose Mourinho fumed, "There was no chance it was an accident … Hunt clearly flexed his leg to catch Petr. He dropped his knee at the 'keeper's head." Hunt adamantly disagreed, claiming, "One hundred per cent my intention was to win the ball. I hope Petr isn't too badly hurt and makes a full recovery."

And the truth is?

(Mark Irwin, *The Sun*, 16/9/06)

into

the

deep

THE 'SORT OF' TRUE STORY

Some stories are based on real events but get embellished. Sometimes we hear a story but reckon it would be far more interesting to add a bit on. This is the kind of story that we wish were true but it's not ... though we keep telling it anyway.

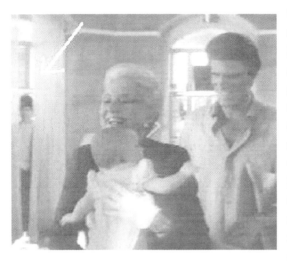

One example of this category of story comes from the film *Three Men and a Baby*. The story goes that in several scenes of the film, the outline of a young boy is seen hovering near a window. Supposedly, it is the ghost of a boy who died in the apartment block where the film was shot. The outline of the boy is clearly visible throughout the film. According to the story, the boy's parents begged the studio bosses to cut the scenes but they refused.

It is said that the truth never stood in the way of a good story, and this is an example. For a start, the film wasn't produced in an apartment block but in a studio. As for the outline of the boy, it is actually a life-size cut-out of Ted Danson, which was left just outside the 'apartment' window. Owing to an odd lighting effect, the white face and shirt appear to glow. Though the effect is startling, the truth is less so. Obviously someone decided to ignore that and just create a good story.

into the deep

ASSIGNMENT

Give examples of stories that have a factual basis to them that have been embellished. Examine how rumours are started and why.

DIFFERENT TYPES OF TRUTH: SCIENTIFIC AND RELIGIOUS

THE DEBATE ABOUT ORIGINS

As we have already seen, truth is not clear-cut and there are different forms of truth. This point is very relevant to the relationship between religion and science because both disciplines are based on different types of truth.

The history of the relationship between religion and science has not always been a happy one. Perhaps one of the reasons for this is a lack of understanding concerning the purpose of each endeavour. Generally speaking, scientists ask questions about *how* things work or *how* things came to be, whereas theologians (religious thinkers) tend to ask *why* things exist or came into being.

A case in point is the debate about the origins of the universe. At a glance, it would appear that science and religion have a completely different opinion of how the universe came into being. According to the book of Genesis, life was created in six days:

 God saw everything that he had made, and indeed, it was very good. And there was evening and there was morning, the sixth day. Thus the heavens and the earth were finished, and all their multitude.

(Genesis 1:31–2:1)

Yet two scientific theories were seriously to challenge the account of the origins of the universe and human life given in the book of Genesis.

Charles Darwin (1809–1882) developed the theory of evolution, whereby species evolved over millions of years. Obviously this challenged the notion of the world created in six days as presented in Genesis. Another scientist, Edwin Hubble, discovered from his observations of the stars that the galaxies were moving away from one another. If the universe is

into
the
deep

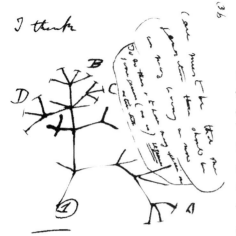

Then between A & B [...]
[...] of [...] C + B [...]
[...] gradation, B & D
rather greater distinction
Then genera would be
formed. — bearing relation

expanding, it suggests that at some point there was an explosion that sent the matter spinning out into space. Such an explosion is now referred to as the 'Big Bang'. According to scientists, this cataclysmic event occurred around 13.7 billion years ago. Yet according to Archbishop James Usher, a religious thinker who examined the Bible, creation occurred on Sunday, 23 October 4004 BCE.

The discrepancy between the scientific age of the universe and the Genesis age of the universe is about 13.7 billion years! So who's right: the scientists or the authors of the book of Genesis?

In 1996, Pope John Paul II announced that evolution was a well-established scientific theory, and the Catholic Church has also accepted the 'Big Bang' theory as a scientific principle. So what's happened? Has the Catholic Church accepted defeat? Is Genesis wrong and science right? Well, it comes down to how we understand truth and, as we noted from our above investigations into truth and story, truth is a very slippery phenomenon.

DISCUSS

1 Why do you think the Church accepted these scientific discoveries, even when they seemed to contradict scriptural passages?
2 Do you think the book of Genesis contained truths other than scientific ones? Explain.

into
the
deep

INSPIRATION AND TRUTH IN SACRED SCRIPTURE

God is the author of Sacred Scripture. 'The divinely revealed realities, which are contained and presented in the text of Sacred Scripture, have been written down under the inspiration of the Holy Spirit.'

(CCC, 105)

The scriptures are understood to be the word of God, but the people whom God used to transmit this word were bound to their own cultures and place in history. The book of Genesis was written around 600 BCE, well before telescopes or advanced scientific techniques. It can't therefore be expected to provide scientific information because that was not available at that time or in that culture. The writers of the book of Genesis did not have access to scientific instrumentation but they were trying to convey the truth about creation within the confines of their own culture. The book of Genesis, while not conveying scientific truths, does contain truths 'for the sake of our salvation' (CCC, 107).

Genesis tells us that God is the creator of all that is. This is the truth contained in the book of Genesis. And when God created, God saw that all was good. Nothing that God made is bad. Humanity has a special place in God's creation, as we are created in the image and likeness of God. Again, these are the truths found in the book of Genesis. Having been created in the image and likeness of God, we too should participate in the act of creation and be creative in our world as a force of goodness. The earth was given to us and so it is our duty to take care of it for each successive generation. The truths in the book of Genesis refer to the nature of God and the nature of humans. The book was not written for mathematicians. The intention of the author was not mathematical or scientific, it was religious.

In order to discover the *sacred authors' intention*, the reader must take into account the conditions of their time and culture, the literary genres in use at that time, and the modes of feeling, speaking and narrating then current.

(CCC, 110)

1 Read Genesis 4:1-17. According to the book of Genesis, Adam and Eve were the parents of all the living. They had two sons, Cain and Abel. If the author of this account wanted to present a detailed description of human origins, what big inconsistency is in this text? What do you think was the intention of the author of this account in the book of Genesis?

'Adam and Eve' by Lucas Cranach the Elder (1526)

into

the

deep

2 Read the short account of Jonah in the book of Jonah in the Old Testament. Jonah is asked by God to go to the city of Ninevah to deliver a warning to the people. They must

repent or the city will be destroyed. Jonah tries to evade his mission to save the people of the city and ends up in the belly of a great fish for three days and nights. Do you

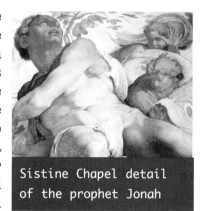

Sistine Chapel detail of the prophet Jonah

think the author of the book wanted people to believe this part of the story? What do you think the intention of the author was? What does the story tell us about God? What does it tell us about our response to God?

ASIDE

Prophecy in the Bible

There are different styles of writing or literary genres in the scriptures. The account of Jonah was a *literary style*, which means it was a fictional account, a story that was made up but with an important religious message. *Prophecy* is another type of writing that can be misunderstood. People today think that prophecy is about foretelling the future and that if the prophecy doesn't happen, then it's not true, but in the Bible the prophets weren't foreseeing future events. In the sacred scriptures, prophecy is often viewed as a way of conveying a message about the nature of our relationship with God and how we are to live our lives.

In the book of Revelation, there are references to the ancient city of Babylon. Some modern readers think this is a reference to Iraq, as the ruins of Babylon lie close to Baghdad. But Babylon, for the readers at the time, was a veiled reference to the Romans, who, like the Babylonians years previous, had invaded and destroyed the Temple.

into the deep

THE BIBLE: TRUTH LEADING TO TRANSFORMATION AND FREEDOM

 Know therefore that the Lord your God is God, the faithful God who maintains covenant loyalty with those who love him and keep his commandments, to a thousand generations.

(Deuteronomy 7:9)

The truth of the Old Testament is that God is shown to be constantly trustworthy and reliable. God responds to those who are imprisoned and suffering. God is constant in relationships and never abandons us. God also reaches out to those who have turned away and is constantly trying to repair broken relationships, as seen through the mission given to Jonah.

In the New Testament, we see the fullest revelation of what God is like. Once again, through the actions of Jesus, his self-sacrifice and resurrection, God saves us and frees us. The Bible is an account of a God who sets the example for what relationships should be like and challenges us to try to constantly live lives that are fulfilling and free. The truth of the Bible concerns right relationships between ourselves and God. Ultimately, as the letter to the Ephesians puts it: 'Jesus is the truth' (Ephesians 4:21).

 … And you will know the truth, and the truth will make you free.

(John 8:32)

A story about freedom and a biblical vision of life

Note: There are some references in the following story that you may need to be reminded about. Many years before the time of Jesus, the Hebrews of old were slaves in the foreign land of Egypt. They cried out to Yahweh to save them from slavery. After the night of the Passover, they were freed from bondage and made their way to the promised land of Israel. The event is known as the Exodus.

Keep on Drivin'

It was evening and the long road ahead seemed to reach itself out to the very end of the world. Peter relaxed back into the old worn leather of his grandfather's convertible and just kept driving. To his left a sleepy sun was slumbering into the west, leaving a shimmering haze of purple and red on the horizon. His journey had all the feel of an apocalypse, his own apocalypse, his own personal end to things that no longer mattered.

He had left a girlfriend in tears. Another time he would have been stunned and shrunken by feelings of guilt and remorse but not now. Not when you eventually learn that some people just use you. She never loved him anyway and for all he cared she could cry her crocodile tears until she got another guy with a car and enough stupidity to bankroll her.

He had left a job too. No more boss, no more taunts of 'slow Peter'. He wasn't slow, he just never cared about a job that paid too little and traded too many insults. He was driving to his own promised land. This was his Exodus.

His grandfather understood. He told him to take the car and drive hard. His grandfather was steeped in old biblical language and imagery. He told him he

into
the
deep

was of the age to find his own Zion, his own sacred place in the world. The old man told him to trust in providence and Peter would do that.

Sometimes, in moments of great clarity, a person breaks free and follows their own true path. Peter had gazed into the tomb of what was once his life and he saw no future there. Tomorrow was a new day. Peter was free.

'

(Tom Gunning, *Driving Through*)

TIME FOR A HAPPY THOUGHT IN YOUR HEAD ...

Take a few moments of silence in the classroom right now. The above text is about breaking free from all that's not good for us in our lives. It's about an open road and a dash for personal freedom. Spend a few moments thinking about sliding into a convertible and driving through a balmy hot evening, with the sun setting in the west. What and who would you choose to leave behind? What would you like to let go of now and just drive away from? Where would you like to drive to? If you could do that, what would your life be like twelve months from now?

into the deep

DISCUSS

1 Why do you think people avoid truth in their lives? Why are people slow to realise they are in bad situations and need to get out of them?
2 Why do some people find it difficult to leave bad relationships when the truth is that they don't work?
3 Why is truth important in human life? Does it really set us free? Give examples in class.

THE BIBLE AS LIVING WORD

One of the major problems with biblical interpretation is that many young people see the Bible as an ancient text for an ancient people. Truthfully, the Bible does indeed seem like an ancient text, but that's because it was written in a particular time in history and in a particular culture. The literal sense of a piece of scripture may be tied to an ancient culture but the scriptures always contain a deeper meaning, a spiritual truth which, like a story, can travel through any time and any culture. The message contained in the scriptures is as relevant now as it was back then, even if the culture or history isn't.

We noticed that urban legends have the ability to travel through time and through different cultures. They can do this because the deeper message of caution that they contain is as relevant to one culture as to another. The test of a great text is its ability to speak to audiences far removed in space and time from its original audience. Yet the scriptures are like no other text. The Bible is a living word that can become alive in the personal story of any person at any time.

AN EXTRAORDINARY TEXT

The endurance of the Bible for so long suggests that it has something extremely important and powerful to say to each successive generation. The challenge is to appreciate how its message is as relevant today as it was for the first audience that read and heard it.

One major aspect of this challenge concerns the fact that the medium it belongs to is the written form. Younger audiences now receive texts or narratives through incredibly stimulating and exciting media, such as computer-generated games, music videos and films replete with special effects. So, what would happen if a couple of filmmakers decided to make a film with a powerful spiritual message for a contemporary audience? What would happen if they decided to represent this important biblical theme through the medium of some of the most exciting and impressive visual and computer-generated effects? Such a film was made, compliments of the Wachowski brothers, and it was called *The Matrix*.

TIME TO GO TO THE MOVIES: THE MATRIX

What is the Matrix?

 The world that has been pulled over your eyes to blind you from the truth.

The principal character in the movie is a computer programmer called Thomas Anderson, played by Keanu Reeves. He works for a corporation called MetaCorTechs. At night, however, Anderson becomes 'Neo' – a very, very good computer hacker. After receiving a strange e-mail, Neo then gets a call on a mobile phone in his office; it is from Morpheus, played by Laurence Fishburne.

Morpheus lets Neo in on a little secret, one that has profound implications. Reality, as he perceives it, is nothing more than a series of computer-generated signals sent directly into his brain. Neo does not actually work for a computer corporation. This is simply the programme that is being fed into his brain and it seems to keep most humans happy. But it is not reality; it's only an appearance of a reality.

Reality is quite different. Neo's body is actually lying in a pod, one among millions, and his life is being used as a battery to feed the energy requirements of the Artificial Intelligence (AI) life-forms that have taken over the world. It is explained to Neo that it has simply been a part of evolution. The machine has taken over. Bodies that die are liquefied and fed back into the humans lying in their pods. The humans are 'happy' because they know

no different. The programme that is fed into their brains gives them the impression that they have a life, but they don't. Morpheus and some others have freed themselves from this Matrix. Morpheus wants Neo to join them, as Morpheus believes that Neo is 'The One'. He believes that Neo can save humankind from the Matrix.

DISCUSS

Is it possible that right now you are in a Matrix and you are simply being fed electrical signals into your brain that totally convince you that what is around you is reality when it's actually not? What proof do you have that you are not in a Matrix?

How to interpret the biblical themes and imagery in 'The Matrix'

The Matrix is first and foremost a Hollywood-produced movie and cannot be viewed as a tool for a reliable interpretation of scripture, but what it does do is present biblical themes and images in a most startling fashion. The biblical message in the film is profound and disturbing. In order to understand the frequent biblical references in the film, the class should first familiarise themselves with the following themes of scripture. Then, and only then, should the film be viewed. (If you try to cheat, remember, God is watching!)

into
the
deep

The Sacred City

The ship, the *Nebuchadnezzar*, and the references to 'Zion' relate to the Old Testament. It is important to note that the central theme of the film is freedom from slavery. One of the central narratives of the Old Testament is the story of the escape of the Hebrews from slavery in Egypt. This event is known as the Exodus and can be researched in the book of Exodus. The Hebrews called out to God to free them from bondage. On the night of the Passover, the angel of death 'passed over' the homes of the

Keanu Reeves as 'The One'

Hebrews because the blood of the lamb that was smeared on their doorposts acted as a marker. The first born male in each Egyptian home died. The Hebrew people were only saved because of the sacrifice of the lamb. They were saved by innocent blood spilt. The lamb is a central image in Old Testament literature and can be found in many churches. It is the symbol of freedom.

Nebuchadnezzar was the king of the Babylonian Empire, while the references to Zion as the ultimate place of refuge are direct allusions to the sacred city of Jerusalem (Zion). King David brought the Ark of the Covenant to Jerusalem and later a Temple was built to house the Ark. The Hebrews believed that God dwelt in the Holy of Holies, the secret chamber where the Ark was kept.

into

the

deep

The Messiah

Throughout the Old Testament, the Hebrew people suffered different forms of oppression and slavery. Yet, as God's chosen people, they believed that God would save them. They believed that God would send someone to liberate them. This person would be 'the anointed one' or 'Messiah'. In Matrix terminology, Jesus was 'The One'. The Hebrew people believed that the Messiah would be a powerful military leader who would overcome their enemies. Jesus understood that he himself was the promised Messiah, as is shown in John's gospel when he meets the woman at the well:

> The woman said to him, "I know the messiah is coming …When he comes he will proclaim all things to us." Jesus said to her, "I am he, the one who is speaking to you."

(John 4:25-26)

In the New Testament, Jesus seems reluctant at times to reveal himself as the Messiah, especially in Mark's gospel. The reason is that people were expecting a military and political Messiah. Jesus, however, would bring spiritual, rather than political, liberation.

Death and Resurrection

The theme of death and resurrection is a recurring one in the gospels. In John's gospel, we read the account of the death of Lazarus (John 11:1-44). Lazarus was a friend of Jesus, but by the time Jesus got to his tomb, some four days had passed since his death and there was already a stench. But Jesus ordered that the stone be rolled back and then he cried out in a loud voice:

> "Lazarus, come out!" The dead man came out, his hands and feet bound with strips of cloth, and his face wrapped in a cloth. Jesus said to them, "Unbind him, and let him go."

(John 11:43-44)

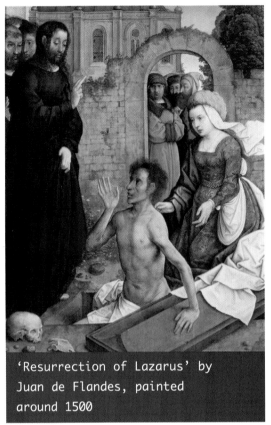

This miracle proved to be a turning point in Jesus' ministry because it attracted so much attention that he was noticed by the Roman authorities and was soon perceived as a threat.

Later in John's gospel, we read about the crucifixion and death of Jesus. Once the Roman authorities were persuaded that Jesus was a threat, he was crucified and died on the cross. His followers dispersed and all seemed to be lost. Yet through the divine intervention of the Father, Jesus was raised from the dead into new life. The Resurrection is the basis of Christian faith. None of Jesus' followers expected him to die or rise from the dead as foretold in the scriptures. In John's gospel, we read of how the followers of Jesus came to believe:

'Resurrection of Lazarus' by Juan de Flandes, painted around 1500

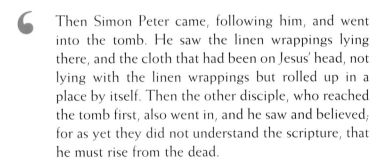

Then Simon Peter came, following him, and went into the tomb. He saw the linen wrappings lying there, and the cloth that had been on Jesus' head, not lying with the linen wrappings but rolled up in a place by itself. Then the other disciple, who reached the tomb first, also went in, and he saw and believed; for as yet they did not understand the scripture, that he must rise from the dead.

(John 20:6-9)

into

the

deep

Death and Sacrifice

As noted above, the Hebrews were saved from slavery by the blood of the Passover lamb. In Christian tradition, Jesus is referred to as the 'Lamb of God'. This reference links Jesus with the Old Testament Passover lamb. In order that we be saved from sin and death, it was necessary for Jesus to die and shed his blood for many. Through his sacrifice, by giving his life for another, Jesus established a new covenant or relationship between humanity and God.

We remember this sacrifice every time we celebrate the Eucharist. In Mark's gospel, Jesus foretells his sacrificial death for others:

> Then he took a cup, and after giving thanks he gave it to them, and all of them drank from it. He said to them, "This is my blood of the covenant, which is poured out for many."

(Mark 14:23-24)

ASIDE

'The Singularity'

The Matrix presents a vision of society where machines have evolved to become more powerful than humans. The machines then take over. According to some scientists, the time will come, probably in the third decade of this century, when computers will be as powerful as the human brain. That moment is referred to as 'The Singularity'. At present, a computer would need to be the size of a football field to be capable of computing the ability and functions of the human mind. Yet advances in computing power suggest that, sooner than we think, smaller computers will be able to process the same amount of information as a human. In an ominous twist, however, some scientists believe that special 'quantum' computers will be far superior in ability and intelligence than the human brain. What such computers decide to do with that power remains to be discovered.

into
the
deep

TIME TO GO TO THE MOVIES ...

Given that class times vary, you can now watch the film *The Matrix* at your own pace. However, the film is far more interesting once the viewer can understand the biblical references and imagery which the film relies heavily on. As you watch the film, keep in mind the following questions, and when you get the answers, you can note them for discussion at the end of the film.

QUESTIONS

1 How soon does the film indicate that Neo has messianic characteristics?

2 During which scene does Neo appear to be in a Lazarus-type scenario?

3 At what stage does Neo appear to 'rise from the dead'?

4 What effect does his 'resurrection' have on those who witness it? Does anyone witness Jesus' resurrection in the gospels?

5 In what way does the 'post-resurrection' Neo seem different? In what way is the post-resurrection Jesus different? (See John 20:24-29 and Luke 24:13-17.)

6 Where does Neo appear to sacrifice his own life for another? What effect does this act have on humanity?

7 Which characters most resemble Judas and John the Baptist?

READING THE BIBLE WITH ADULT EYES

> God is with us to liberate us from the darkness of sin and death and raise us up to eternal life.

(Dei Verbum, 4)

Scripture is part of God's self-communication or revelation to us. Yet God's revelation and God's saving activity are inseparable.

The scriptures free us from the darkness that can envelop our lives. The message is one of true liberation to lead happier and more fulfilling lives. Jesus reveals God's plan for us, which is designed to help us to live in good and right relationship with one another. Sometimes, it becomes apparent that we're not very good at doing just that …

On being nasty …

When a group of students were asked to identify the ways in which teenagers can be nasty to one another, they produced this list:

- Gossiping

- Spreading rumours

- Violence

- Laughing at a person because they're different

- Discriminating against someone because they dress differently

- Not accepting people from other groups

- Flirting with a friend's boyfriend/girlfriend because you're jealous

- Leaving people out of plans

- Sexual pressure

- Back-stabbing, being two-faced

- Not getting on with people we've fallen out with

into the deep

DISCUSS

1 Do you think teenagers, as opposed to adults, are particularly nasty to one another? Why is that?

2 Do you think teenagers need help with understanding the implications of some aspects of their behaviour towards others? What sort of advice would you give some students you know?

The scriptures are designed to transform our lives and the lives of those around us. An adult approach to the Bible doesn't read the text in a literal manner but instead understands the modes of expression and narrative at the time. The adult approach understands that it is not a mathematical or scientific text but a religious one that offers us truths about our salvation and freedom in Jesus Christ. The scriptures, unlike any other text or story, must be allowed to root themselves in our lives so we can be enriched. The adult reader of the Bible reflects on the implications of the text and message for their own lives.

On right relationships ...

Read the text below from Matthew's gospel and then answer the questions that follow.

> You have heard that it was said, "An eye for an eye and a tooth for a tooth." But I say to you, Do not resist an evildoer. But if anyone strikes you on the right cheek, turn the other also; and if anyone wants to sue you and take your coat, give your cloak as well; and if anyone forces you to go one mile, go also the second mile. Give to everyone who begs from you, and do not refuse anyone who wants to borrow from you.
>
> You have heard that it was said, "You shall love your neighbour and hate your enemy." But I say to you, Love your enemies and pray for those who persecute you, so that you may be children of your Father in heaven ... for if you love those who love you, what reward do you have?

(Matthew 5:38-46)

DISCUSS

1. Do you think the first part of this text is meant to be understood literally, or is there a deeper meaning to it?
2. What difference would taking the advice in the second paragraph make to your life and to society as a whole? Is it relevant to the nasty people? Why?
3. Would you be willing to follow any of this advice in your own life? If you did, how would it change how you live? What effect would it have on those around you?

The above piece of scripture may seem to be very demanding and challenging and that is exactly what it is intended to be. The images probably startle most: give and forgive without preconditions. Now it is unlikely that anyone will ever ask you for your coat or to 'walk a second mile', but Jesus recognised that we need to evaluate radically the way we treat others, and it's not to be a piecemeal effort but a thorough overhaul of our relationships.

As evidenced above, we can be quite nasty to one another at times and we have the ability to inflict real and lasting damage. This, quite simply, is not acceptable for anyone who claims to be anything resembling an adult. Pettiness, vindictiveness, back-stabbing and bullying, whether subtle or otherwise, damage others. The scriptural text above demands that we all abandon such narrowminded behaviour. It is not acceptable to define right relationships as that which exists among my small group of friends who make me feel good. Being nice to the small group of friends that we have is really a form of self-protection … 'I'll be nice to you … you be nice to me. Couldn't care less about anybody else.'

into the deep

The scriptures demand that we transform our lives and, most importantly, that we transform how we treat others. By so doing, we will be a happier and safer people.

Chapter Twenty

GOD'S UNFOLDING STORY

> After a long time the king of Egypt died. The Israelites groaned under their slavery, and cried out. Out of the slavery their cry for help rose up to God.
> God heard their groaning, and God remembered his covenant with Abraham, Isaac, and Jacob. God looked upon the Israelites and God took notice of them.

(Exodus 2:23-25)

THIN PLACES

An ancient Celtic tradition that has survived down through the ages involves people journeying to sacred sites associated with saints, burial grounds and significant spiritual events. The journey to the sacred site was often arduous, but something strange happened at various points along the way. The journeymen and women of old were extremely perceptive and believed that some places along the way were spiritually significant. Stone crosses were placed at these sites and those who stopped there believed that they felt a close presence with the spiritual world. They felt they were close to God, that the veil between this world and the next was lifted, and things felt different at these places. They were called 'thin places'.

In life, sometimes, we encounter 'thin places', where it would appear somebody is looking out for us. A saving presence feels close.

DISCUSS

Do you know of any places that seem to have a special power and in some way seem to be linked to God's presence? Describe them in class.

A Deadly Date

A number of years ago when my niece Cynthia was living with her parents as a fifteen-year-old teenager, she hitchhiked a car ride home from a young man in his twenties. During the ride, they exchanged pleasantries, and the man, named Michael, revealed that he was in the insurance business. Michael asked Cynthia for a dinner date and she accepted.

When she told her parents an insurance man had asked her for a date, even though they didn't want her to go out with boys until age sixteen, they were delighted. Her mom had been anxious about the calibre of people that Cynthia chose to associate with. It was a typical concern that moms often have for teenage daughters, especially those that are as attractive as Cynthia was at this age. Her mom had seen Cynthia dropped off before by long-haired, tough guys on motorcycles, known for late nights and drinking. Getting a date with a guy who wore a suit and tie was a very welcome sign.

When Michael arrived for the date, he was met by Cynthia's mother and father and was escorted into the living room to wait for Cynthia to finish getting ready. The parents were very impressed with Michael and were trying their best to make a good impression on him.

When Cynthia finally joined everyone, before she could utter a word, her eye caught Michael's eye. She immediately retreated to her bedroom. Her confused parents tried to smooth over the social infraction, writing it off to the immature behaviour of a teenager.

Michael Ross on
Death Row

After an uncomfortable ten minutes, her dad went to find Cynthia in her bedroom and encourage her to speed it up, as it was starting to get embarrassing. Cynthia said she was not going anywhere with Michael. She told her father there was something wrong with Michael, and she would not be alone with him. Her father pleaded with her, pressurising her to fulfil her commitment to the date. He finally demanded that she come out and tell her date directly. Cynthia composed herself and approached Michael with extended hand. She told him frankly that, while he was probably a very nice guy, she was sorry but there was something about him that made her very uncomfortable, and she didn't want to go with him. Michael left and never returned.

Cynthia, who never locked or even closed her bedroom door before, locked the door and windows that night. Several years later, Micheal was on the front page of all the Connecticut papers. He was Michael Ross, the serial killer who murdered four young women in eastern Connecticut before he was caught.

(from Sally Rhine Feather and Michael Schmicker,
The Gift)

into

the

deep

DISCUSS

1 Why do you think Cynthia decided not to accept the date?
2 Some students who read this story believed that the girl was being guided or protected by a spiritual power. Why do you think they might have said that?
3 Do you have any stories whereby someone you know seemed to have been guided in making an important decision? Tell the story to the class.

JUST A COINCIDENCE?

> The angels went on to say that all things, in fact the smallest of all things, are directed by the Lord's Providence, down to the very steps taken by the feet.

(Emanuel Swedenborg)

> On March 1, 1950, a gas explosion ripped through a church in Nebraska. The blast occurred at 7.27 p.m., exactly three minutes before a choir practice was about to begin. The explosion blew the church apart and was located just under the choir stands. Every member of the choir would have been killed except for a peculiar set of events.
>
> The choir were understandably very punctual and should ordinarily have been on time and seated above the blast zone. Ten to twenty minutes after the blast, the shaken members of the choir huddled outside the carnage and began to relate strange stories of delays and watches that had stopped. Others unusually became engrossed in TV and radio programmes back at home. Every single member of the choir turned up late that evening and not one was injured. All were convinced that some divine hand had engineered their salvation that night.

(from G.S. Eckersley, *Out of the Blue*)

DISCUSS

1 Do you think the above events were just a coincidence or do you believe that they were saved by divine intervention? Give reasons for your answer?

2 Do you know of any events where someone believes that they were saved from danger through divine intervention? Tell the story to the class.

into

the

deep

> No one comes to the Father except through me. If you know me, you will know my Father also.

(John 14:6)

Throughout Christian tradition, God has been revealed to humanity. In the Old Testament, God was revealed first to the prophets and leaders of the Hebrews, God's chosen people. Yet one thing became clear from early on: God was intimately involved in the lives of those who worshipped the one true God. The Hebrews who were slaves in Egypt cried out to God to save them. God intervened in their history and led them to freedom. Ultimately, the fullest revelation of God was through the life and death of God's son, Jesus Christ.

Throughout the gospels, we read accounts of Jesus performing miracles, forgiving sins and reaching out to those who were marginalised and abandoned by society. Jesus shows a path to freedom in life, where we are encouraged to turn away from materialism and instead focus our attention on others. He came to serve others, not to have his needs served. Jesus outlines a true path towards personal happiness and fulfilment through his teaching in the gospels. God has been ultimately revealed to us through Jesus and subsequently through the scriptures, but revelation doesn't end there. And this is the interesting bit. In St Paul's letter to the Corinthians we are told something that, if we accept it, has important implications for how we view our lives. He poses a question: 'Do you not know that you are God's temple and that God's spirit dwells in you?' (1 Corinthians 3:16)

Because the spirit of God is inside us, God is continually revealed throughout our lives and in our experiences. In this chapter, we will try to identify where God is revealed in human life.

> God, in his greatness, uses a pedagogy to reveal himself to the human person: he uses human events and words to communicate his plan; he does so progressively and in stages, so as to draw even closer to [the human person].

(General Directory for Catechesis, 38)

DISCUSS

We have mentioned some examples of where God was perhaps revealed in people's experiences through events where they made the right decision or where they avoided harm. Can you think of other examples? Share them with the class.

SEEING THROUGH THE LIES

 ... and you will know the truth, and the truth will make you free.

(John 8:32)

The spiritual pathway leads to truth and away from lies. We have a natural leaning towards truth, and teenagers are particularly good at figuring out the lies that society tells them, even if they find it hard to follow the truth. God is truth and when we find the truth we find God. When a group of students was asked what lies they thought society and the media were telling them, they identified the following:

- You have to look a certain way in order to be accepted.

- You have to achieve certain grades and results in order to be considered a success.

- Adults tell you materialism isn't everything but then they boast about their kids who have gone on to 'do well', which means make lots of money.

DISCUSS

1 What other lies are presented to young people as the truth? Do young people live their lives by the truth when they find it? Discuss your answers with the class.
2 What are the sources of truth in life? Who tells the truth? Who inspires you as a teller of the truth?

into
the
deep

THE PURPOSE OF YOUR LIFE

> " I am the way, and the truth, and the life. "
>
> (John 14:6)

" I kept having this feeling that there was something I had to do with my life. It was like unease inside. There were things that I thought would stop that feeling: exam results, boyfriends and first car, but they didn't. It wasn't there the whole time but sometimes. Then after college I volunteered to do work with an Irish aid agency. I hadn't noticed it until someone started a conversation about the purpose of your life. I didn't enter into the conversation but I realised that while I was out there I was completely happy. I'm doing things for others now and I've never been happier. "

(Female, 22)

A Catholic saint, called Augustine, identified the unease that the female student spoke about above almost fifteen hundred years ago. He spoke about a restlessness at the heart of the human spirit. One thing that teenagers are interested in finding out about is their true selves, their authentic self. Often, we pretend to be someone we're actually not, just to be accepted by parents and others. The real person can be far beneath all the layers. Christian teaching tells us that there is a deeper and inner self, which only we can discover. The true self knows the purpose of life. The truth about who we really are sets us free to be the

into the deep

person we want to be and to do the things we want to do. Often, people are most happy when helping others, fighting for truth and justice. The truest part of ourselves, our inner selves, is where we find God. Find the truth about yourself and you'll find another presence there too, one that is characterised by purpose and happiness.

ASIDE

Some years ago, a group of researchers decided to find out who were the happiest people around on Christmas day. They checked the children first, but a lot of them were playing with the boxes that their presents from 'Santa' had come in. Not the happiest. They then checked with people who received presents. They were happy but many were too influenced by alcohol, so a true reading couldn't be established. They then went along to the shelters where people had decided to give up their Christmas dinner and instead make one and serve it to the homeless. In their widely published findings, it was this group of volunteers who were the happiest people on Christmas day.

DISCUSS

1 Do you know any shallow people? Why do you think some young people pretend to be something that they're actually not? Why do they put on false accents, mannerisms and personalities?

2 Why do you think it's difficult to find your true self? Why do some people stand in the way of that search for truth?

3 In what way do religion or religious rituals allow you to reflect on who you really are and what your true purpose may be?

into

the

deep

INTO THE DARKNESS

❝ I had never thought about religion much to be honest. It was something there that I knew was probably important but I was not sure how important. I had never rejected it but I never really had the time to do anything about it. But then everything changed. My two best friends were killed in a car crash eighteen months ago after a night out. I was supposed to be with them but was at home with the flu. I always kept thinking that if I had been there, would things have been different. Would we have been a bit later? The timing of everything would have been different. That wrecked my head for ages and I felt responsible for not being there. I realised also that really you've only a few good friends and the rest are just there. I began to go into a very, very dark place after the lads' funeral and was lucky enough that the school chaplain took time to help me talk about the whole thing. I don't see myself as a religious person and would never say this in front of my classmates but I only got it together when I

started to pray to whoever it is we pray to. I don't know how to describe what happened but just one morning I woke up, went outside and things were different. The weight was lifted. The world was a better place. I go up to the lads' grave every so often. I can do that now. I always bring something with me and leave it there. On a night out when something funny happens I think that the lads would have enjoyed that. I have a great girlfriend now who I can talk to about stuff. Life is OK again now and I pray regularly but, as I say, I would never say this openly. '

(Male student, 19)

One of the characteristics of Christianity has been its approach to darkness, tragedy and suffering in life. It's a unique position in world religions. Christianity is rooted in the death and resurrection of Jesus. Death was overcome, darkness was overcome, and God is revealed to us in life when we emerge from bad times. Bad stuff happens to everyone but the challenge of Christianity is to move on and reach a better place. We're not supposed to stay in the tomb. There's no one there. Hope, fulfilment and happiness are the goal of the Christian life.

In the ritual of Baptism, we are told that we go into the tomb with Christ and emerge with him. The strange fact is that many people have to go into the tomb or end up in a dark place before they see God in their lives or develop a relationship with God.

> **DISCUSS**
>
> 1 Why do you think the student above wouldn't admit in front of his classmates how he felt about God? What is the difficulty in talking about such things?
> 2 Why do you think a person's religion and their faith becomes important during dark or difficult times? Why don't people turn to God when they win the lottery?

into
the
deep

ONE FINAL STORY...

We began this book with a piece about music and the quest for an authentic life. We end now with one final story which we received soon before publishing. It's the story of a young musician and how an experience of darkness and loss in his life was to change it forever. It's a story about revelations...

      6 Music is an outburst of the soul. **9**

(Frederick Delius)

6 In all of our lives we go through times that are hard, times that are good, times that are uncertain, times that we just don't know who to turn to. We've all been there at some stage. Some people use drugs, some use alcohol, some just blame fate and go through their lives feeling the same way every day. Me ... I use music.

Many great things come from terrible happenings in a person's life. My love of songwriting and music came from tragedy but gave me the inspiration I needed to keep on going. In 1999 my older brother Gary passed away. I was almost twelve years old. I was so young and felt so lost, so angry and upset. I needed something to comfort me, something that could help me project my feelings. I found that something in music and in song.

My love of music began as far back as the age of two or three but at the age of eleven (only months before my brother's passing) after hearing a Thin Lizzy record on my Dad's record player I heard something I hadn't heard before – the real song. The guitar immediately seduced me. I remember sitting in awe, knowing that I had to have a guitar and I had to try to sing. After saving my pocket money religiously for what seemed like years (but was only a few months!) I eventually bought an old classical guitar from the local music shop. I remember the

into the deep

excitement as I brought it home, thinking it would be as easy as strumming my tennis racket in the mirror. How wrong I was! After a couple of fruitless weeks of sheer frustration and noise making, my Mam's friend's son offered to teach me. I jumped at the chance. I learned how to play the guitar for quite a few months and decided that I was sick of learning songs and sifting through tablature books at the edge of my bed – I just wanted to write songs!

My brother's passing was what brought about my songwriting. I was, like most enthusiastic people who are learning to play the guitar, very focused on becoming the next Jimi Hendrix – but ultimately I wasn't good or patient enough! It was a tough grieving process that I was going through when I was twelve and I felt that I needed an escape from reality when I got home from school. The other pupils in my class didn't have any idea of what I was experiencing and so I felt quite lonely at times. I needed something that I had total control over and that let me talk about my feelings, my thoughts and my life.

You might say that songwriting was my resurrection from my grief. I've never thought of myself as a particularly spiritual person. Songwriting, however, helped me to get in touch with my spirit, my own sense of self. It can be extremely hard for young people (or indeed anyone) to just believe in something. After all, much of what we held to be our beliefs as children were just false. I asked difficult questions at this time in my life. Was there a God? If there was, then why would he take my brother? God and my sense of spirit became more real to me during the times when I felt like I just couldn't keep on going. I found God in every song I wrote, in each note I played. You see, spirituality and holiness is more than going to church every Sunday or saying a prayer every night. God is inside all of us and I found him in the comfort I felt when I could write my feelings down in song.

So my bedroom became my place to be, my sanctuary. I'd sit there every day for hours just trying to write my own songs. My first song was called 'Losing you again'. I was nearly thirteen when I wrote it. Some lines from it include:

The light in your eyes turns my heart to gold,
Your glistening smile makes me bleed,
I never thought that this would be the case,
Oh Lord how I'm going to miss your face.
        But most of all I want to forget the pain,
The pain of losing you again.
I want to laugh, I want to sing with you again.

Even now I write about my feelings and how I wish every day I could write songs to celebrate the things that give me hope in life. I want to revel in the people who have made me be the person I am today.

Wish I could write a song for you
That would celebrate your life in the way you
wanted it to
No sad refrain or gentle tune
Could reflect clearly
The memories I have of you.

I remember the feeling of how proud and relieved I felt when I wrote it. I played it to my family and friends and saw the effect it had on them. I even got to play in the local pub in town. When people heard my song and clapped, I knew then and there that I wanted to do this for the rest of my life.

I then went to secondary school in St Peter's College, Wexford. Every day I still kept coming home to my bedroom to write something. I was beginning to look to play more gigs now but was finding it hard because most of the gigs I was playing were on in pubs where I had to be out by nine! My songs were now starting to look at different topics such as love and drugs and things I saw on television.

into
the
deep

God's Unfolding Story

The lyrics were improving and my craft was developing constantly. But it wasn't about how good the songs were – it was me being myself, telling everyone that I was comfortable being me and that was what mattered the most (and still does).

A lot of young people nowadays (you included) have to cope with challenging issues such as drugs, alcohol, bullying, teenage pregnancy, etc. People from older generations, such as your parents and indeed your grandparents, didn't face a lot of these things as early as you will face them. I'm not saying that you should pick up a guitar or play the piano and hide away from the world writing songs all day every day – I'm saying that you should find ways to enjoy life without endangering yourself. Find the thing in life that makes living worthwhile and never

let go of it. That's what I've done – and that's what life is all about ... living.

Still to this day writing music and songs and playing them to as many people as I can is what I live for. It's in everything I do. It's what I think about when I'm at home or bored in a lecture (did I say bored?). It's what makes me the person I am today –

an individual, not some product of a peer group or a plastic celebrity. Listening to the music that I love is what makes me feel happy. I don't just listen to what my friends like or tell me to like. I listen to what strikes a chord with me and means something to me. We all have a soundtrack to our lives. The sooner we find our own and not just someone else's, the sooner we find music that becomes more than just music. It becomes a healer and a friend for life. For me, God is – as the Queens of the Stone Age aptly put it – 'in the radio'. He's in everything I commit to paper and to record. I hope you find your own sense of self and spirit because I know that in music I've found mine.

People will pass on, but a song is ever lasting. **'**

Stephen Somers
www.myspace.com/milliondollarshoes
milliondollarshoes.bebo.com

DISCUSS

1 What was Stephen's experience of darkness and what got him through it?

2 In what way was God revealed to Stephen as he experienced this difficult time?

3 Do you think he emerged a stronger and better person after the loss of his brother? Give reasons for your answer?

4 In what way do you think it changed his religious outlook on life?

into the deep

God's Unfolding Story